A WAXING MOON

A
Waxing
Moon

The Modern Gaelic Revival

ROGER HUTCHINSON

EDINBURGH AND LONDON

First published in Great Britain in 2005 by
MAINSTREAM PUBLISHING COMPANY
(EDINBURGH) LTD
7 Albany Street
Edinburgh EH1 3UG

ISBN 1 84018 794 8

A catalogue record for this book is available
from the British Library

Typeset in Goudy Catalogue

Printed in Great Britain by
Creative Print and Design, Wales

The Publisher acknowledges support from the
Scottish Arts Council towards the publication of this title

Contents

Gealach an Fhais os cionn Shleite

Dùn Sgathaich 'na chàrnaich luim
'S an Caisteal Uaine fo eidheann,
is samhlaidhean na falachd 's a' bhàis
a' tathaich am mur matbha laga;
Luibhean is blathan an rùin
mu Shabhal Ostaig; agus solus,
Deò-greine dòchas nan Gàidheal
Mu bhallachan ùra 's seana.
Mo dhùrachd gu robh math is buaidh
Air obair luachmhoir an t-Sabhail.

Somhairle MacGill-Eain

A Waxing Moon above Sleat

Dunscaith a bare cairn of stones
and the Green Castle under ivy,
and the ghosts of feuding and death
haunting their weak dead ramparts;
the herbs and flowers of aspirations
about Sabhal Ostaig; and a light,
sunbeam of the Gael's hope,
about its old and new walls.
May good fortune and success
be with the great work of the Sabhal.

Sorley Maclean

Introduction

The words 'revival' and 'renaissance' have many implications. They suggest, among other things, the resuscitation of someone or something which has been dead or, at the very least, comatose.

That is itself sufficient reason to beware of planting the terms on Scottish Gaelic. It may be remarkable but it is nonetheless true to say that this language, which evolved on the western seaboard of northern Europe 1,500 years ago, has never died, or even fallen into a morbid sleep. It is still, early in the twenty-first century, the first, the default, language of tens of thousands of people, some of them children. In Scotland alone, it has still almost 100,000 cognisants, or people who are familiar enough with it to understand and enjoy Gaelic radio and television, and are even able to read passages of the written word. And we should never forget the global Gaelic diaspora. From Nova Scotia to New South Wales by way of Coventry and London, there may no longer be many Gaelic-speaking communities, but there are certainly tens of thousands of scattered Gaels who show up on nobody's census figures.

This does not represent anything so insignificant as a 'survival' or a corpus in need of a defibrillator. It is actually no more nor less than an assertion of place, culture and identity as successful in the contemporary world as it was in the medieval. If modern legislators were to adopt this understanding a little more and the concept of benevolent bestowal a little less, then their relationship with Gaelic and Gaels might become more constructive.

None of which is to say that Gaelic does not, early in the twenty-first century, require 'help' and 'assistance' – although, once again, the condescending words can be misleading and reflective of a dangerous attitude. Gaelic does not demand charity from a modern state and society. What Gaelic does require is its due.

Not for several hundred years has Gaelic been the first or the majority language of any state. In the course of the careless twentieth century its core constituents, its fluent users, slipped – not so dramatically or chronically as many would suggest, but substantially – from a quarter of a million to sixty thousand in Scotland. There have been many, many reasons for this decline, some of which are explored in the following pages. However, the fact is that despite the negligence of the 1872 and subsequent Education Acts; despite anglophone radio, newspapers, television and pop music; despite all the blandishments of the American century, we are not talking here of the worthy invalids that are Cornish or Manx. We are talking instead of a vivid daily vernacular which has seen off Norse, Norman French, Doric, Scots and even English to welcome in the twenty-first century.

Gaelic begins the third millennium as a language that is no less patently, provenly alive for having a province of tens, rather than hundreds, of thousands of speakers. The first Gaelic revival did in fact commence when, in the last third of the nineteenth century, there were 250,000 Gaelic speakers. Its success or failure should not solely be judged by the fact that within 20 years of the start of the twentieth century, that number had almost halved. We would do well here to consider a parallel universe, an alternative history of a period which had never contained a great many energetic people who established pressure groups, publications and Gaelic societies, constantly relating those efforts to the economic and social well-being of the Scottish *Gaidhealtachd* – what, in 1921, would the statistics have shown if those people had never raised a hand?

The same point is doubly true of this second renaissance a

century later. Anybody who chooses to decry its validity or effectiveness on the grounds that between 1971 and 2001 the number of Gaelic speakers in Scotland fell from 90,000 to 60,000 is either misguided or malicious. Without both movements, and without the connecting thread of courageous activity between them, there might have been no Gaelic census at all – in 1881 or in 2001. And without them, by the latter date such a survey might have been quite redundant.

Gaelic is undeniably changing. Anybody who visits Eriskay, South Uist or the west side of Lewis in 2005 will hear less of the language than in 1975. It is too early as yet to predict with any certainty a Scottish Gaidhealtachd with no surviving Gaelic communities, but they are fewer by the decade and only investment in and fierce commitment to Gaelic-medium education will do much to alter that course of events. All recent trends described by the National Census indicate that Gaelic, which once lived almost exclusively in the north-west of Scotland, is in recent times to be heard as much in Glasgow as in Gairloch – muted as it may be by the noise of foreign traffic.

But change is not death. It is rather the Darwinian alternative to extinction. For a number of chiefly self-indulgent reasons, this writer dearly hopes that the vernacular Gaelic of the Hebrides and the north-western seaboard communities retains and improves upon its twentieth-century strength in the twenty-first century. That may require a Scottish Gaidhealtachd policy of exclusively Gaelic-medium primary and secondary education in designated islands and parishes, to which few could object.

Bilingualism, hailed by the world of educational theory as the redeemer of minority languages, is now their future. It is an easy enough future to envisage; indeed, it has already been with us for decades, and anybody in need of proof of its efficacy can do no better than visit the small primary school a mile north of the Gaelic college in Sleat, Skye – before, of course, visiting Sabhal Mòr Ostaig itself.

This book began as a history of that Gaelic college, before stumbling along the arterial roads to its friends and relatives in the modern Gaelic revival. The author is most grateful to all who have staffed and supported Sabhal Mòr on its short journey from ruined steading to 'jewel in Scotland's crown'.

I am not an autodidact in this subject; I was taught. The people who did most of the teaching, and to whom I am consequently grateful beyond English words, were, in alphabetical order: Joni Buchanan, Alan Campbell, Alastair Campbell, Torcuil Crichton, Norman Gillies, Jim Hunter, Revd Jack MacArthur, Martin MacDonald, Farquhar MacIntosh, Ken MacKinnon, Cailean Maclean, Father Calum MacLellan, Donald Angie MacLennan, Janet MacLeod, John Norman MacLeod, Revd Roddy MacLeod, Duncan MacQuarrie, Anne Martin, Donnie Munro, Ishbel Murray, Iain Noble, Seán O Drisceoil, Roy Pedersen, Iain Taylor and Brian Wilson. It goes without saying that they will expect students such as myself to be imperfect receptacles. Without the patience and skill of Joan MacIntyre, this book would have been impossible.

Roger Hutchinson,
Isle of Raasay, 2005

One

The English man of letters Samuel Johnson and his Scottish amanuensis James Boswell spent the whole of September 1773 – the month and the year would two centuries later seem to be strangely auspicious – in the island of Skye.

Johnson and Boswell entered and departed Skye at the same harbour in Armadale Bay on the east coast of Sleat, the most southerly of the island's peninsulas. Upon first arriving on 2 September, they were guests of the hereditary landowner Sir Alexander Macdonald at his family seat. This was at the time a large stone house with a walled orchard in the low hills behind Armadale Bay. They enjoyed neither their host nor his stiff Etonian hospitality.

On their return journey at the end of the month, they chose more convivial surroundings. Instead of lodging once more with the difficult Macdonald, the two men accepted the hospitality of a Church of Scotland minister, the Revd Mr Martin MacPherson of the parishes of Sleat and Knoydart, who lived with his wife Mary in a house on a farm a mile or two north of Armadale at a small settlement which both Johnson and Boswell knew as 'Ostig'.

Samuel Johnson enjoyed himself at Ostig between 28 September and 1 October (when they were informed that Sir Alexander Macdonald had left for Edinburgh and it was now safe to decamp to

Armadale and await a boat to Coll). The minister's sister was in residence, and Miss MacPherson 'pleased Dr Johnson much' by singing Gaelic songs to a guitar accompaniment.

Despite Miss MacPherson's delightful entertainments, his presence at Ostig inspired Johnson to some of his more brutal assessments of Scottish Gaelic, or 'Erse', as the language was widely described in England and the south of Scotland until the early twentieth century. This now redundant but once commonplace term seems to derive from early Lowland Scots renderings of the Old English or Old Norse for 'Irish', which were respectively 'Irisc' and 'Irskr'. It was used as early as the fourteenth century by the Archdeacon of Aberdeen John Barbour, whose historical poem 'The Bruce' refers to 'all the erischry . . . of Argyle and the Ilis alsua'. By the 1500s, William Dunbar was writing of 'Erschemen' and other people talking 'Fful lowd in Ersche'. A *Penny Cyclopaedia* in 1838 declared that 'The language spoken by the Scottish Highlanders is familiarly known among the Lowlanders by the name of the Erse, or according to the more usual pronunciation the Ersh, that is plainly the Eirish or Irish.' Under concerted pressure from respectable Gaelic societies, the word lost ground rapidly at the end of the nineteenth century, but survived as a literary curiosity as late as 1917, when P.G. Wodehouse featured in his novel *Uneasy Money* a parlour-maid who in times of stress reverted to speaking 'what appeared to be Erse'.

Having conceded that his or her use of 'Erse' was what in 1773 defined a Highlander ('Under the denomination of Highlander are comprehended in Scotland all that now speak the Erse language') and that he himself knew nothing but what he was told of the subject, Samuel Johnson proceeded nonetheless to unload himself of a series of prejudiced and – given their illustrious source – damaging judgements of Scottish Gaelic:

> It is the rude speech of a barbarous people . . . The Welsh
> and the Irish are cultivated tongues . . . while the Earse
> merely floated in the breath of the people, and could
> therefore receive little improvement . . . That the [Gaelic]

> Bards could not read more than the rest of their countrymen,
> it is reasonable to suppose . . . the Bard was a barbarian
> among barbarians, who, knowing nothing himself, lived with
> others that knew no more.

Those and other comments, which would have a discernible influence on succeeding generations of educated Britons and their treatment of the 'rude speech' (the word 'Erse' itself, which was a simple, unloaded noun on Samuel Johnson's lips, rapidly became a signal of mockery and scorn), were actually delivered as a salvo in a literary duel.

Johnson had staked his reputation on his conviction that James Macpherson's English 'translations' of the Ossianic Gaelic legends, which were in the 1760s and 1770s taking the fashionable parlours and coffee houses of Europe by storm, were faked. The cornerstone of Macpherson's defence was that the 'Ossian' poems were a broad translation of antique Scottish Gaelic texts. The cornerstone of Johnson's prosecution was that this was impossible, as Scottish Gaelic had never been written down. Both men were wrong (although only one was a fraud). Neither man suffered. Macpherson died rich and Johnson died in the odour of celebrity. Only Scottish Gaelic, their innocent punchbag, was left torn and frayed.

In fact, his musings at Ostig did not perfectly reflect Samuel Johnson's opinion of old languages in general and Gaelic in particular. Johnson was a keen philologist, a lexicographer and autodidactic student of languages who was offended more by James Macpherson's historical deceit than by the claim to survival of Scottish Gaelic. He had a track record from several years earlier, as we shall see, of supporting the right of the Gael to a translation of the Bible in his own language. He had been known to muse sympathetically on the Scottish Highlander: 'Of what they had before the late conquest of their country [following the Battle of Culloden in 1746] there remains only their language and their poverty. Their language is attacked on every side. Schools are erected in which English only is taught.'

Before turning up at Martin MacPherson's manse in Sleat,

Johnson and Boswell had spent several enjoyable hours in the company of another local Church of Scotland minister, the Revd Mr Donald MacQueen.

MacQueen was a classicist and Gaelic scholar who was interested to establish connections between his native Celtic culture and the realms of antiquity. He had been recommended to the travelling friends as 'the most intelligent man in Skye'.

James Boswell watched with interest a series of respectful debates between MacQueen and Johnson. At one point Donald MacQueen suggested that there was a link between Skye and the ancient civilisation of Scythia in Asia Minor, because the Scythians 'were the ancestors of the Celts'. According to Boswell this provoked from Samuel Johnson one of his most celebrated – and misinterpreted – aperçus. He said:

> What can a nation that has not letters tell of its original? I have always difficulty to be patient when I hear authours quoted, as giving accounts of savage nations, which accounts they had from the savages themselves. What can the McRaas tell us about themselves a thousand years ago? There is no tracing the connection of ancient nations, but by language; and therefore I am always sorry when any language is lost, because languages are the pedigree of nations.

Samuel Johnson left Ostig and Skye for the last time, early in October 1773, reinforced in three convictions. One, which need not detain us, was that James Macpherson was a scoundrel and his 'Ossian' an elaborate fake. Another was that Scottish Gaelic, if it was to enter the academies of civilised nations, must become a fully literate language, taught in schools and preserved in print. And the third was that if it failed so to establish itself then it would die, and its death would distress Johnson, who was 'always sorry when any language is lost, because languages are the pedigree of nations'. His first conviction would be justified. His second would, over the succeeding centuries, be conceded torpidly, grudgingly and piecemeal, but sufficiently and probably just about in time to save

Samuel Johnson's ghost from wanly mourning the sad truth of his third, depressing conviction.

Several years after Johnson's departure from Skye, some small developments occurred in the township of Ostig. In the late 1790s or the early 1800s, the tourist's old host and hostess, Revd Martin MacPherson and his wife Mary, gave up the lease of their holding there and moved to retirement a few miles further north at Knock Bay. Ostig or Ostaig Farm (the name means 'East Bay' and derives from Old Norse, like so many others in the Scottish *Gaidhealtachd* – the term originally employed to describe the Gaelic-speaking areas of Scotland, but which is now commonly used to describe the Highlands and Islands as a geographical rather than linguistic entity) was then taken over by Mrs Mary MacPherson's sister, Jean MacKinnon of Corry.

Jean MacKinnon married a Macdonald of Clanranald from Arisaig on the Scottish mainland. In 1823, her son, Major Allan Macdonald, in his turn took over the lease of Ostaig.

And at some time between 1823 and 1831 (in which year he was requesting a reduction in his lease payments to the Macdonald Estate as compensation for building improvements carried out at Ostaig) Major Allan Macdonald hired men to erect in vernacular style and stone around a spacious courtyard a substantial, sturdy complex of barns and byres. In their native language, the local people came to know this building as Sabhal Mòr Ostaig, which means 'the large steading at Ostaig'.

This steading served firstly Ostaig Farm and latterly the Macdonald Estate for a further 150 years. Then another Lord Macdonald of the blood Donald sold it, along with most of the rest of his inheritance.

And exactly 200 years after Samuel Johnson had deliberated on the patrimony of Scottish Gaelic at Ostaig – two centuries to the week, perhaps the day, possibly the hour, since the stout philosopher had paused to tell the Revd Mr Donald MacQueen that languages were the pedigree of nations – a young journalist named Brian Wilson sat at a desk in Skye and typed the following news story. The *West Highland Free Press* of 21 September 1973 announced:

Sabhal Mòr Ostaig in Sleat is to be established as a charitable foundation and plans are well advanced for establishing it as an educational institute, with a special emphasis on Gaelic educational functions.

Four *urrasairean* or sponsors have been adopted – they are Gordon Barr, D.R. Macdonald, Sorley Maclean and Iain Noble.

As educational institutes go, Ostaig will be unusual in that it will cater for every age group from toddlers and schoolchildren to graduates, postgraduates and people of all ages. In addition to its role within Skye and the islands, the sponsors hope that it will act as a place where people from all parts of the globe can further their interest in Gaelic.

Already 90 books have been donated to the library, which it is intended will become the first comprehensive Gaelic library in the west of Scotland.

An early development of local interest will be the holding of Gaelic night classes at Ostaig. A spokesman for Sabhal Mòr Ostaig said that Inverness County Council had been 'less than enthusiastic' about supporting this development, indicating that if there were to be any night classes in Sleat under their auspices they would be held on council premises . . .

Other activities envisaged are the holding of short courses and eventually full-length one-year courses, perhaps with diploma status. A link with the Celtic departments of the Scottish universities will also be sought.

These developments have arisen within less than a year of Sabhal Mòr Ostaig opening its doors as an occasional social centre. It would seem a safe bet that further points of interest will continue to emerge as this unique experiment continues.

We do not know how many Gaelic speakers lived in Scotland at the time of Samuel Johnson's visit in 1773. The language had by then been established in the country for more than 1,000 years. It had mutated gently but inexorably from its Irish roots, from the original tongue which had been imported along with Christianity in fast, seagoing currachs by monks and tradesmen, nobles and soldiers throughout the fourth, fifth, sixth and seventh centuries AD.

It would never lose its Irish grammatical and lexicographical base. Scottish 'gallowglasses' (*gall-òglaigh*, or foreign soldiers) would receive and issue Gaelic military commands while serving the common Celtic cause beyond the English-speaking Dublin pale in medieval Ireland. Lowland Scotsmen raided by Rob Roy MacGregor's gang in the early eighteenth century would report that their attackers used 'the Irish tongue'. Hebridean fishermen working the waters west of Connemara in the nineteenth century would discover themselves capable of swapping with the locals stories of land struggle. Irish men and women from their own west coast *Gaeltacht* (the Gaelic-speaking areas of Ireland) would settle easily in the primarily Gaelic Roman Catholic society of South Uist in the 1950s. Students from Galway and Ross-shire would debate in Belfast or Skye with a minimum of interpretation in the twenty-first century.

But the language which became the first language of Scotland by the twelfth century was no longer Irish, just as the languages of Italy and Spain were no longer Roman Latin. Its key words and expressions of everyday usage were mostly recognisable if not identical on either side of the North Channel. The literature of the two languages remained broadly unified. But this was not a literate society, and its vernacular was growing away from the tongue which landed half a millennium before in Galloway (Gall-Gaidhealaibh, the place of the foreigner), Kintyre (Ceann-tìre, the head of the peninsula) and Argyll (Earra Ghaidheal, the high land of the Gael, or Oirer Ghaidheal, the coastline of the Gael, or Ara Ghaidheal, the boundary of the Gael). It had evolved, as living languages must, to deal with fresh circumstances in changing times in a different country.

As even the twentieth century's anglophone maps indicate, Scottish Gaelic became and remained for some centuries the first language of hearth, home and neighbourhood from Caithness (Gallaibh) in the far north-east to Stranraer (An t-Sròn Reamhar) in

17

the south-west, from Tiree (Tiriodh) to Gleneagles (Gleann na h-Eaglais). Wherever a Dun, a Knock, an Ath or a Muck exists, it marks the spot where some medieval Gael built a castle, climbed a hill, forded a stream or established a piggery. It failed to sink deep roots only in the Teutonic Lothians – where they spoke a form of Saxon English – Doric Banff and Buchan, and the Norse northern islands of Orkney and Shetland.

By way of compensation, Gaelic was certainly used in medieval Cumbria and Northumberland. A Durham monk named Simeon, writing of certain events in the 1060s, mentions a powerful (and, it should be said, troublesome) man north of the River Tyne who bore the distinctly Gaelic name of Gillemichael (Michael's son). It is equally telling that Simeon himself understood enough Gaelic to make a play on the usage – Gillemichael, he quipped, would have been better christened 'son of the devil' for his want of respect for clerics. A list of men living around 1200 AD in Peebles, south of Edinburgh, contains two Gillemechails, two Gille-Christs, two Gille-Moires, two Crisdeins, two Padruigs, a Gille-Caluim and others. Those Gaelic Christophers, Peters and Calums outnumbered in that particular Tweeddale settlement 800 years ago their Norse, Saxon and southern Brythonic Celtic neighbours.

Here, between the retreat of the Romans and the accession of the Normans, Scottish Gaelic became for the first and only time the language of a state. Its population was small. The whole of northern Britain may have contained no more than 500,000 people. But the majority of them will have been native Gaelic speakers, or have understood a Gaelic dialect, or at the least recognised Gaelic as the language of trade, power and administration. Even the obdurate Norsemen, who left their place and family names across the land, who held sovereignty over a large swathe of the insular Gaidhealtachd until 1266 and whose own language could still faintly be heard in the distant Hebrides as late as the fifteenth century, were assimilated – all those Torcuils and Nicolsons and MacLeods – into the mainstream of Gaelic culture.

The remarkable thing is not that the language retreated as the Middle Ages progressed, as French and then English-speaking barons achieved hegemony in both Scotland and Ireland, but that it retreated so slowly. What became known as the Highland Line served as a boundary for centuries. The physical and cultural fault-line meanders down from Speyside, running a long way south. It dips almost to the southern mouth of Loch Lomond. There, in the small agricultural townships which litter the shoreline, within sight and easy walking distance of the great southern conurbations of Dumbarton and Clydebank, there were to be found native Gaelic speakers in the first half of the twentieth century. Galloway Gaelic, with its close historical association to Manx and Irish dialects, cut off from the rest of Scotland and within clear view of England, survived in a few lonely pockets as far south on the map as Newcastle-upon-Tyne until the eighteenth century and possibly later. When the parish of Barr in Carrick in modern Ayrshire advertised for a schoolmaster in 1762, the elders specified that the successful applicant 'budst be able to speak Gaelic' (the lucky appointee 'was fae aboot the Lennox' in Dunbartonshire). Frontier towns such as Inverness accepted early the advent of English as the new language of power and money but retained healthy bilingual populations throughout the Middle Ages, into the twentieth century and even beyond. (As late as 1881, almost a third of the urban population of Inverness was Gaelic speaking.) And in the northern and western glens, on the seaboard and in the island fastnesses, whole families, whole communities continued into the reign of the second Queen Elizabeth, in the most advanced technological society on earth, into the era of space travel and television, using and hearing in daily life no language other than the Gaelic which their ancestors had passed down for over 1,000 years. It was an extraordinary survival.

While we cannot know for sure how many Gaelic speakers there were in Samuel Johnson's time, because there was no official census, we can make an educated guess. It is reliably estimated that Scotland at the time of the Union of Parliaments in 1707 had a population of a little over a million, most of whom lived in rural communities and almost half of whom lived north of the River Tay. Subtracting the Doric communities of Banff and Aberdeen, and the Norse of the northern isles from this 500,000, we are left with a Gaelic population in 1707 of perhaps 350,000, or between a quarter and a third of the entire population.

The first National Census was taken in 1801. It enumerated a Scottish population of 1,608,420. During the preceding century, incipient industrialisation and the growth of urban communities had increased the overall population by 60 per cent. But despite some rural – and especially Highland – decline, despite the depredations which followed the failed Jacobite uprising of 1745, despite the dissolution of traditional Highland society and the advent of clearance and widespread emigration, the number of Gaelic speakers in Scotland is estimated to have fallen only to around 300,000. There were, in short, probably as many speakers of Gaelic in Scotland in 1700, and even in 1800, as there had been in a more sparsely populated land during the heyday of the language's ascendancy 600 years before.

The balance of power had, however, irrevocably shifted. A language with 300,000 or 350,000 native speakers is not immediately threatened. A language whose 300,000 or 350,000 speakers comprise the majority, or a half, or a third or even a quarter of its country's population is still in a position of strength. But a language whose speakers total 15 per cent and falling of any given polity is a language that should watch its back.

The population of the rural Highlands and Islands grew by as much as 50 per cent during the decades which spanned the end of the eighteenth and the beginning of the nineteenth centuries. This was not quite in line with the population of the whole of Scotland, which in the same period increased by 80 per cent. But in certain Gaelic homelands the establishment of a form of crofting, the development of fisheries and the kelp industry (which depended on harvested Atlantic seaweed) brought an even larger growth. The medium-sized island of Skye, to take one not untypical example of a virtually monoglot Gaelic community, contained 11,252 people in 1755 and 15,788 people in 1801, but had expanded to 23,074 by 1841. In the same period, the population of Harris grew by 98 per cent, the population of North Uist by 141 per cent and the population of South Uist by 211 per cent. Given the nature of Skye, Harris and Uist society in particular and the Highlands in general at that time, almost all of the additional population would have been native Gaelic speakers. It is therefore possible to surmise that there was a striking demographic increase in the entire Scottish Gaidhealtachd between 1800 and 1840, which perhaps took the number of Gaelic speakers by mid-century as high as 400,000. If that was the case, it could represent the language's numerical mountain-top.

This estimated peak can be well illustrated in the tiniest of microcosms. In 1954, the Gaelic writer Sorley Maclean published in the magazine *Gairm* a poem called 'Hallaig'. Its 14 defiant, tragic stanzas would come to be recognised internationally as the masterpiece of twentieth-century Gaelic literature. Hallaig was a township on the east coast of Maclean's native island of Raasay. In the first decades of the nineteenth century, Hallaig's population increased so rapidly, from a few dozen people to well over a hundred, that in 1830 the people of the village built a school and in 1833 petitioned the Gaelic Schools Society in Edinburgh to provide a teacher. 'There are [in Hallaig] upwards of 24 families paying rents, besides a number of cottars,' attested their petition. 'No less than 60 scholars could be got to attend School.'

The 1841 census revealed Hallaig to have a population of 129, every single one of whom would have been a Gaelic speaker, and few of whom would have enjoyed much facility in any other language. Two or three years later, Upper Hallaig was cleared of people by its last MacLeod landowner. The 1851 census declared what remained of Hallaig to have a population of 72. In 1854, most of those men, women and children were evicted by a new landowner to make way for a sheep run. They were put on a ship called the *Edward Johnstone* and sent to Australia. By 1861, this busy place had been reduced to a shepherd and a labourer. By the time of the National Census for 1891, the returns from Hallaig in Raasay amounted to one eloquent word: 'Nil'. Its place name did not even survive in everyday use for long enough to be mauled into phonetic English on Inverness Council's road signs – Hallaig remains Hallaig, in both languages. This emblematic Gaelic community had experienced an unnaturally brief flowering on the green east coast of Raasay. It would never be repopulated.

After that early-nineteenth-century zenith, the four horsemen of famine, clearance, disease and emigration struck the whole of the north-western seaboard. Populations scattered and fled, declining as sharply as they had risen. By 1881, the number of people in Skye had fallen back to 17,680. This reduction was perfectly representative of most of the rest of the Scottish Gaidhealtachd. It did not, however, reflect the fortunes of the industrial Central Belt or the north-east of the country, which continued to thrive and to grow by between 7 and 10 per cent each decade, widening at an alarming rate the fissure between what was clearly an ailing Gaelic society and its equally clearly robust Lowland cousin.

This period in the middle of the nineteenth century can be identified as the start of Gaelic's modern malaise. Not the fall of the Gaelic-speaking Royal House of Canmore, not the collapse of the Lordship of the Isles, not the Battle of Culloden – significant as they all were to the language and the culture. In the famine and clearance years of the 1840s, when the kelp industry had all but collapsed, the Highland economy and population began a downward spiral of decline which would last for over a century. At the same time, the Lowlands of Scotland accelerated their extraordinary development, which by the 1900s would see Glasgow processing more capital per head than any other city in the British Empire. The 1840s were the watershed years, when the Lowland road and the Highland road, which, whatever their comparative size, had hitherto run a roughly parallel course, forked and dramatically diverged. After that decade, one led to apparently infinite prosperity while the other descended into decay, into a social and cultural deterioration so rapid and inexorable that it began to appear terminal. And inevitably it took its language, its standard, its means of interpreting the world, down with it.

The decline of the second half of the nineteenth century came just in time for the first official census of Gaelic speakers to be taken in Scotland.

Questions designed to ascertain the number of Irish Gaelic speakers in Ireland had been introduced to the National Census of 1861 (it indicated that there were, 150 years ago, just over 1,000,000 Irish speakers in a total post-famine population of 3,400,000). In August 1880, Charles Fraser-Mackintosh, the Gaelic-speaking MP for Inverness Burghs, asked the House of Commons to consider extending the same courtesy to Scottish Gaels in the 1881 census. Such a gesture was the least that might be offered, Fraser-Mackintosh said, to an ethnic group who were, unlike the Irish, 'a peaceable and orderly people who seldom obtruded their wishes on the House'.

Highland modesty cut no ice. The Home Secretary, Sir William Harcourt, rejected that suggestion and a second one. In January 1881, by which time the 1881 census schedules had already been printed without reference to Gaelic, the ten-year-old Gaelic Society of Inverness (GSI) threw its bulk behind Fraser-Mackintosh's campaign. The GSI wrote to the Home Office:

> A census of the Gaelic speaking population of Scotland, such as has more than once been taken of the Irish speaking population of Ireland, would be of great practical value in connection with several important questions affecting the Highlands, and would hereafter be considered a valuable historical record.

William Harcourt relented. It was too late to alter the census questionnaires, but the survey on 4 April was mostly taken orally, and the 1881 National Census enumerators were instructed to ask people resident in Scotland if they were 'habitual' speakers of Gaelic. Following further pressure from Charles Fraser-Mackintosh, who considered that the term 'habitual' might exclude the many thousands of bilingual Gaels who lived and worked in English-speaking environments, the enumerators were told to forget 'habitual' and instead ask Scots if they could speak Gaelic 'fluently'.

This was still imperfect – it naturally discounted such borderline cases as the very young and the Edinburgh undergraduate at his

Celtic studies, or even the overmodest bilingual Gael – but it would have to do. The 1881 census results reported that 231,594 people out of a total Scottish population of 3,735,573 declared themselves to be 'fluent' speakers of Gaelic. Almost all of these – 88 per cent of them – lived in the Highland crofting counties of Argyllshire, Inverness-shire, Sutherlandshire, and Ross and Cromarty, which between them then incorporated all of the Hebrides. At some point in the previous 40 years an important boundary had been crossed. Most probably during the two decades between 1850 and 1870, Gaelic speakers in Scotland had for the first time in a millennium fallen to below 10 per cent of the population.

The Gaelic Society of Inverness protested that both the question and the method of asking it had been flawed, and that the total number of Gaelic speakers in 1881 was closer to 300,000. The number of Gaels in Glasgow, for instance, was enumerated as only 6,085 out of 500,000. In 1881, there were probably more than 6,000 Gaelic-speaking policemen in Glasgow. The GSI had good reason to believe that the true total figure was closer to 50,000 and that the census takers had somehow managed after all to confuse 'habitual' speakers with 'fluent' speakers. The same confusion would have explained the absurdly low numbers of Gaels declared in other anglophone environments such as Edinburgh (supposedly only 2,142 in a total of 389,164) and Aberdeen (607 among 267,990). In such places, not even the most fluent Gael was a habitual user of his native language.

The Gaelic Society of Inverness was right, but not so right as it wished. Ten years later in 1891, the question was refined and rephrased and dignified by inclusion on the printed census schedule. The number of self-confessed Gaels duly rose, but only to 254,415. Just over one-sixth, or 43,738 people in that total, spoke Gaelic and no other language. The total Scottish population in 1891 was just over 4,000,000. In 100 years of hardship and oppression, the number of Scottish-Gaelic speakers had fallen by only 15 per cent. But the proportion of Gaels to non-Gaels in the whole of the burgeoning, vibrant country had in the same period collapsed by 150 per cent.

It was the last time but one that a National Census would record a rise of any kind in the number of Gaelic speakers in Scotland. A century later people would look back in awe at those statistics and wonder what the late-Victorian Gaelic Society of Inverness had to worry about.

The answer would be: a lot. The last third of the nineteenth century saw what might be termed the first Gaelic renaissance. There had been earlier Gaelic organisations and Gaelic lobbies. The oldest surviving of these groups, the Gaelic Society of London, was formed in 1777, just 31 years after Culloden, and in those unpromising times managed to help repeal the Disarming Acts which had outlawed the tartan plaid and the Highland pipes.

Anti-Gaelic attitudes in the educational and religious establishments proved less easy to reform. Throughout the eighteenth century the Protestant Society in Scotland for Propagating Christian Knowledge (SSPCK) had established missionary schools mostly in Presbyterian areas of the Gaidhealtachd. Catholic districts depended on hedge-schools run by priests, which traditionally embraced and employed Gaelic; but between its foundation in 1701 and its reformation in 1767, the SSPCK specifically banned the use of the Scottish and Irish languages from its institutions.

The after-effects of this prohibition lingered in some unfortunate schools into the following century. They were vividly chronicled by the author and minister to Edinburgh's Gaelic Church Revd Donald Masson, who in 1889 recalled his boyhood in such an institution:

> Another curse of this absurd practice [of refusing to allow Gaelic in SSPCK schools] in the hands of an ignorant, pedantic teacher, was the utter hopelessness, on the part of really thoughtful boys, of the most earnest attempts at learning.
>
> I well remember one nice, bright boy, who was thus sat upon with crushing effect. He was kept for more than a year at the alphabet. All that time he was made the sport of the

school. His shy attempts at English were mimicked and grossly caricatured. Hours were spent in making game of him, for minutes given to any honest attempt to teach him. To crown all, he was almost daily made to wear the fool's cap – a huge erection of goatskin, with the hair outwards, and the tail hanging down behind . . . to this day my blood boils when I recall the cruel and grossly absurd 'teaching' of which he was the helpless victim.

The SSPCK even resisted the publication of a Gaelic New Testament which was prepared in the middle of the eighteenth century by the Revd Mr James Stewart, a long-serving and highly respected Protestant minister at the overwhelmingly Gaelic-speaking frontier parish of Killin in western Perthshire.

The SSPCK's hostility to Revd Stewart's labours provoked, seven full years before his visit to Scotland and sojourn among the educated Gaels of Ostaig, a fierce broadside from that unlikely friend of the Highlander, Dr Samuel Johnson. According to James Boswell, Johnson was told in the summer of 1766 that 'some of the members of the society in Scotland for propagating Christian knowledge, had opposed the scheme of translating the Holy Scriptures into the Erse or Gaelick language, from political considerations of the disadvantage of keeping up the distinction between the Highlanders and the other inhabitants of North Britain'. Johnson was furious. He vented his anger in an open letter to the Edinburgh bookseller William Drummond:

I did not expect to hear that it could be, in an assembly convened for the propagation of Christian knowledge, a question whether any nation uninstructed in religion should receive instruction; or whether that instruction should be imparted to them by a translation of the holy books into their own language . . . I am not very willing that any language should be totally extinguished . . . My zeal for languages may seem, perhaps, rather over-heated, even to those by whom I desire to be well-esteemed. To those who have nothing in their thoughts but trade or policy, present power, or present money, I should not think it necessary to defend my opinions . . . the translation of the Bible is most to be desired . . . When the Highlanders read the Bible, they will naturally wish to have its obscurities cleared, and to know the history, collateral or appendant. Knowledge always desires increase: it is like fire, which must first be kindled by some external agent, but which will afterwards propagate itself.

Shortly afterwards Samuel Johnson heard, to his 'great pleasure', that his arguments had helped to persuade the SSPCK to change its collective mind. Revd Stewart's lifetime's work would after all be set in type. The Scottish Gaelic New Testament was duly published in 1767. Despite some criticism that the Killin minister had 'retained too much of the Irish dialect of O'Donnell's Irish New Testament', it proved to be a success. Revd Stewart's son, the Revd Dr John Stewart of Luss on Loch Lomondside, was promptly commissioned by a repentant SSPCK to translate the Old Testament, which joined the Gospels in print in 1801.

In that same year of grace 1767, the SSPCK resolved that:

the Society's regulations enjoining the schoolmasters not to teach the scholars Earse be altered and that in time coming schoolmasters in those places in the Highlands where the Earse language is generally spoken be enjoined to teach their scholars to read both Earse and English.

As we have heard from Revd Donald Masson, some schoolmasters were slower than others to get the message.

Johnson's role in this affair may in fact have been marginal, but there is no doubting the central importance of those publications. The Edinburgh Society for the Support of Gaelic Schools (ESSGS) – the Gaelic Schools Society which in 1833 received a request from the village of Hallaig – was established in 1811, almost in contradistinction to the old SSPCK. Upon its 50th anniversary in

1861, the ESSGS estimated that its Sgoilean Chrìosd (Christian Schools) had distributed 200,000 Gaelic bibles and taught 100,000 Gaels to read. Apart from encouraging this degree of Gaelic literacy and fluency in Highland and Island schools and among the churchgoing Highland community in general, the Gaelic translations of the Bible helped the dissenting Free Church of Scotland, which swept to prominence throughout the Protestant Gaidhealtachd following the Disruption of 1843, to take a focal position at the heart of the Gaelic community.

It immediately made its position clear. Despite a first decade of precarious existence, during which it was denied church buildings, manses, funds and even dry land upon which to hold services, by 1851, the Free Church had been adopted by most of the Highland and Hebridean Sgoilean Chrìosd and was supporting between 600 and 700 schools, in many if not most of which Gaelic was the primary medium of instruction. Had the Free Church not taken the language to its bosom and deployed it as the first instrument of worship, Gaelic would have sunk further in the esteem and usage of its deeply religious Victorian Highland native speakers. The Free Church introduced, and sustained throughout the length of the twentieth century, 'Gaelic-essential' posts into which no purely anglophone minister could be called. The established Church of Scotland was obliged to follow suit and, after 1893, the breakaway Free Presbyterian Church willingly adopted the same policy. A free marketplace in denominations worked for Gaelic where the monopoly of the established Church had failed. If one church successfully appealed to people in their own language, others were obliged to copy their marketing strategy. They would even occasionally try to out-Gaelic each other. From the middle of the nineteenth century onwards, virtually every Highland community was served by a parish priest or minister who could not only speak but also read and often write in Gaelic and whose denomination actively encouraged the language. The result was several generations of Gaels who were literate in Gaelic to an unprecedented degree and whose deployment of their native tongue was as sonorous, sophisticated and compelling as any Old Testament prophet.

Despite the efforts of the Free Church of Scotland, education was slow to follow the Kirk in admitting the language. Ironically, this situation was made infinitely worse by that otherwise irreproachable reform: the 1872 Education Act.

Like its predecessor of two years earlier in England and Wales, the Education (Scotland) Act of 1872 was designed chiefly to bring elementary schooling under the arm of the state and to make it both universally accessible and compulsory. It would, in other words, bring education and opportunity to the labouring classes. This initiative, which could and should have brought unprecedented benefits to the Highlands and Islands, became instead a historical ogre. A distinguished Scottish educationalist, Farquhar MacIntosh, would a century later deplore 'the fact that Gaelic was excluded from the school curriculum by the Education Act of 1872. That was probably the most serious blow that Gaelic suffered, more than it did by the clearances or even by the terrible toll that was taken of Gaelic speakers in the First World War.'

Because sadly and almost inexplicably, the framers of the 1872 legislation either overlooked the sons and daughters of the Highland labouring classes or, which is much more likely, they accepted the common nostrum that it would be better for all concerned if young Gaels were educated out of their native language and into the vocabulary of Empire as quickly and unsentimentally as possible. Aside from anything else, it was solemnly announced, 'Gaelic interfered with the pronunciation of English'.

Whatever the reasons, the 1872 Scottish Education Act contained no provision for, or even mention of, Gaelic. Given the developments of the previous few decades, this omission represented a large backwards step. Almost all of the hedge-schools which had with varying degrees of reluctance come to accept and use Gaelic – the Free Church, SSPCK, Church of Scotland, Catholic and the Sgoilean Chrìosd set up by the Edinburgh Gaelic Schools Society – were effectively nationalised under the central aegis of Her Majesty's Inspectorate (which paid absolute fealty to the terms of the 1872 Act) and the local authority of newly created school boards (which depended for guidance and grant aid upon the judgements of Her Majesty's Inspectors).

The result was a sudden decline in the use of Gaelic in elementary schools. Children who had previously received some kind of teaching in Gaelic, however occasional or unqualified that teaching may have been, were pitched into an alien environment in which even their Gaelic-speaking teachers – in many cases the very tutors who had during the previous term been communicating with them in their shared language – were instructing them in English and little else. Not only was there, except in cases of the most obvious need (in some of the stronger Gaelic heartlands and where new pupils from monoglot Gaelic homes required crash courses in how to survive this place called school), no more teaching through the medium of Gaelic, there was no teaching of Gaelic as an individual language subject.

The Gaelic Society of Inverness and other lobbyists addressed this second issue first. A century later it might seem unambitious to campaign for a couple of hours a week of tuition in Gaelic grammar for children in Lewis or Sutherland who used no other language the moment they stepped out of the classroom door, but the Gaelic Society of Inverness in the 1870s was comparatively unambitious. The GSI was happy in a condition of dignified and sustainable minority. It had no desire to reinstate Gaelic as a national, official state language of Scotland. It was academically aware of the possibility of terminal decline, but with 250,000 fluent native speakers, 43,000 Gaels who spoke nothing else and entire large islands such as North and South Uist where three-quarters of the population could not pass the time of day in English, that unpleasant prospect seemed – as indeed it was – a long way off. Their most pressing concern was to achieve recognition of the language.

So the Gaelic societies and other campaigners sought not so much to challenge the new English-language hegemony in Highland schools as to find for Gaelic a place on the curriculum. Those men and women were content for the Gael in future to become – as they were themselves – bilingual. Their anxiety was as much for the preservation in written form of Gaelic 'poetry, sentiments and philosophy' as for the sustenance of the living language.

That, ironically, was not too far from the position of their opponents in the educational sphere. Those opponents were, as would ever be the case, plentiful, vocal, well connected and often to be found in Edinburgh. One of the most strident was a self-made publisher named William Chambers. As a Lord Provost of Edinburgh, Chambers had devoted himself to medieval-slum clearance and the improvement of public health. As a publisher he had produced cheap and accessible educational books and encyclopedias. In recognition of such good deeds, his statue now stands in Chambers Street in the capital. In septuagenarian semi-retirement, William Chambers became one of the new Inspectors of Education, and in this capacity he published (in his own magazine, *Chambers Journal*) in November 1877 an article entitled 'The Gaelic Nuisance'. Arch and condescending in tone but murderously hostile in intent, this essay became a celebrated example of official Lowland adversity to the language. Gaelic should give way gracefully, the Edinburgh grandee argued, to its Darwinian fate as an ancient tongue irrelevant to the modern world. It was a constraint on the betterment of its speakers. Far from surviving even as a conversational vernacular in the Outer Hebrides, it should be consigned as quickly as possible to the dead languages departments of Scottish universities, 'to be cultivated among the higher aims of philology'.

In the teeth of such influential opposition (Chambers' essay was quoted approvingly as far away as the United States, where in 1878 a correspondent to the *Scottish-American Journal* insisted that: 'The continuance of Gaelic as a conversational language, apart from a knowledge of English, is rightly considered by no less a man than William Chambers as a nuisance. Even nuisance is too light a word; it is cruelty.'), the Gaelic activists of the 1870s did rather well.

Some of them still requested a return to the Gaelic-medium elementary education of earlier in the nineteenth century. Their argument was what a later generation would describe as 'child-centred'. Mr H.C. Gillies turned the established anglophone manifesto on its head when he told the Gaelic Society of Inverness in November 1876 that it was tuition in English, not Gaelic, that constrained the young Highlander:

> through Gaelic, and Gaelic only, can we have rational, intelligent teaching in Highland schools. At present Gaelic is not much used, and the result is that boys and girls leave school knowing nothing of man or of the world they are about to enter. They go forth, their only recommendation being ignorance of what they should know. This is our education – and it will remain so as long as the native language is not used as a means of culture and an instrument of teaching. The understanding of a Highland child cannot be reached without using Gaelic as a medium for that purpose.

H.C. Gillies' requests were clear and practical. He, and others like him, did not ask for the moon. He wanted Gaelic to be 'the only medium' used to instruct Gaelic-speaking juniors in English and other subjects. Thereafter English could take over as the main channel of communication, with Gaelic reserved as a 'special subject' by the Education Code which established the parameters of state instruction in Scotland, taught to advanced classes of older pupils. He also requested that all examinations and intelligence tests should be available in Gaelic and conducted by Gaelic-speaking inspectors.

The Scottish Privy Council was persuaded in 1876 to establish an inquiry into the demand for and potential use of Gaelic in Highland schools. The Scottish Education Department (SED) consequently circulated a list of relevant questions to all one hundred and two locally elected school boards in the Gaidhealtachd. Ninety of them replied to the circular. Sixty-five, including a strong representation from the Hebrides, insisted that they were in favour of teaching in – not only of – Gaelic. Fifty-three insisted that they were already able to provide Gaelic teachers, while only fourteen admitted to a possible difficulty in recruiting fluent Gaelic instructors.

There have been suggestions that the SED hoped and expected to discover a crippling shortage of qualified Gaelic teachers, which would have enabled them to smother the project at birth. If so, they were disappointed. They received instead a mandate from the majority of school boards north of the Highland Line (in some areas an overwhelming majority) to re-establish Gaelic as both a subject and a medium of instruction in schools. Charles Fraser-Mackintosh commented: 'From the returns it appeared that there were upwards of 20,000 children who ought to be instructed in Gaelic, but who are at present deprived of the great advantages which would accrue from such instruction.'

Their deprivation would continue. The SED's response was slow and reluctant. In 1878, Gaelic was recognised by the Scottish Education Code, which meant that henceforth it could be taught as a school subject – but only if the hard-pressed local school boards found the money from within their existing budgets. The result, as one educationalist would later write, was that 'Gaelic continued to be virtually ignored in the school curriculum . . . It was scarcely surprising that teachers should hesitate to provide for the teaching of a subject not recognised for the award of grants.'

In 1879, the teachers' union, the Educational Institute of Scotland, editorialised in its house journal *Educational News*:

> It is to betray the grossest ignorance of all true education to say that we ought to ignore Gaelic, and teach English from the very beginning. We cannot do this even if we would, and we should not do it even if we could . . . It is utterly impossible to teach these Highland children except through the medium of their own tongue.

The Education Department provided no additional grant for Gaelic instruction until 1885, when the language was elevated to a 'specific subject' and ten shillings a year was made available to boost the stipend of any teacher who taught it.

But the emphasis was by then, as it would remain for a further century, firmly on teaching the language, rather than teaching in the language. It was a crucial distinction. Gaelic became and remained a 'subject', like French or arithmetic, to which a couple of hours tuition might be devoted every week. The notion of Gaelic as a legitimate native language, through which – as countless politicians, educationalists, teachers, ministers, priests and parents had by then argued – French, arithmetic and English could more easily be taught to young children who spoke nothing else, was more or less abandoned. In the Highlands and Islands, the new state elementary schools became forcing schools, devoted initially to squeezing their pupils out of one comfortable, familiar language and into the straitjacket of another. Changes and improvements to the educational status of Gaelic would gradually be made over the course of the twentieth century, but until the 1980s, they would be so slight and occasional as to be almost imperceptible. Primary schools in the Gaidhealtachd would become, on the whole, startlingly good and well-staffed institutions while remaining strangely artificial environments, linguistically alienated from their communities.

Following the passing of the Education Act, adults and children who in the evening and at weekends, in the street, in each others' homes or on the croft might converse in nothing but Gaelic would, upon crossing the schoolroom threshold as teacher and pupil at nine o'clock on Monday morning, switch like automatons to English. This generation, and many succeeding generations, would not quickly lose their language as a result: it was still too strong outside the schoolroom door. But they were indisputably educated out of Gaelic rather than educated in it.

In such circumstances, Gaelic was not only projected by the education authorities as irrelevant, it was made to be irrelevant. The perfect incongruity of teaching children to regard a strange second language as their first and then re-teaching their native language to them as though it was as foreign as German or Latin was not lost on teachers, parents, school boards or the children themselves. Even those compensatory few hours of Gaelic grammar lessons frequently disappeared from Highland elementary and primary curricula.

The importance of elementary education was understood by the middle-class men and women of the late-Victorian Gaelic renaissance, but it did not dominate their toil. The nineteenth century saw starbursts of activity in all areas of Gaelic interest. Exiles established Island societies in the major cities. Glasgow, Greenock, Aberdeen and Dundee followed London and Inverness in forming their own Gaelic societies. A Chair of Gaelic was created at Edinburgh University. Educated Gaels in the Scottish Lowlands and in England embarked on a flurry of literary and journalistic endeavour. Men such as John Francis Campbell, Alexander Carmichael and John Stuart Blackie tramped the Highlands and Islands collecting and recording the folklore of an ancient oral tradition – and occasionally meeting each other on windswept outcrops to swap quatrains and tales of Hebridean hospitality. It has been estimated that between 1830 and 1900 approximately 900 secular Gaelic titles (chiefly translations but including some original work) were published in Scotland. Late-Victorian English-language periodicals, such as John Murdoch's *The Highlander* and John MacKay's *Celtic Monthly*, which specialised in the broad panoply of Highland life from land struggle to shinty, featured Gaelic in their columns and proselytised passionately for the language. The 1885 report of the Napier Commission, set up by William Gladstone's government to examine land hunger and crofting conditions in the Highlands and Islands, diverged from its specific remit to recommend Gaelic-medium education in Highland schools.

Gaelic was no longer voiceless. If anything, it had too many megaphones. In 1891, the first pan-Gaelic organisation – since a short-lived attempt in 1878 to create a Federation of Celtic Societies – was formed. An Comunn Gaidhealach perceived itself as taking a holistic view of the language's health. It would be non-party political (and would, if feasible, have preferred to declare itself above and beyond all forms of politics). It would draw into its warm blanket each and every person – Gael or non-Gael, Tory or Liberal, land raider or landlord – who professed an interest in Gaelic. It would lobby and campaign. But most of all it would create and organise a Gaelic cultural festival of music and verse on the lines of the Welsh Eisteddfod.

An Comunn's first Mòd Nàiseanta, or National Mod, was held a year later in 1892 at Oban. Its rolling revue of Island-society choirs, Ross-shire tenors, Uist pipers and children's recitation would take place every peacetime year thereafter, through and beyond the twentieth century, in cities, towns and islands across Scotland. An Comunn was quick to exploit the House of Battenberg's romantic association with Highland life – a link which stretched unbroken from Queen Victoria's building of a Schloss at Balmoral to the late-twentieth-century Prince of Wales holidaying with a crofter on the small island of Berneray. HM Queen Elizabeth II became the patron of An Comunn Gaidhealach and Am Mòd Nàiseanta evolved into the Royal National Mod. An Comunn would become itself the aristocrat of the Gaelic movement; albeit an aristocrat with a turbulent youth and an occasional tendency even in benign maturity to relapse into strident advocacy of its chosen cause.

Most of the founding members of such bodies as An Comunn Gaidhealach and the Gaelic Society of Inverness saw a large, even a fundamental part of their task as rescuing Gaelic from the infamy of earlier centuries and making it respectable. They were aware, more aware than most, of the slurs which had attached to 'Erse': that it was a mongrel dialect of literary Irish; that it was Samuel Johnson's 'rude speech of a barbarous people'; that it had no pedigree; that it somehow 'held back' its people; that it was guilty by association with Jacobite rebels, recusant Roman Catholics, outlawed cattle-raiders and worse.

They consequently set themselves to restore dignity to the language. They could do this best by retrieving its past from the condescension of posterity. With the reverberations from James Macpherson's Ossian controversy still ringing in their ears, educated Victorian Highlanders walked cautiously into what the Gaelic Society of Inverness called 'the world of letters and philosophy' holding aloft the claims of Gaeldom to its own 'traditions, legends, poetry, sentiments and philosophy'. The immense folklore collections of such a tireless researcher as Alexander Carmichael, an exciseman from the island of Lismore who between 1845 and 1890 travelled 'from Arran to Caithness, from Perth to St Kilda' with his notebooks in his saddlebags, were typically dedicated to the reputation of his people and their culture. After publication of the first two volumes of his *Carmina Gadelica*, Carmichael would write:

> I am profoundly thankful that I have been able to do a little, if but a little, for my much beloved and maligned people. Everything Highland is becoming of interest. Let us show the world that our dearly beloved people were not the rude, barbarous, creedless, Godless, ignorant men and women that prejudiced writers have represented them. It is to me, heart-breaking to see the spiteful manner in which Highlanders have been spoken of.

If there was a drawback to this obsession with restoring the past, it might not have been evident in the 1890s. It was that by placing so much emphasis on tradition, the good people of An Comunn and the Gaelic Society of Inverness were effectively conceding the twentieth century before it had begun. They played out of the hands of their old enemies, who had claimed that Gaelic had no past worth recording, but into the hands of their new enemies, who said that Gaelic had only a past of rural superstitions, sagas and incantation, and that in the past was where it should stay.

They were also sending a dubious message to ordinary Gaels. If their inherited knowledge, language and culture were traditional, what could they say about the modern world? If they were chronically endangered, then what was the common person with common family aspirations (as opposed to the Gaelic evangelist) to do but withdraw? Traditional culture could, it seemed, be only retained or lost – it had no discernible useful future outside the Celtic Department of Edinburgh University. Gaelic, in this light, was a historical romance – as beautiful and artistically valid as any other medieval tapestry, but impractical and suitable only for display at the Mòd Nàiseanta in Inverness or Perth.

As the nineteenth century ended, there were still well over a million native Gaelic-speaking Gaels in the old homelands of Ireland

and Scotland. Two hundred thousand of them were to be found between the Isle of Arran and the Butt of Lewis, up the mountainous seaboard from Kintyre to Cape Wrath and across to Dingwall, Glenmoriston and Strathspey.

The remainder – the residue of the 300,000 or 400,000 Scottish Gaels from the early half of the nineteenth century – had not disappeared from the face of the earth. Nor had they died and gone unreplaced. They were simply no longer within reach of the Scottish National Census. Like the people of Hallaig, they were overseas. They were in townships named Kilmore in south Australia and Sutherland in Nebraska, USA. They were in Dunedin (the Gaelic rendition of Edinburgh) in New Zealand and Glencoe in South Africa. They were in places called Dunvegan and Skye Glen in the Atlantic provinces of Canada, where in 1890 the Canadian House of Commons was told that 75,000 Gaelic speakers lived on Cape Breton alone, and where between 1892 and 1904 the world's first Gaelic-language weekly newspaper, *Mac-Talla* (Echo), was published by a young man named Jonathan MacKinnon who had been born in 1869 to Skye emigrants in the Nova Scotian county of Inverness. Most of this diaspora had scattered during the nineteenth century and very few of its constituents would ever return. The exiles would have their numbers boosted as the twentieth century took hold.

Those who remained decreased in number. The early twentieth century saw the steady increase of a new demographic phenomenon: the Scottish Gael who did not speak Gaelic. The linguistic Highland Line was pushed back, north and west, up to and beyond Lochaber and the Inverness-shire glens. The population of the crofting counties declined, but not so rapidly as the number of Gaelic speakers. Between 1901 and 1931, the total of native Gaelic speakers living in Scotland fell from 202,700 (4.5 per cent of the population) to 129,419 (2.7 per cent). They were mostly to be found in the Hebridean islands north of Islay and in the thin littoral of Argyllshire, Inverness-shire, Ross and Sutherland. The old frontier, which just 50 years previously had still roughly shadowed the geographic Highland boundary, had been irrecoverably breached.

The linguistic despoliation of certain key areas could occur within a single lifetime. When Calum Iain Maclean, a Gaelic folklorist who had been born as a younger brother of Sorley on the island of Raasay in 1915, visited Lochaber in the early 1950s, he discovered, as he recorded in *The Highlands*, that:

> A new culture had penetrated the Rough Bounds (Garbhchrìochan) of the Gael and was sweeping before it all traces, all memories of the past . . . The culture of Hollywood has certainly influenced youth in Lochaber today. Formal education during the past seventy years did not help much to instil into Highland youth a pride or interest in their native districts. There is hardly one child in any school in Lochaber today who will be able to read, write or even speak Gaelic on reaching school-leaving age. Yet English was a completely foreign language in Lochaber until the advent of the West Highland Railway in the final decade of last century.

Calum Iain Maclean employed some forgivable exaggeration. English had been a force in some urbanised districts of Lochaber before the 1890s. The celebrated Father Allan McDonald of Eriskay, for instance, was born in Fort William in 1859 to working-class Highland parents but was raised in English and, as a Gaelic learner in the Hebrides, would often bemoan the accident of birth which had landed him in an anglophone town rather than in the open countryside two miles north, south, east or west, where Gaelic would have come as naturally to him as it did to his Eriskay flock.

But the twentieth-century drift was inescapable and the essence of Calum Iain's observations were sound. In the 1950s, he discovered a Lochaber in which Gaelic might not yet be dead, but was rarely used. Yet just 70 years earlier, the large Lochaber parishes of Kilmonivaig, Kilmallie and Laggan had contained a total of 5,561 people, 4,488 of whom were native, habitual Gaelic speakers.

Some efforts were made to cater for the language. The Education (Scotland) Bill of 1918 included a Gaelic amendment which would supposedly allow Gaelic to be taught at all levels of education within the Gaidhealtachd. By the 1930s, 284 schools, chiefly in the Highlands and Islands, were offering the language to 7,000 pupils – but as a separate subject, as a curriculum item, rather than as a primary medium of instruction. Young Gaels were still first being educated out of Gaelic and then, almost as an afterthought, being taught it in class through the medium of English.

Gaelic had become what it would remain for most of the twentieth century: the everyday vernacular of an indigenous rural working class; the default tongue when speaking among themselves of their sons and daughters in the city universities or working the herring fleets off Lowestoft; and the special interest of a handful of concerned academics and professionals in Edinburgh, Glasgow and London. The latter two groups would not alone have sustained the language. Its bulwark against extinction was the marvellous, thousand-year-old attachment to their native Gaelic of the north-western crofting community. As this crofting class declined, reaped in the thousands by two world wars and in peacetime by the relative stagnation of the Highland economy, so too did its language.

The academics and professionals whose self-appointed task it was to monitor such things were naturally aware of the problem. But times had changed dramatically since the 1890s, for Edinburgh professors and Hebridean islanders alike. The peaceful, self-absorbed domestic world of the *fin de siècle* exploded in 1914. The international cataclysms of the first half of the twentieth century, the mountainous demands of global ideologies and conflicts, reduced the cares of Scottish Gaelic even among users of the language to a hill of beans.

The apparent irrelevance of the language began, most shockingly, to be reflected in the Highland home. In 1936, An Comunn Gaidhealach stirred itself to commission a report on the language through the prism of a focus group of 14 pupils and their parents. An Comunn concluded that: 'The majority of Gaelic-speaking parents are averse to the speaking of Gaelic to their children; they discourage the use of it so that their children have very imperfect English and no Gaelic.'

This was evidently an unrepresentative sample group, which resulted in an overly pessimistic conclusion. If the 'majority' of Gaelic-speaking parents in 1936 refused to speak the language to their sons and daughters there would have been vanishingly few Gaelic speakers left by 1971, when in fact there were still 89,000 of them – almost all of whom, it should be added, were also perfectly fluent in English.

But An Comunn had identified an undeniable trend. The rise of English as a global lingua franca, the arrival of the British Broadcasting Corporation's radio services in the furthermost corners of the United Kingdom, the education system's continuing relegation of Gaelic to fourth-class citizenry – all these factors meant that, to a rural Highland Gaelic community which seemed to regress in steady counterpoint as the rest of Britain developed, urbanised and expanded, the beauty and ease of their mother language appeared to be an expensive consolation. They and even their children might never be wholly comfortable in English; no language but Gaelic could ever properly frame or express their culture, environment and character. But if – when they got off the ferry in Oban or the bus at Fort William – Gaelic was as useless as a peat-iron, what price was being paid for that ancient attachment?

The price was in fact substantial. When Christine A. Smith came to examine the effect of an English education on Gaelic-speaking children in rural Lewis in 1943 and 1944, she unsurprisingly discovered that one was quite unsuited to the other. By the middle of the twentieth century the stock cultural content of much of the state-school curriculum was foreign to the young Gael. Such common-or-garden features of southern primary textbooks as circuses, railway stations, lamp-posts and cricket bats were unrecognisable in the Lewis townships of Ness and Lochs. Christine Smith could have continued almost indefinitely to include dogs on leads, taxi cabs, coalmen and dustmen and a hundred other everyday features of life in Glasgow, Kilmarnock or Brighton which would have been as baffling to a Hebridean schoolchild as an illustration of a peat-stack or a shinty stick to her urban equivalent.

The result was that the educational performances of many Gaelic children were unnaturally depressed. They often scored badly in IQ tests and were stigmatised by Lowland teachers and external inspectors as shy, slow, reticent, unambitious and even genetically lazy.

It seemed a downward spiral with one inevitable destination. In 1951, the first National Census for 20 years recorded 93,269 Gaelic speakers, which was probably the first time in over 1,000 years that the number had fallen below 100,000.

They were fewer than 2 per cent of the Scottish population, and the dry rot had reached even the Western Isles. Between 1957 and 1959, the Bilingualism Committee of the Scottish Council for Research in Education reported from the Hebrides:

> The process of Anglicisation begins historically around the official centres of transport on the east side of the island opposite the mainland. Thereafter, an English 'pale' develops inland from the bridge or pierhead. It may be some time before the development makes any marked advance inland. This is still true of Stornoway in Lewis . . . In Skye, on the other hand, as can be seen around Portree and Kyleakin, the development once begun soon spread. Before the 'breakthrough' occurs there are signs of the times to be seen here and there. What happens is that localities, such as Elgol in Skye at the present time [late 1950s], that were traditionally Gaelic, tend to become Anglicised for various local reasons, and then the whole front proceeds to break up. That process is now nearing completion in Mull and Islay.

If by 'completion' the Bilingualism Committee meant the extermination of Gaelic, it was not so near as they thought. The language would hang on in pockets of Mull and Islay and in Elgol.

Its tenacity, its ability to stay alive, even as a minority tongue in its own homeland, would be a notable feature of Gaelic in the twentieth century. But its erosion was indisputable.

The Bilingualism Committee's 1959 report effectively identified this erosion of community. If English was the vehicle of commerce, and commerce brought with it tradespeople from abroad, and those tradespeople found themselves in an island or a parish where it was no longer necessary to achieve fluency in Gaelic because everybody else spoke English, then they and their families were so much less likely to adopt the language. Those qualifications may not have been in place 50 years before, and certainly did not apply in the middle of the nineteenth century, but by the National Census of 1971, only 477 persons in the whole of Scotland were identified as speaking only Gaelic – and many of those would have been pre-school-aged Hebridean children. The result was not the quick death of the language, as many people presupposed, but its relegation to a secondary tongue in communities where the 'default' language – a category, much loved by linguists, which means in this case the language first used in open company by people who are fluent in Gaelic and English – ceased to be Gaelic and became English. Gaelic did not consequently disappear. It merely ceased to be the medium of the shop and the pierhead as it had already ceased to be that of the school. It retreated to the home and the sheep fank.

And in time it might even be banished from those sanctuaries. The ebb and flow of people, the social mobility which accelerated throughout the twentieth century, was slow to reach the mainland Scottish Gaidhealtachd and even slower to reach the islands. As late as 1974 some 90 per cent of the married couples of Back, a heavily populated crofting community a few miles up the east coast of Lewis from Stornoway, had selected their spouses from within a five-mile radius. In other words, Gaelic speakers had married Gaelic speakers. If a man and a woman from Back or anywhere else first conversed in Gaelic, they would more often than not continue their relationship in Gaelic. If they married, Gaelic would become the language of their home and, ineluctably, of their children.

But as the twentieth century passed, as car ferries were introduced to Stornoway and Lochmaddy and passenger aeroplane services arrived, young men and women from such islands as Lewis and the Uists increasingly married people from outside the shrinking Gaidhealtachd – from Kent, or Glasgow, or Inverness, or even Kyle of Lochalsh. Their default language, and consequently the language of their home in Back or Daliburgh as much as in Canterbury, would be English.

In a free society, there was clearly no way of forcibly halting this trend, or of slowing it down. The Gaelic language would have to learn to live with social mobility – the same social mobility which had, after all, first introduced it to Scotland 1,500 years earlier. That required above all else a renewal.

Two

By the 1970s, as we have seen, there remained in Scotland a small handful of adults who spoke only Gaelic. In his introduction to an anthology of the verse of Father Allan McDonald of Eriskay, the author and scholar Ronald Black described the implications for himself of meeting one of those precious souls in Maighstir Ailein's island in 1966.

Eriskay people then in their 70s, Black discovered, had learned their catechism from Father Allan at the turn of the century:

> Liveliest of all were the recollections of a delightful old lady at Acarsaid who spoke no English. Would that there were still monoglots like her around in the twenty-first century to encourage our young people to dig deep for their Gaelic in the way I had to do that day!
>
> When I came back four years later [in 1970] . . . Eriskay had begun to change. A café had appeared, and I no longer met ponies being led off the hill with panniers of peats. But the old lady was still in Acarsaid.

That charming *cailleach*, surviving into the age of moon landings and outliving the use of Eriskay ponies to fetch home peats, embodied nonetheless the end of another era for her native language. When she was born there had been over 40,000 monoglot Gaels in Scotland. Her own parish of South Uist, Benbecula and Eriskay had in the 1890s a total population of 5,821, of whom 5,532 spoke Gaelic, 3,430 spoke only Gaelic and just 289 spoke no Gaelic. (They must, suggested the Hebridean historian John Lorne Campbell, have been tourists or visiting fishermen: 'Very few persons then resident in Uist can have been entirely ignorant of Gaelic, which was then essential for anyone doing business on the island.' In fact, as Campbell knew well, at least 3 of the 289 anglophones were a headteacher and his family who had arrived at Garrynamonie School in South Uist from Birmingham.)

When Ronnie Black's 'delightful old lady' died, she took her perfect vernacular Gaelic, honed and embellished by a lifetime's use as a first and only language, away with her. It could not, as Ronnie Black discerned, be replaced. There were still in the 1970s almost 90,000 native speakers left, most of them with enviable fluency and many of them using nothing but Gaelic from one week's end to the next. Enough work had been done by enough scholars to ensure that the finer details of the language and the more arcane features of its lexicography would be saved for posterity. But by the end of the 1970s, there was not a township or a peat cutting in the loneliest of Hebridean islands at which English could not be used. Gaelic was no longer essential for anyone doing any form of business anywhere.

Such bilingual environments were not new. They had prevailed for centuries on the shifting frontier between Highland and Lowland Scotland, in the Celtic departments and the Celtic societies and in the Minch ports. But they had never previously occurred throughout all of the language's innermost redoubts, from the west coast of Lewis to the southern shores of Uist.

The educated Gaels of the early twentieth century saw the spread of bilingualism coming. Recognition and use of Gaelic by the state school system continued to be piecemeal and churlish. The Education Act of 1908 ignored the language, and consequently shored up the inadequate status quo. During the First World War, in 1915, some teenaged students benefited from the introduction of a Gaelic Higher-grade paper. As we have seen, a 'Gaelic clause' was inserted into the 1918 Education Act, but it merely obliged education authorities to prepare 'adequate provision for teaching Gaelic in Gaelic-speaking areas', without defining the word 'adequate' or the demographics of a 'Gaelic-speaking area' and once again without recognising the demand or requirement for teaching through the medium of Gaelic.

The Schools Gaelic Supervisor Murdo MacLeod wrote in 1963:

> These concessions helped to promote the teaching of Gaelic to older pupils, often in an arid, academic fashion through the medium of English, but they did nothing to improve the position in the primary school, where Gaelic as a teaching medium would have proved most valuable . . . As a result . . . more emphasis was placed on the teaching of Gaelic as a subject, but this instruction was mainly confined to secondary departments and advanced divisions. The general pattern in the education of Gaelic speaking children continued to be one of using Gaelic only when necessity dictated its use. As soon as the Gaelic speaking child had acquired a modest acquaintance with English, Gaelic was almost completely discarded until its study was taken up in a desultory manner in the upper primary classes.
>
> This peremptory exclusion of the Highland pupil's native language persisted despite an increasingly sympathetic outlook on the part of the Scottish Education Department. It is, perhaps, not surprising that the bias against Gaelic, which was for so many years the official attitude, should have communicated itself to the schools, and should have produced in many native Gaelic speakers an apparently irrational but quite understandable prejudice, which shows itself either in indifference or in a conscious determination that their children are not to be exposed to the 'disadvantages' of bilingualism.

That 'apparently irrational prejudice' of some Gaelic-speaking adults against their own language would be a feature of the twentieth-century debate. It was far from being a new phenomenon. In 1889, Revd Donald Masson claimed that earlier in the nineteenth century, some church schools which had in theory been prepared to use Gaelic rarely in practice did so because 'the parents in many cases, even those of them who themselves knew little or no English, were dead against the teaching of Gaelic; they wished their children to learn English, that they might get on in the world.'

Such Gaelic refuseniks would become part of the ammunition of such strident anti-Gaelic campaigners as William Chambers and his successors down to the twenty-first century. It has been, in endless repetition, decade after decade, an effective but wholly dishonest argument. It has echoed through the years: 'Why should I bother about/my taxes pay for/my television be cluttered up with Gaelic speakers/schools/broadcasts when Gaelic speakers themselves can't be bothered with the stuff?' But Highland parents, from the Middle Ages onwards, who wished their children to learn English were neither rare nor disloyal to Gaelic. Many if not most of them had already ensured that their children were fluent Gaelic speakers; they merely wished the schools to give them fluency in a second or a third language. In the first half of the twentieth century, when schools and all other agencies of the state effectively ignored or actively blacklisted Gaelic, if parents had adopted a similar attitude to the language, it would have died before the end of the second millennium.

In fact, Highland parents were uniquely successful in and almost solely responsible for keeping Gaelic alive, even in the adverse circumstances of the growing towns and business centres. The journalist and broadcaster Martin MacDonald was born in Achachork, some two miles outside Portree, and recalls the late 1930s and early 1940s in the Skye capital and its hinterlands.

'I don't think we thought a lot about the survival of the language,' he says. 'In the crofting communities, everybody spoke it at that time, so you had to speak it if you were going to work in the fank. If you were going to do anything with sheep, everybody around you spoke Gaelic and if you didn't speak Gaelic you felt rather strange and out of it. Conversation in all the houses outside Portree –

Penifiler, Drumuie, Achachork, Torvaig – the domestic language was Gaelic actually. It changed slightly in the streets of Portree. You would challenge people and they would say, "Och well, probably there's no great future for it."

'We were Gaelic speaking – most of Portree was Gaelic speaking, but we didn't realise it at the time. A lot of my schoolmates from Portree were Gaelic speaking, but we didn't realise that until we left school. They didn't use it at school, they used it at home, it wasn't encouraged at school – it wasn't the bad old days where you got belted if you spoke it, but I think the education system had decided to do without Gaelic. Some of the lads, like Ian MacDougall and I, we always talked Gaelic to each other down by the shore there.

'Looking back, and I've got a photograph of my primary qualifying class, my last year – primary five it was in my day, it's now seven – looking back at these kids, more than 50 per cent of us from the village of Portree were Gaelic speakers, we just didn't realise it at the time. Only three or four of us realised it, because we were either related or were next-door neighbours and the families spoke Gaelic to each other, so we spoke Gaelic to each other.

'We didn't realise that the other kids also spoke Gaelic at home. In fact, I was in the ludicrous position, in 1986, when I was back at the BBC as manager of Radio Highland, I think it was a Gaelic current affairs programme, and we'd been doing the news schedule in the morning, and I said, "How are you getting on? Have you got a spokesman for the Department of Social Security?" or something like that. They said, "Yes, we've found one. She's from Portree, Christine MacDonald." I said, "Christine MacDonald from Portree? She doesn't speak Gaelic." They said, "Yes, she does." I said, "No, she doesn't. I sat beside her until primary five." There was an imbalance between boys and girls so Christine and I had sat together in the back seat. My colleagues at the BBC said, "Well, she's got Gaelic." You know, this was 1986 and I'd sat beside the girl for day after day in class in 1949 – and she was a fluent Gaelic speaker and I'd never known it.

'I remember, having left school in Portree, roaming the local dances in the early 1960s, actually when I'd gone back to Skye and was working as a freelancer, I was suddenly struck by the number of young people who didn't speak Gaelic. But Gaelic was quite prevalent at the dances – the Skeabost dances, Uig dances, Kilmuir, and Portree in the Skye Gathering. And there was a number of people who would use a few phrases in Gaelic who actually didn't speak the language, but to be part of the company you would hear them say "A *bhalaich*" – boy. You know, people like that who are pro-Gaelic and are saying: "Look, we are part of this even if we don't speak the language."

'I was quite struck by that, and the other thing that always occurred to me was that people, maybe in their 20s, from a Gaelic background can feel deprived of the language. I have spoken to a number of people who say: "I just feel deprived, there's something missing in my life," or "There's some part of me that's missing" and it's something to do with identity. I think that's why education is important, even more important than the survival of the language in itself. People should never be put in that place, in that situation of feeling that part of their identity is missing, somehow or other – you know, because they can't handle this language.

'I remember a girl in Portree, Louise MacLeod, she was brought up in Portree and married Ally Ruadh from Bernisdale. Ally of course had Gaelic, and Louise told me that she said to her mother, "Why didn't you teach me Gaelic when I was young?" Her mother said, "We tried to, but you wouldn't listen." A lot of kids would say their parents were using it as a private language, blaming the parents. The parents were probably using their old familiar language, but the kids and their peer group were into other things. So they probably didn't speak Gaelic. And the school didn't encourage it. So, for one reason or another, it fell out of use.'

The wonder was not that some twentieth-century Gaels wanted their children to learn English, but that so many of them continued to ensure that the next generation spoke Gaelic. In an age of bilingualism, it would have been feasible for whole Hebridean communities – and certainly for a majority of households within those communities – to switch wholesale into English and by doing so discomfort only a handful of old-age pensioners. The twentieth-century education system clearly wished them to do so. The twentieth-century media almost demanded it of them. The twentieth-century businesses and industries which beckoned their people made no allowance at all for their language.

It was surprising not that some parents expressed reservations about the usefulness of Gaelic to school-leavers in the space age but that hundreds of thousands of parents throughout the twentieth century held on to their language with proud obstinacy even while radio and television were filling their homes with the vocabulary of an ascendant tongue. The tenacity of the Gaelic language during a hundred years of harsh and stony soil is more remarkable by far than its decline – and its grip on life is owed almost entirely to the mothers and fathers of successive generations of Scottish Highlanders. Far from encouraging the Scottish Education Department's extirpation of Gaelic, those parents flew in the face of authoritative advice and kept the language alive.

In the twentieth century, it survived almost as an underground demotic. Gaelic had not for a very long time been the majority language of Scotland. Unlike Welsh and Irish, it was not regarded as a political banner by its country's governing classes. Historical divisions in Scottish society between Highlander and Lowlander, Protestant and Catholic had on the contrary bred a powerful atavistic mistrust among many Central Belt opinion-formers and bureaucrats of the culture of Irish-speaking cattle-raiders from north of Stirlingshire.

Gaelic did not, in consequence, have a high profile within Scotland, let alone south of the border. It was rarely heard except in its north-western redoubts or under the 'Hielanman's Umbrella' (the railway bridge in Glasgow's Argyle Street beneath which exiled Gaels congregated) or in the Gaelic churches and societies of the southern cities. The true condition of the language, its level of usage and importance, was therefore opaque to foreign eyes. When an observer of British social and political life as astute and sensitive as George Orwell went to live on the island of Jura in 1946, he arrived in almost total ignorance of the language of his new neighbours. It took first-hand experience to lead him to prepare, in February 1947, a supportive essay. He wrote with an uncertain grasp of the precise facts but a characteristically sure feel for the kernel of the matter:

> In the Gaelic-speaking areas, Gaelic is not taught in the schools.
>
> I am speaking from limited experience, but I should say that this is beginning to cause resentment. Also, the BBC only broadcasts two or three half-hour Gaelic [radio] programmes a week, and they give the impression of being rather amateurish programmes. Even so they are eagerly listened to. How easy it would be to buy a little goodwill by putting on a Gaelic programme at least once daily.
>
> At one time I would have said that it is absurd to keep alive an archaic language like Gaelic, spoken by only a few hundred thousand people [the 1951 census in fact recorded 93,269 Scottish Gaelic speakers]. Now I am not so sure. To begin with, if people feel that they have a special culture which ought to be preserved, and that the language is part of it, difficulties should not be put in their way when they want their children to learn it properly. Secondly, it is probable that the effort of being bilingual is a valuable education in itself. The Scottish Gaelic-speaking peasants speak beautiful English, partly, I think, because English is an almost foreign language which they sometimes do not use for days together. Probably they benefit intellectually by having to be aware of dictionaries and grammatical rules, as their English opposite numbers would not be.

There was a touch of Victorian condescension to Orwell's advice; surely the point of keeping Gaelic alive was not to enable Gaels to speak more precise English. But his comments about the value of bilingualism were more percipient than he can have known.

George Orwell encountered in the late 1940s a Scottish Gaidhealtachd which was – albeit in small pockets – healthier than it had a right to be. Farquhar MacIntosh was born in 1923 in one of those pockets. Elgol in Skye would, in the 1950s, be identified by the Scottish Council for Research in Education as a district of rapid Anglicisation. But in the 1920s and '30s, 'We always spoke Gaelic at home and I often say that when I went to school, I had two words of English, "yes" and "no", and probably used them wrongly. So all my English was acquired at school where Gaelic was hardly ever used. The headmaster was a chap, R.E. Dunoon, who was not a Gaelic speaker, and his assistant, who came from Broadford in Skye, was a Robertson. She spoke Gaelic but hardly ever used it in school, and we were not encouraged to use it. But we used it in the playground – everybody at Elgol Primary School was a Gaelic speaker, over 40 pupils, and it was Gaelic that was the language of the playground, down by the sea there.'

There was no Gaelic whatsoever in Farquhar MacIntosh's formal education until he left Elgol to attend Portree High School, where he would later be headmaster, in 1935. 'To get there, you had to win a bursary, because my parents couldn't have afforded to pay the hostel – you had to live in a hostel then. I might as well have gone to school in Edinburgh or Glasgow! I'd be twelve and a half. I got a county bursary which paid the cost of the hostel and I got a MacLeod of Skeabost Scholarship which helped to make up for any deficit, so that it was more or less free education as far as my parents were concerned.'

And his education for the very first time, not untypically, began to include Gaelic. 'I did Higher Gaelic at Portree School. That was when I became literate in Gaelic. In fact, at that time, you had to do Latin as one of your languages – I don't think it mattered which school you went to at that time, you had to do Latin in secondary school, or grammar school or whatever you like to call them, academies – and I went to do French along with it and I was a week in the French. You got no guidance; certain subjects you had to do, mathematics you had to do, a science, and you had to do either history or geography and for the first three years you had to do a bit of both.

'So I went there and after a week John Steele, who was head of Gaelic at that time, as he was when I went back to Portree High School as headmaster, came into the French teacher's room and he said, "Excuse me, there are a numbers of pupils here who ought to be in my class because they come from parts of Skye where they are fluent Gaelic speakers," and he marched three or four of us out into his class. I was sorry later on because you weren't allowed to do three languages, and I would have liked to have done French. I didn't regret doing Gaelic at all, but I wish I had been able to do French as well.'

Farquhar MacIntosh's odyssey through the Scottish educational system was interrupted by the Second World War. After service in the Royal Navy, he returned to Edinburgh University to read history. 'But I also did two years doing Celtic studies as well because I wasn't sure what I wanted to do; I hadn't done history at school because it wasn't offered as a Higher in my time.

'Celtic studies was taken by a Professor Dillon from Ireland, who was the Edinburgh University professor at the time, and a chap called Kenneth Craig, who was killed in an earthquake in Yugoslavia later on. The two of them didn't get on terribly well because Craig was a rather ardent Protestant and he thought he would have got the Chair himself when Professor Carmichael Watson, who was drowned in the navy in the Mediterranean during the war, when his Chair was filled – in 1946 it would be, it was after the war was over anyway. Kenneth Craig applied for it and didn't get it, and they took on this Professor Michael Dillon, whom I liked. He came over from Ireland, and of course he was a Catholic as well. I remember Craig going round a number of us and asking us to sign a petition saying that he had been promised the Chair by Professor Carmichael Watson and I said, "But the Chair is not in the gift of the outgoing professor – that's the duty of the university authorities to appoint," so I think we all refused to sign. But it wasn't a happy period. I might indeed have chosen to do Honours in Celtic studies rather than in history if the department had been a more friendly place. The course consisted largely of academic study of Scottish Gaelic, both the language itself from a linguistic point of view and Scottish Gaelic literature, also you had to do a little Welsh and, in the second year, quite a lot of Irish. I had done a little Irish at school.'

Such was the journey of the educated Gael through the middle of the twentieth century. Teachers, such as Farquhar MacIntosh's John Steele, who remained fiercely loyal to and protective of their shared heritage played a disproportionate role in elevating the language out of the indifference of the education system.

In some cases, the role of those people was above and beyond the call of duty. Thanks to a curious set of circumstances in the early 1960s, Duncan MacQuarrie found himself one of the first Mull schoolchildren since the Middle Ages to be taught Latin through the medium of Gaelic!

MacQuarrie's family experience embodied much of what was lost in this period in the southern and Inner Hebrides. He was born in the middle of the 1940s into one of the richest social and cultural traditions in the Scottish Gaidhealtachd. His father's family was from Bunessan on the Ross of Mull, a crofting peninsula which reaches out to Columba's island of Iona, and from the offshore island of Ulva, the erstwhile home of the parents of the Victorian explorer David Livingstone.

'My MacQuarrie grandfather was Lachlan MacQuarrie and my MacLean grandfather was Duncan MacLean, and Duncan gave testimony to the Napier Commission at Kilfinichen Church. This was on Duke of Argyll territory of course, and that testimony traditionally was given at midnight so that they could escape the Duke's baillies, and the people giving testimonies had people with them to protect them from the baillies.

'This same Duncan's father, who was my great-grandfather, was a first cousin of Mary MacDonald, who wrote the Gaelic hymn "Child in a Manger". Duncan looked after her after she was widowed, because the Duke of Argyll, in these days, evicted widowed women from their crofts or parcels of land, and he gave that testimony to the Napier Commission. My MacQuarrie grandfather was evicted from Ulva in November 1849 by Francis Clark, the owner of Ulva who had bought it from the last MacQuarrie chief. Legend has it that when they went to pay their rents the previous May Day, the rents were taken but they were not given receipts. When they went to pay their rents on November rent day, they were accused of not having paid their previous sums of money and, of course, had no proof.

'As a result, the cattle and the houses and suchlike were confiscated and virtually all of Ulva, 400 to 500 people, ended up on a point of land which is known to this day as Starvation Point, Rubh' an Acrais. I got back to Ulva recently for the very first time. I am the first of my family to be able to get back, because the island was closed all these years by the landlord trouble. So that was the first time any of our family has been back in that time. So my roots on that side go very deep indeed in the traditions and history of Mull and of its language.

'My mother was from Harris and she and my father met when they were both working in John Brown's in Clydebank, of all romantic places, just before the war and during the war, and they married during the war. Her family are still in Harris, she has two sisters still alive, and I have a legion of cousins on that side. I have very few relations on the Mull side, and the only close relation is a first cousin of my father who is eighty-five, which is quite sad in a way, but that was the way, of two families of eight, only three men appeared, and that was the way of things.

'And so I'm imbued with the traditions of both the Outer Isles and the Inner Isles although probably the Inner Isles traditions are the stronger in that I was brought up there, in Tobermory, and this was in the '50s.

'At that time, if you wanted to go on to education to do certificate work at either O grade or Higher, you had to leave home and go off to Oban High School or anywhere else, but Oban High School was the usual destination. At that time there were three schools of such kind in Argyll – Campbeltown Grammar, Dunoon Grammar, Oban High School – and when I was in Oban High School, a couple of years behind me in Dunoon Grammar was the future founder of the *West Highland Free Press*, Brian Wilson. We used to debate against each other!

'I went into lodgings in Oban. I left home in August and went home at Christmas, which was much the same experience as people from Uist and Harris and suchlike had in Inverness-shire, and the whole thing was controlled by an iniquitous system of IQ exams, 11-pluses and 14-pluses. Your reward for succeeding was to be sent away from home and your reward for failing was to be able to stay at home. So the whole process was, in many ways, one of de-culturalisation, and I believe, I don't know if there is any research evidence to back this up, that one of the strongest periods in which young people acquire cultural values is between the ages of 12 and 15 or 16, and the cultural values of rural Gaeldom and of the language itself and of the ideas of poets and authors and artists of all kinds were, in many respects, lost to these people because they were wrenched from the background in which they could have learnt these in the community.

'I was very fortunate, in my personal circumstances, in that my father and mother were late in marrying and I was brought up without any English, and I don't think I had any when I went to school – not that I can remember, but so I'm told. My father's mother was still alive as an old lady and she had two brothers, one of whom survived until I was well into my 20s, so I had a huge resource of Gaelic *dualchas*, of heritage, and they themselves, in their time, had been key contributors to the School of Scottish Studies. Their collectors such as Calum Maclean and Alan Bruford were frequent visitors to our house, because my grandparents came to live with us in their old age and they were both born in Victorian times. My grandmother died at the age of 95 in 1965, and her brother Archie was 92 in the early '70s when he died.

'So, Archie, for example, met a man who met a man who had been at Culloden, which just shows you how short history is. He had a fantastic memory and all the songs he knew, he knew who taught him the song, who he heard it from and who that person heard it from – he could give the genealogy of the song. I remember being fascinated by him telling me, not that I can remember it just now, a Mac Mhaighstir Alasdair song and the three steps, three points of human contact, between him hearing it personally and the poet originally reciting it.

'But I had no Gaelic education until the middle of primary six, when I was transferred to a little school that my father had become schoolmaster of in Salen. He had taught us at home, my brother and sister as well, to read and write Gaelic and then he taught us formally in the school in short lessons.

'When I went to Tobermory Secondary, I did Gaelic as a subject and, at that point, there was a teacher from the Isle of Scarp, a fascinating man by the name of Alan Norman MacLean, who was a brilliant teacher, and it ended up that I was the only person doing Latin in the whole of my year group, and once a couple of other people who were there had gone, Alan switched to teaching me Latin through the medium of Gaelic. That was informally and it was, as it were, at that time, an eccentricity of Alan's. But it did me the world of good.

'From there I went on to Oban High School, where I was taught Gaelic by the legendary Donald Thompson and the equally legendary John Maclean, Sorley's brother, who was Rector. Then I went to Glasgow University to study under, again, the legendary Derick Thomson. I did Celtic studies plus some history and some English – Celtic studies took in Scots Gaelic, Irish and Welsh, and you had to work in all three languages, plus history and linguistics and things of that kind. I did my four years there and elected to go to Jordanhill to train as a teacher.'

Mull was no minor outpost of the Scottish Gaidhealtachd. It was, in living memory, a fulcrum of the culture. In view of its proximity to the anglophone south, it is remarkable that so much survived there for so long. The idiosyncratic beauty of Mull Gaelic – refined over centuries in a big landmass which lay, unlike the larger northern islands, at the geographical heart of the Gaelic world of the islands and north-western seaboard – was a precious asset, held close to their breaking hearts by people such Duncan MacQuarrie's parents. The island's main town of Tobermory had living links not only with the mainland railhead of Oban and the historically vital Gaelic district of Argyllshire, but with Islay, Coll, Tiree, Barra and Lochaber. The pipe bands travelled to and fro, alongside the fishermen and ferrymen and intermarried families. Tobermory had also a vast, sustaining hinterland; a relationship with its Gaelic countryside which would survive in greater isolation and different degree between Stornoway and Lewis, between Portree and Skye.

But this was not Lewis: this was Mull. It was a separate, a vital and essential component of the Gaidhealtachd, the third-largest landmass in the Hebrides. In the 1820s, the 3 parishes of Mull contained a total of 10,500 people, almost every one of whom was a Gaelic speaker. By 1881, when Duncan MacQuarrie's grandmother was a girl, the island's population had fallen to 5,600, 95 per cent of whom spoke Gaelic. When the young Duncan MacQuarrie was being taught Latin through Gaelic by Alan Norman MacLean at Tobermory High School in 1961, only 2,024 people still lived in Mull. And as native Gaelic speakers, Duncan and Alan were then part of a minority in the largest and most important of all the Inner Hebrides. By 2003, when Duncan MacQuarrie became the first member of his family since 1849 to revisit their ancestral seat at Ulva, the population of Mull had risen again slightly to 2,821. Just 564 of them had any fluency in Gaelic.

Many of the technological advances of the twentieth century were slow to reach the Scottish Highlands and Islands. Car ferries, for instance, did not begin to serve the Uists until the early 1960s. Radio was widely if sporadically available, as George Orwell learned, from the 1930s onwards, but television did not arrive in some north-western homes until the 1970s (and in a very few until the advent of satellite broadcasting in the 1980s). When the ferries did begin to dock and the TV programmes were beamed in, they brought with them a virtually hegemonous diet of English. Even that apparently innocuous device, the telephone, subverted the social habits of a pre-industrial society.

Alan Campbell, who would become a prominent Gaelic activist, was born in the Skye township of Colbost in 1948. 'My early memories,' he recalls, 'are of a very busy, bustling village, everybody Gaelic speaking. Everyone walked everywhere, there wasn't even a bicycle, there were no cars. My father subsequently got a motorcycle, and he was unique in the sense that he was one of these people who enjoyed any form of mechanical conveyance. I remember very clearly how we then still had the tradition of community cooperation, and things like sheep-shearing, dipping and gathering, peat-cutting and potato-planting, harvest time, it was the done thing to work with your neighbour. They had a saying in Gaelic: *lìonmhorachd do làmh* – many hands make light work – and that was very much the philosophy of the village.

'The other thing that I suppose with hindsight I am very conscious of was that, after a day's work, it didn't matter how long that day was, it was quite common for a neighbour to take a stroll and visit another neighbour and just blether for an hour or whatever. You frequently got, let's say, if you can imagine a house say halfway through the village, you would get people coming from both ends of the village and meeting there – it might be just an individual from each end, but if there was any news of importance, that was how that news was immediately transmitted through that village because the two recipients of that news from the central point then distributed it as they went. News of a death, a funeral, some event in the village, something that had to be done.

'It was years later, maybe in the late '50s and early '60s, that the telephone became common to us and every house had a phone. I think ours was one of the first houses in the village to have a phone, and people used to come to make a telephone call because our house was nearer than the post office, which was one and a half miles away, or a public kiosk further down the village which was a mile away. Then people started getting the telephone in their homes and, almost without anyone being aware of it, the ceilidh, this casual dropping in, just stopped.

'I believe that the telephone was the real killer of the ceilidh, of what was the means of distributing news – that was long before television came – and the attitude of people was that maybe you had to realise that people were getting a bit older then as well, and if you had had a hard day, you just wanted to put your feet up and you didn't want to walk a mile and then a mile back, or half a mile or whatever it was, just to visit a neighbour.

'The other factor was that people took this attitude that if there was news, you would hear about it because the means was there in the telephone of somebody contacting you. So there was an assumption that if the phone didn't ring, there was no news, and I suppose that was true, that was a fact. But hitherto, you didn't know whether there was news, so you went to check, you made that visit, you made that effort and having made that effort, if you got there and you found there was no news, you didn't just immediately leave, you would start a little conversation and, quite often, because people were good storytellers and because they enjoyed the camaraderie, the *craic*, they would start swapping anecdotes and memories, and those of us who were younger would hear that, and we were, if you like, given that precious cultural heritage of what was anecdotal to the village and to the community.

'I remember a lot of that yet – it never ceases to amaze me that when my own father was on his deathbed, six years ago at eighty years old, he was still retelling, for the umpteenth time, some anecdotes of people who certainly were dead long before my time, some of them I suspect might have been dead before my father's own time. That was an extraordinary thing – because it was witty or because it was pithy, people remembered it and they retold it: "I remember the day John MacDonald, somebody said so-and-so to him and he replied . . ." and whatever John replied was so good that people would want to tell everyone, and sometimes these little things got a little embellished, as you can imagine.

'In fact, a cousin of my grandfather was something of a malapropist and he was never stuck for a word, and his Gaelic was without a shadow of a doubt better than his English. That didn't stop him, and if he wasn't sure of your name, he just gave you the one that he seemed to think suited. For example [the feudal superior] Dame Flora MacLeod of Dunvegan Castle, I think at some stage in her life was a Mrs Walters, and Murdo MacLeod was wanting to get in on the MacLeod act in case there might be a dram going or something so he barged into her company and stuck out his hand and said "Mrs Waters" because he couldn't quite grasp this Walter bit, that was the kind of guy he was. People like Murdo made life fun in the village, he was something of a rogue.

'When sheep subsidies came in (he was a very keen crofter), he couldn't actually believe that a situation could arise where somebody would give you money for any sheep you had. So, with some doubt, he filled in the form and away it went, and he got money. He was really impressed with this so, by some magic, his flock increased somewhat the following year as he tested the system, and he gained, money came. So, year three, Murdo thought, "Right, this is it, I've arrived at the end of a rainbow." He increased his flock quite dramatically and was somewhat pissed off when this guy appeared from Portree and very politely said that he was from the DAFS, or whatever they were called then, and he was so impressed with the way Murdo's flock had increased that he wanted to talk to him. He said, "We reserve the right to do a spot check and we need to count them," and Murdo said, "Oh, you've got to be joking, they're scattered all over the hills." The guy said, "That's fine, I realise that, what I'd like to do is fix a date with you when you've got a gathering." Murdo said, "Oh, I don't have another gathering now until autumn."

'"You don't get the message, Mr MacLeod, I'm telling you – the next couple of weeks – just you get them together."

'So Murdo, without consulting his neighbours obviously, rounded up every sheep in the village and struggled to make the quantity he put in his subsidy form. But, of course, he had them all in a field and his neighbours knew what was going on, or had some idea, they knew that he'd rounded up all the sheep. When the man from Portree came and looked them over and counted them and they were almost there numerically, he turned to Murdo and he said, "OK, Mr MacLeod, the one thing that puzzles me is why have they all got different colours on them?"

'"Oh," said Murdo, "that's so that I'll know which field they're in."

'These stories were part of the whole culture of the village, and, without a doubt, people like Murdo MacLeod had stories attributed to them which they actually had probably never had anything to do with, it was just that these stories seemed appropriate to the character. There was no harm in that, it was good fun.'

Gaels in the twentieth century did not stand still in the face of the dramatic erosion of their language. Some key battlegrounds were drawn. Gaelic publishing had never and would never again experience an event so influential as the translation of the King James Bible. But many small advances continued to be made on the back of the late-nineteenth-century Gaelic revival and several of them were the initiative of the second son of a Scottish nobleman who was born in Brighton in 1869.

The Hon. Ruaraidh Stuart Joseph Erskine of Marr was a son of the fifth Lord Erskine. Given his birthplace and his family, he was one of the least likely native Gaelic speakers in the modern history of the language. But Ruaraidh was nannied on the south coast of England by a woman from Lewis. He grew up bilingual and, with all of the time and resources traditionally available to the 'spare' second son of a peer, his nursery language became his life's first love.

As a young man, Erskine of Marr became a committed Home-Ruler. There was at the end of the nineteenth century no Scottish National Party and very few Scottish nationalists. As vice-president of the Scottish Home Rule Association in 1892, when he was just 23 years old, Erskine committed himself to supporting a Scottish assembly within a federal United Kingdom. Unlike most of his colleagues, however, Erskine was at this time devoted not so much to the notion of a parliament in Edinburgh as to the renewal of Gaelic Scotland. Ruaraidh (he was christened Robert) Erskine of Marr felt not only that the Home Rule movement should assist the Celtic Highlands but he also believed that the whole of Scotland should be re-Gaelicised. 'To confine the Gaelic movement to the "Highlands",' he suggested with remarkable prescience, 'would be, even if it were practicable – which it is not – a truly suicidal policy.'

So he became Ruaraidh Arascain is Mhàirr, left-wing nobleman, prototypical Scottish nationalist, unreconstructed Jacobite, pan-Celtic agitator, Leninist revolutionary, anti-war demagogue and Gaelic visionary. Within the Home Rule Association of the early 1890s, Erskine befriended John Stuart Blackie, who combined a personal enthusiasm for devolution with his foundation of the first Chair of Celtic studies at Edinburgh University, and Alexander MacKenzie, the publisher of two of the era's most prominent – if chiefly anglophone – Highland exile periodicals: the *Celtic Magazine* and the *Scottish Highlander*.

As the new century dawned, so Ruaraidh Erskine's politics and activities wandered to the Edwardian extremes. In 1904, he began publishing a quarterly entitled *Guth na Bliadhna* (*Voice of the Year*). *Guth*, which would run until 1925, featured both Gaelic and English prose and verse, and Erskine's own political polemics urging Scots to follow the example of their Irish cousins and establish a Caledonian republican movement. By the third issue of *Guth*, he had swung towards the heady idea of a Gaelic confederation, a political union firstly of Ireland and Scotland which would shortly expand to include the other Celtic nations of Wales, Cornwall and Brittany.

At the root of Erskine's vision lay always the Gaelic language of his Lewis nanny. A union between Ireland and Scotland was not, in his view, a precursor of language revival – it would be the result! 'The drawing together,' he wrote, 'of the Gaels of Scotland and Ireland is a natural consequence of the language movements of both countries.'

In 1907, he called for the 'restoration' of the Highlands as a Gaelic-speaking community, and insisted that every civil servant, politician and other holder of state office in the whole of Scotland should be compelled to have a qualification in the Gaelic language. He coined the phrase 'No Language, No Nation!' and sideswiped An Comunn Gaidhealach writing that:

> [they] regard the language movement as something that may be played with – as a hobby suitable for dull winter evenings, or as an excuse for 'social gatherings' at which tea and gossip (for the most part in English) may be indulged in to the weak heart's unbounded content . . . It is now full time that we ceased junketing – that we put an end for ever to all our sentimental do-nothing twaddle about clans and 'Bonnie Prince Charlie' and seriously addressed ourselves to business.

And he published like a man possessed. *Guth na Bliadhna* was joined in 1908 by his short-lived Gaelic weekly newspaper, *Alba* (*Scotland*). When *Alba* folded a year later in 1909, Erskine launched a monthly magazine of fiction entitled *An Sgeulaiche* (*The Storyteller*), which he sustained until 1911. Finally, his irregular publication *An Ròsarnach* (*The Rose*) appeared between 1917 and 1930. *Guth na Bliadhna* in particular, with its eclectic mix of journalism, fiction, commentary and verse, would be praised much later by the Gaelic scholar and academic Donald John MacLeod as 'the true beginnings of journalism in Gaelic'. Before the climacteric of the First World War, Erskine of Marr even found time to establish two literary institutions, Ard Chomhairle na Gàidhlig (The Scottish Gaelic Academy) and Comann Litreachas na h-Albann (The Society of Scottish Letters). They did not survive for long, but they set a certain precedent.

In the late 1920s, Ruaraidh Erskine of Marr fell out with his newfound political stablemates in the young National Party of Scotland over their insistence on standing for Parliament. Erskine – who by then had drifted off towards the fascism and dreams of racial purity that would afflict so many mid-century nationalists – wrote a final bitter polemic accusing them of 'collaborationism' with the Anglo-Saxon enemy, closed down *An Ròsarnach* and in 1930 moved to the south of France. He lived there, in Riviera solitude, for a further 30 years until his death at the age of 91 in 1960 but never again said a single public word for Gaelic or for Scotland.

In 1952, three decades after *Guth na Bliadhna*, Derick Thomson and Finlay J. Macdonald founded between them a Gaelic-language cultural magazine named *Gairm* (the word means a proclamation or a cock-crow). *Gairm* would run for half a century. The periodical was closed by Professor Thomson only in the early months of 2003 (its substantial book-publishing arm remains active). For a small-circulation quarterly publication, *Gairm* was extraordinarily influential. Much of Sorley Maclean's work, most notably the classic 'Hallaig' (a single achievement which would in itself justify the existence of any magazine), was first published in *Gairm*, along with works by writers of the calibre of Iain Crichton Smith,

Aonghas MacNeacail and Angus Peter Campbell. Hardly a single
Gaelic writer of the second half of the twentieth century was not
published in *Gairm* and not many literate Gaels did not at some
time encounter the magazine. During the lean years of the 1950s and
1960s, when few other initiatives were launched in any medium and
when its lifeblood seemed to be sapping from the language, *Gairm*
kept a precious standard flying for published, literary Gaelic.

'*Gairm* was a very important influence from the 1950s onwards,'
remembers Martin MacDonald. 'It disseminated a lot of work that
we weren't aware of and tried to cover a wide range of things, from
the purely parochial to the intellectual, to a women's page and
things like that. It did have an influence even if it didn't have a very
big circulation, and I think that was important in terms of a
continuity of some kind. Of course, in the '50s everyone was still
recovering from the Second World War and that was true of Gaelic
as well as everything else. You've got to consider that two world
wars in the space of 20 years interrupted everybody's life.'

'*Gairm* was very much a one-man show with Professor Derick
Thomson,' says Alan Campbell, 'and he sustained something very
valuable for a long period of time. I think it's always sad when you
have the professional doing something over many years who doesn't
have an apprentice to carry it forward. That's always sad because
you tend to lose so many skills along the way.'

Television and radio in the mid-twentieth-century trough was solely
the preserve of the public service British Broadcasting Corporation.
The first-ever broadcast in Gaelic was heard on radios all over
Scotland on Sunday, 2 December 1923, when Revd John Bain
issued to the microphone a fifteen-minute religious address from the
High United Free Church in Aberdeen. Two weeks later, BBC
Radio broadcast a recital of Gaelic song, which was introduced to
listeners in English.

In the remainder of the 1920s, one regular Gaelic radio
programme established itself. The celebrated Gaelic singer Neil
MacLean's *Sgeulachdan agus Oran* (*Stories and Songs*), which issued
from the Aberdeen studio, might have been little more than lip-

service to the 150,000 Gaelic speakers in the Scotland of his time, but it was progress of a kind. In 1933, the first Gaelic radio play, *Dùnach*, was broadcast. *Dùnach* was produced by a BBC employee named Gordon Gildard who neither spoke nor understood Gaelic.

In 1935, Hugh MacPhee became the BBC's first Gaelic assistant and in 1938, the head of the corporation's first Gaelic department. MacPhee presided over a period in which the language began to inch its way out of a broadcasting ghetto. In 1939, a weekly Gaelic news review was launched to supplement the established diet of song, story and sermon.

After the interregnum of the Second World War, the future co-founder of *Gairm* Finlay J. Macdonald joined Hugh MacPhee in the Glasgow studios. Gaelic airtime crept up to about ninety minutes a week, including the ten minute Friday night news slot which attracted the attention of George Orwell in Jura. Orwell's comments about its 'amateurishness' were well advised: even those involved would later characterise the post-war Gaelic news as cheerfully chaotic, larded with unscripted comment, reminiscence and 'scholarly talk', and occasionally relieved by field trips into the Gaidhealtachd in search of raw material.

Fred MacAulay replaced Finlay J. Macdonald at Hugh MacPhee's side in 1954, and in August 1957 found himself facing a small crisis when BBC cost surveys resulted in the Gaelic news slot being relegated from once a week to once a month. To the corporation's amazement, a previously docile and receptive Gaelic community protested at this slight. Audience research was carried out in the Gaelic-speaking areas of north-western Scotland. Its results indicated what later surveys would slowly confirm: that a huge majority of bilingual Gaelic speakers preferred to get the broadcast news in Gaelic and that the Scottish Gaidhealtachd contained a large and growing number of people who claimed not to be fluent Gaelic speakers, but who understood the language well enough and who also better trusted the BBC's news in Gaelic than in English. The Gaelic news service was reinstated to once a week.

In the bilingual north and west, the support of the mid-twentieth-century Gaelic community for broadcasting provision in their own language was not only a matter of comprehension. It was a question of identity. Gaelic broadcasters from necessity were sons and (occasionally) daughters of the Gaidhealtachd, miraculously transmitted back into the kitchens and living rooms of their homeland. 'My early days of listening to the BBC,' says Alan Campbell, 'were with Fred MacAulay and James Ross. Now, if you were growing up as I was in Glendale, in Skye, in the Colbost area, James Ross of course was a son of the community, a brother of Mairead Ross, he has a brother still living, Alasdair, who had the Misty Isle Hotel. James Ross died in a car crash. He was a very, very good broadcaster, he had a good voice and something tells me he worked in the School of Scottish Studies. James Ross the broadcaster was a famous son and, you know, people still do tend to think about broadcasting as being terribly glamorous and if you know a broadcaster or whatever, it gives you some kind of "edge". If you had a broadcaster in your family, then that was incredible; in your village, I suppose there was a measure of borrowed greatness.

'So when James Ross was on, everyone in Glendale tried to listen because he was one of their own and quite often he produced programmes about the area, about the Glendale Estate, about the Land League, all that sort of thing and he talked to people locally so they might just hear not only James but other folk as well.

'I remember when the postman used to walk round the village and the postman also carried news verbally, you know like a funeral would be at such a time, the gathering will be at such a time and place, the shearing will be here or there – the postman was the email of that time! I remember the postman coming one day and saying, "Remember James Ross is on tonight at half past seven." That's how important it was. It ranked up there with the shearing and the gathering, so James on the radio was important.'

By 1962, about two hours of Gaelic radio programmes were broadcast by the BBC every seven days, including a fifteen-minute newscast. As a result, perhaps, of the fact that until 1963 very few areas on the west coast of the Highland mainland, let alone the islands, could receive TV signals, both the BBC and independent television effectively ignored the language until 1964, when the

BBC's light-entertainment department produced *'Se Ur Beatha* (*You're Welcome*). 'The first Gaelic TV shows were musical programmes,' recalls Martin MacDonald. 'Gaelic songs introduced in English in case you alienated the majority audience. Subsequently, we found out that putting on a Gaelic show entirely in Gaelic got a larger audience, even if some of them were quite irritated and said they wished they knew what it was about. The early ones were songs all the way, which the late Finlay J. produced, Gaelic songs introduced in English. Then Fred MacAulay produced *'Se Ur Beatha* and it expanded from there.'

Broadcasting on television or radio delivered an unexpected benefit. It united linguistically a Gaelic community which had previously been considered to be divided to the point of mutual incomprehension.

'All the Gaelic that was taught in Argyll in the 1960s,' recalls Farquhar MacIntosh, 'was concentrated in Oban High School, where they had two Gaelic teachers, Donald Thompson and Dan Morrison, who both came from Lewis. I remember the headmaster from Inveraray School on one occasion, when we were at an EIS [Educational Institute of Scotland] meeting together, said, "I'm glad you have a Gaelic Department in Oban, but I'm sorry that good old Argyllshire Gaelic is being polluted by Lewisisms"!

'The fact is, though, that the more Gaelic broadcasting there was, the more people got used to each other's dialects. Fred MacAulay asked me to do Gaelic interviews on television for the current affairs programme *Bonn Còmhraidh* [The Conversation Topic] that began in 1970. It was just a conversation really. He chose a number of topics each week and the programme went out from Aberdeen, so I had to travel up from Oban to Aberdeen every Friday. The programme went out about 10 p.m. or later and each week we had three or four people with me. I chaired the panel and we discussed the topic that Fred had chosen.

'In the third one, one way or another I landed with three Lewis people on quite a difficult topic to talk about in Gaelic – it was the air medical or ambulance service for the Islands, which they had introduced, and we were discussing it. Well, on Tuesday the week afterwards, I had a number of letters from people in Argyll. But the one I remember most clearly was from somebody in Tiree. It was in Gaelic and translated it said: "I have been listening to your programmes, *Bonn Còmhraidh*, since they started and I'm getting quite used to your own Skye Gaelic, but last Friday, when you had these three Lewis people with you, I might as well have been listening to three dogs barking."

'So I said to Fred, who had got a pile of complaints too, "Before the series finishes, Fred, get me three people from Argyll on the programme." So he chose as easy a topic as we could have – crofting and the future of crofting. If I remember, I had one from Islay, one from mainland Argyll and one from Tiree. Well, I can't remember getting more than two letters of complaint this time but Fred had a pile, many from Lewis people in Glasgow, and the recurring phrase was: "That was such tinker language!"

'Now that wouldn't happen today. We're getting used to each other's dialects and I think they're merging. [Professor] Donald Meek and I were discussing last year the effects of Gaelic broadcasting and Willie Gillies, the Professor of Celtic in Edinburgh, had written a paper where he looked at the influence of increased Gaelic broadcasting on the development of Gaelic itself – he compared broadcasting in that sense to the influence of the Gaelic Bible. I mentioned that to Donald and he said, "That's right, I think we're moving towards *Gàidhlig choitcheann*" – common Gaelic, what you might call standard Gaelic. We're moving towards a form of standard Gaelic in speech as well as in writing.

'When I was chairman of the Examination Board we had a committee set up to decide on Gaelic orthography for the Gaelic examinations at school level, to have an agreed orthography. Eventually we hammered it out and agreed, and it's been the basis now of the spellings ever since, although they've made some changes. But now the effect of broadcasting on spoken Gaelic is such that we are coming closer to a situation where all Gaelic communities use a similar dialect. I spent almost nine years in Glasgow living with a Lewis landlady, so I had no problem – although sometimes I got into trouble because the word for hair is the word we have for pubic hair in Skye. You've got to be careful sometimes!'

For a further three decades, the focus of Gaelic broadcasting would remain on radio. The wireless remained the staple broadcasting medium of the post-war Gaidhealtachd. Alan Campbell remembers from north-west Skye 'the post-war radios with the liquid accumulators, as they were called – you know, the batteries. Every home had a radio. We didn't have mains electricity, but every home had a radio and everyone had an accumulator. It was a glass container with a metal handle and two terminals on the top and you could see this acid swashing around inside it. When one went flat and you changed it over, you then arranged as quickly as possible to get the other one recharged – that meant, in our case, going to Dunvegan with it, which was five miles away. We went to someone there who obviously had a generator and something tells me it was a blacksmith in Dunvegan, down near the castle.

'I remember on one occasion a cousin of my father was home on holiday and he had a dinghy, and it was a lovely day so we'd sailed across from Colbost to Dunvegan and we landed at the slip just west of the castle, put the accumulator in to get charged and walked up to the village and when we came back down a few hours later, the accumulator was ready to go back home. You probably heard the well-known sort of wartime joke about not every home had a radio and the people were very anxious to keep themselves abreast of the news because almost everyone had relatives or sons and daughters away in the war, and a lot of them at sea. The story was told that this old man met a neighbour on the road, an old lady, and she said, "What's the news of the war, John?" because he had a radio and he said, "Oh, I don't know, the accumulator went down last night." The old lady said: "Oh, dear, many a poor lad lost his life on that one."'

In 1964, the legendary Hugh MacPhee retired and was succeeded as head of the BBC's Gaelic department by Fred MacAulay. Assisted by the fact that the new head of BBC Radio Scotland, Alasdair Milne, was a Gaelic learner and unabashed enthusiast for most things Highland (in 1968, Milne would give a ten minute speech in Gaelic at the close of the National Mod in Dunoon), and in keeping with the spirit of the times, MacAulay attempted a small linguistic broadcasting revolution.

He hired a number of Young Turks. 'When, many years later, I became manager of the BBC in Inverness,' says Alan Campbell, 'about a couple of weeks into my new job, Fred MacAulay appeared in to see me. He sat down in front of my desk and said, "Well, now that you're there, Alan, you'll maybe understand" – and I'm paraphrasing here – "the hellish difficulty I found myself in back in the late 1960s and early 1970s. There I was, senior producer of Gaelic at the BBC in Glasgow, on my own, where the only support I had was three young limbs of Satan, the worst buggers you could possibly imagine that any poor person would ever have the misfortune of having to work with – yes, you probably guessed it – Neil Fraser, Martin MacDonald and Seonaidh Ailig MacPherson." And I think they would all say the same of Fred.'

'Broadcasting began to bite in the 1960s,' says Martin MacDonald. 'Gaelic broadcasting had been there to some degree since radio broadcasting started in the 1920s, there was at least early tokenism and Gaelic was expanding very, very slowly. In the 1960s, there was a major expansion and people like the late Fred MacAulay were at the heart of it. Fred actually was a very quiet radical, the BBC didn't realise that he was quite as radical as he was, he fought very hard and it was exciting because they were trying new things in broadcasting – television was coming in as well then.

'I suppose in the early 1960s you had someone like John Alick [Seonaidh Ailig] MacPherson. He was a schoolmaster in Uist at the time and he set up a pirate radio station in Gaelic. I think he was basing that on the fact that the BBC were doing very, very little, that progress wasn't fast enough and he was aware that Ráidió na Gaeltachta in Ireland had been set up through a protest movement. A couple of us in Skye were talking to him and he was saying, "Well, you've got to start what we started." We didn't get too far in that direction, I must say, mainly because all of a sudden John Alick and myself found ourselves in the BBC.'

In 1965, the BBC's Gaelic news went daily, with a five-minute current affairs round-up at noon, followed by ten minutes of song. Evening cultural programmes brought the corporation's Gaelic provision up to six and a half hours a month – which was supplemented by a weekly magazine programme broadcast only on north-western transmitters. In 1970, BBC (Scotland) Television commenced *Bonn Còmhraidh*, the first-ever Gaelic current affairs TV slot.

On 5 March 1973, BBC Radio transmitted *Roinn na Gàidhlig* (The Gaelic Portion), a programme celebrating 50 years of Gaelic broadcasting. It was a necessarily top-heavy celebration. More Gaelic had been broadcast in the previous year than in the whole of the 1940s and 1950s, and more in the previous week than in the entire span of the 1920s. In 1973, some 90,000 people in Scotland were able to hear *Roinn na Gàidhlig* as native Gaelic speakers.

The attachment of so many small Gaelic communities to their language during the first 70 years of the twentieth century may have masked its chronic decay. People raised in Skye and the Inner Hebrides, Argyll and Wester Ross or even the Western Isles in the 1950s and 1960s could not ignore the census figures, or the apparent worthlessness of Gaelic within the education system, or the painful reluctance of the broadcasting authorities to do much more than play a Calum Kennedy record and deliver a few minutes of national news translated directly from English. They could not deceive themselves about the steady erosion of their everyday tongue. But still, to the vast majority in Staffin, Colbost, Elgol and Sleat as much as in Daliburgh and Carloway, the language was still there.

For many, it was a strange and slightly unreal position, as if a language and culture were sleepwalking into oblivion. 'It never really occurred to us in the 1950s,' says Alan Campbell, 'that Gaelic might be in terminal decline. And even if it had, the perceived wisdom in the community at that time was not to be bothered about it.

'I remember so clearly, in my teenage years, when I was at Portree School and was fairly successful in anything related to Gaelic, and spoke the language at home and in the community – I remember the common buzzword at that time was: "Gaelic won't take you beyond the Kyle of Lochalsh. It's wonderful, it's fine, it's nice to have it but don't waste your time on it. If you want to get on, forget Gaelic."

'I came through a primary school system where, for five of my seven years there, I had a very excellent teacher who was from the village, she was a relative of mine as well, but it wasn't until the last few months of my primary education that I got a single word of Gaelic in school. Although all but one family in the school were Gaelic speakers and in the latter part of my school life, every person there was a Gaelic speaker.'

At the same time in the north Skye township of Flodigarry, a boy named Norman Gillies 'came across English first of all when we went to Sunday School. That was quite strange because the woman who was taking it, certainly her first language was not English. Then another guy started taking Sunday School who was a Gaelic speaker and that was great fun because he used to tell us stories about his days in the merchant navy and his life at sea and a whole variety of other things.

'That was my first coming across English and I was rather flummoxed by it, to be quite honest. I would be about three or four but my brother and sister sorted me out because by that stage they were quite conversant with English. But Gaelic was very much the language of the village and the language of the home and everything was done through the medium of Gaelic, and it was very natural. School, of course, was a completely different matter – it was a reversal of what happens now. We went in and got taught in English and went out and played in Gaelic – what tends to happen now is that you get taught in Gaelic and go out and play in English. Gaelic was very much the language of the school playground, and I think it was very rarely we had somebody in the school who was not a Gaelic speaker. It might not have been the first language of somebody but they had enough of a knowledge to pick it up quite quickly.'

Between total fluency in Gaelic and total ignorance of Gaelic, there were infinite degrees of ability. Since the multilingual Middle Ages there had always been Lowland and Highland Scots who combined a workaday knowledge of Gaelic or English (and French and Latin and Dutch and a dozen others) with their first tongue. Tradespeople on the south side of the nineteenth-century Highland Line often required some proficiency in Gaelic, without perceiving themselves as Gaelic speakers. Many Gaels raised by mixed families in frontier communities had reached adulthood with a working comprehension of Gaelic but neither the will nor the confidence to translate that understanding into fluency.

In the middle of the twentieth century, at the same time as the last monoglot Gaelic speakers – such as the old lady encountered in 1966 by Ronald Black in Eriskay – were counted merely in their hundreds, the heartlands of the Scottish Gaidhealtachd itself began to produce such children. They were boys and girls, men and women, with more than an occasional phrase of Gaelic, often with heads full of the received language, who had been born and bred with Gaelic in the air, who could understand conversations overheard, who could and did listen to and enjoy Gaelic radio, who could occasionally even read Gaelic – but who lacked the practice and the confidence to speak it. They would come to be regarded as a missing generation, and they would be counted in their tens of thousands.

In 2003, the journalist Alasdair Campbell spoke to seven such people who had been born in the second half of the twentieth century. They included John MacDonald, a 48-year-old man from Strath Kanaird on the north-western mainland near Ullapool:

> [John] had a Gaelic speaking parent as he grew up in an area with an obvious island influence from across the Minch. 'My father spoke occasionally in Gaelic, and a few people in the community used Gaelic – there were a lot of people from the Islands, Lewis in particular, who had moved to the area,' he said. John admits to having a fairly good understanding of the language. 'I think I could make more of an effort myself, I have a Gaelic-speaking partner and I don't have an excuse not to be fluent myself. Also getting confidence could help,' he added.

Mairi Stewart, a 42-year-old teacher from Grimsay in Uist:

is another who has one parent who spoke Gaelic – her father who was from Harris. In her case her father's job had an impact on how fluent herself and her two sisters were. He was a policeman and the family had to move with his job.

Her older sister Catherine spent the first six years of her life in Sleat, surrounded by Gaelic speakers and so had a grounding in the language, whereas Mairi was brought up and schooled in the Fort William area.

Her younger sister, however, grew up in Harris and as a result is a fluent speaker. And so, a victim of circumstance as much as anything else, Mairi finds today that she understands plenty of Gaelic, but would not see herself as a speaker.

'It depends on your personal circumstances and background and has a lot to do with your parents,' Mairi said. 'Culture impinges upon the individual, it makes a difference if there is a Gaelic speaking culture in the area. Usage in the home is a linchpin.'

Mairi also felt that the education system at the time had an impact on her grasp of Gaelic. 'The other problem in Fort William was that you couldn't do Gaelic and French, and you were told that you needed a modern foreign language if you wanted to go on to further education. There's a whole generation of islanders who didn't do Gaelic but did French.'

Her 45-year-old sister Catherine MacLeod, who lives in Loch Eport, North Uist, would perhaps have classed herself in the same category as Mairi a few years ago, but has since made the transition to spoken fluency. 'I moved here about 20 years ago, and like a lot of people that moved here I went to classes. I had also gone to evening classes as a student on the mainland,' she said. 'I now teach a bilingual class in Lochmaddy Primary 1–3. The council have a bilingual policy and we are encouraged to promote that. [I gained fluency] partly through the job and my own children.'

Catherine's children both went through the Gaelic Medium Education system at nearby Carinish School. 'We put the kids into Gaelic Medium. People want their children to have the opportunities that they missed out on,' she said.

Thirty-five-year-old Marion Steele from Benbecula also felt unable to describe herself as a Gaelic speaker. 'My younger brother was disabled and my parents knew from a young age that they would have to send him to Glasgow and so they spoke English. He was two years younger than me,' she said.

Two of Marion's older brothers are fluent speakers. But as Marion explains: 'There wasn't any Gaelic medium then, and I wasn't interested when I went to secondary school – it wasn't cool to speak Gaelic then.'

Marion, who is a Home Economics teacher at Paible and Daliburgh secondary schools, also had this feeling that Gaelic wasn't much use. 'I suppose I didn't think it would help, Gaelic was frowned upon. It now pays to speak Gaelic, there are good employment opportunities with teaching and television,' she said.

The climate has now changed, thinks Marion, with the advent of Gaelic Medium Education and other initiatives which have raised the profile of Gaelic. She explained: 'I'm putting my own kids through Gaelic Medium Education. And I'm growing in confidence in speaking it. It's the confidence thing that's the major obstacle. I would like something informal, not with complete learners – that's off-putting. I have it all in my head. I've been to Gaelic classes in the past, and I've felt they have been a waste of time.'

A new social category had emerged in the Scottish Highlands and Islands. Where less than a century earlier there had been 44,000 Gaels who spoke only Gaelic, there were by the early 1970s tens of thousands of Gaels who did not speak any Gaelic. Dr Johnson's dictum had altered irrevocably: 'Under the denomination of Highlander are comprehended in Scotland all that now speak the

Erse language' no longer applied. There was a Gaelic-speaking Gaidhealtachd and an English-speaking Gaidhealtachd. The former was shrinking by the year, while the latter continued its seemingly inexorable advance.

Three

Ambivalence about the current health and the future of the Gaelic language was heightened when, remarkably, in 1971, its long decline appeared to stall.

The 1961 Scottish census had declared 80,004 Gaelic speakers; by 1971, the number had apparently risen by more than 10 per cent, to 88,892. This was only the second recorded increase in the history of the Gaelic census. The results attracted a good deal of sceptical comment. Practical experience suggested that the number of Gaelic speakers in Scotland had continued to decline throughout the 1960s. All previous projections had suggested a fall in numbers to around 70,000 by 1971.

There had also been a change in the 1971 questionnaire which may have induced confusion. In previous censuses, householders had been asked merely to write the letter 'G' opposite the names of people who spoke Gaelic only, and 'GE' to signify those who spoke both Gaelic and English. But in 1971, a separate section devised only for Gaelic speakers was introduced. In this form, householders were asked to tick a box denoting that a person 'speaks Gaelic and English'. 'We feel that some people may not have noticed the cross-heading saying the section was only for Gaelic speakers,' said a census official in 1974. 'They may have been confused and chose the "speaks Gaelic and English" box when in fact they couldn't speak Gaelic.'

But if there was any kind of stabilisation, or even increase, it may also have been partly due to a small change of direction in a corner of the education system.

In 1960, Inverness County Council – which at that time incorporated the heavily Gaelic-speaking islands of Harris, North and South Uist, Benbecula, Barra and their smaller inhabited Hebridean satellites such as Vatersay, Eriskay and Berneray, as well as Skye, Lochalsh and the Gaelic-speaking districts of Wester Ross – presented its schools with a Gaelic Education Scheme.

It was emphatically not a centrally imposed directive in favour of Gaelic education. The Inverness Gaelic 'scheme of work' was drafted from suggestions made by teachers in the Gaelic-speaking islands. It was entirely voluntary in practice. As one of its progenitors, the celebrated schools inspector and tireless campaigner for Gaelic education Murdo MacLeod, put it:

> It was emphasised, when the scheme of work was issued, and subsequently at teachers' conferences held to discuss its implications, that teachers were at liberty always to select the provisions which they felt were appropriate to the peculiar situation of their own schools and, by the same token, to reject those which they felt to be irrelevant.

The Inverness Gaelic Education Scheme of the early 1960s was not much more than a green light to teachers at primary and secondary schools in bilingual areas of the north-west Highlands and Islands to apply Gaelic in the classroom as and when they saw fit to do so. Gaelic could, depending on the abilities and sympathies of the teachers concerned, continue to be used hardly at all, or become the main medium of instruction, or find itself somewhere in between. As the first had previously been the prevailing status quo, the possibility of the second and third represented an important step forward.

Early in 1963, two full years after the institution of the Gaelic Education Scheme in Inverness-shire, in an address to the Gaelic Society of Inverness, Murdo MacLeod claimed:

It is now true to say that the introduction of the scheme of work has ensured that Gaelic is now being taught at all stages in all the schools in Skye and the Outer Isles, from Harris to Barra. The language is being used in a much wider context than was formerly the case. More emphasis is now being placed on the teaching of Gaelic as a subject, and in certain schools a limited use is being made of Gaelic as a medium of instruction.

One of the chief difficulties facing the scheme, said Murdo MacLeod, had been overcoming a century of perceived inferiority:

> The established tradition that Gaelic belongs to the home and the playground and that the classroom is the exclusive province of English has steadily debased the status of the language. The difficulty of securing for Gaelic a parity with English can only gradually be overcome . . . In most schools [where the Gaelic Education Scheme had been adopted] there is evidence that Gaelic has gained a new improved status in the eyes of the pupils . . .
>
> This enhanced prestige of the language is closely connected with the more enlightened and imaginative approach to the presentation of formal Gaelic lessons, which is probably the most important advance that has been made. The Gaelic lesson was in the past almost invariably conducted in English, and this unrealistic procedure detracted greatly from the appeal and value of the teaching and from the standing of the language.
>
> The basis of the Gaelic lesson was formerly a mechanical reading of a passage from the textbook, followed by translation into English and transcription exercises of doubtful value. The emphasis is now on interpretation rather than translation, and the Gaelic lesson is generally conducted in Gaelic. The distraction of the second language is thus removed, and the lesson proceeds more freely and naturally and with more effect and purpose.

However imperfect and belated were those 1960s reforms, Murdo MacLeod considered that they finally enshrined within at least one part of the state education system an important principle:

> that a child is effectively taught only if adequate use is made of his native language. This axiom has very important implications with regard to those children – of whom [in 1963] there is still a considerable though rapidly diminishing number – who come to school with no knowledge of English.

Attempts to introduce a scheme of exclusively Gaelic teaching for all Gaelic-speaking infants in Inverness-shire had been made but rejected. The idea had not, insisted Murdo MacLeod, been entirely abandoned. The current scheme encouraged schools 'to exercise their own discretion in this matter as in all others, and it was hoped that this new development would gradually evolve from the general operation of the scheme. These hopes are gradually being realised.'

But Gaelic-medium education faced practical as well as ideological difficulties, even where teachers and schools were sympathetic to the idea, as in many parts of the Western Isles:

> To retain the traditional methods of teaching, which are reinforced by a plentiful volume of teaching aids and textbooks, is a strong temptation for many teachers. There is certainly a distressing shortage of printed teaching material in Gaelic, and a teacher wishing to teach the reading skill to infants in Gaelic would require to exercise skill and ingenuity in improvising suitable teaching aids.
>
> Those teachers who have made the attempt are certain that their efforts have been fully justified. Not only do the children acquire the ability to read more easily and naturally in a medium which they understand, but when they are later introduced to English their progress is more rapid, and achieved with much less strain than was formerly the case.

Murdo MacLeod reported that there were in 1963 a few island schools:

> which have deliberately postponed the reading of English until the children have been reading Gaelic for one or two years . . . Invariably it has been found that the introduction of Gaelic reading has both simplified the learning process and aroused a desire for reading generally.
>
> Progress in English reading has not been retarded, and there is some evidence to show that it has been enhanced. In one school in Harris, children of six and seven years of age read and write Gaelic and English with equal facility, and the 12-year-old pupils in the same school, who are also taught by the parallel use of Gaelic and English, now read with understanding and enjoyment English books which are not normally read until the age of 15 . . . In more general terms, it may be stated quite confidently that where Gaelic reading has been introduced early the transition to English has been more easily achieved than in the past, and progress in the acquisition of English has been more rapid and more effective.

However limited, underfunded and understaffed (the Inverness-shire scheme included no extra budgetary provision for Gaelic books or teaching aids and was dependent for its success on the existence in Gaidhealtachd schools of teachers who also happened to be Gaelic speakers), this represented a large step forward. The scheme seems to have played a real part in the improved census figures of 1971, when, as Professor Kenneth MacKinnon observed in an academic analysis of the trends in the Gaelic-speaking population, 'some slight increase in Gaelic speakers occurred amongst children. By 1981 this had become more pronounced amongst ten to fourteen year olds. This effect can be shown to relate specifically to those areas with primary Gaelic teaching schemes.'

Whether or not the Inverness-shire scheme increased by much the number of Gaelic-speaking children in Skye and the Western

Isles throughout the 1960s and early 1970s, it must have increased their fluency and, perhaps, their language awareness to the extent that they were declared as Gaelic speakers where once they might have failed to register. John Norman MacLeod, the future head of studies at Sabhal Mòr Ostaig, was born in 1955 and brought up in Staffin in northern Skye. He began attending the small primary school at Digg in 1960, just as the Inverness-shire scheme was beginning to affect island education. Where Alan Campbell seven years earlier could receive his entire primary education in the north of Skye from Gaelic-speaking teachers among other Gaelic-speaking pupils 'without a single word of Gaelic in school', John Norman MacLeod was at least given an educational grounding – and some personal consolidation – in his native language.

It was far from bilingual education. 'In school, the teacher spoke to you formally in English, and outside school, she spoke to you in Gaelic. It was English immersion in a sense. Day one, you go to school as a Gaelic speaker, and you just learn English and everything is through English. But I think it was a feature of Digg School that, if anything, we got a good grounding in Gaelic, and I always remember when I went to Portree School, a lot of the texts we were using we had used in the primary school as well. And we were encouraged, certainly in our latter years at Digg School, to be involved in Mods and so on. I was not only a Gaelic speaker but was also literate in Gaelic when I went to Portree High School, thanks to Mrs MacLeod at Digg Primary School.'

In fact, the long battle to educate Gaelic-speaking primary children through the medium of Gaelic would be won only as monoglot Gaelic-speaking children began to disappear even from the last redoubts of the language. The slow retreat of Gaelic as a community vernacular was in many areas commensurate with the decline of crofting as a community activity. When the rural Highland working class which sustained Gaelic for centuries began finally to fragment, when most rather than merely an educated few of its children began to look for a life beyond the land and the neighbouring sea, then the home base of the language – which preserved and enriched it as an everyday demotic – would be eroded.

This social dissolution, as much as the damage done to Gaelic by indifferent education authorities since 1872, was a political problem. But Gaelic was traditionally weak in the political arena. Before the wide enfranchisement of many crofter males by the Third Reform Act of 1884, most Highland Parliamentary seats were filled either by men who did not speak Gaelic, or by men who did not much care about Gaelic. Before and after the 1884 Act – which catapulted a number of Gaelic-speaking 'crofter candidates' into the House of Commons – genuine tribunes of the people, such as Charles Fraser-Mackintosh, correctly perceived themselves as elected more to settle the question of land hunger than to agitate for Gaelic. Radicals such as Fraser-Mackintosh and John Murdoch were undeniably sympathetic to the language and saw its status as vital to the regeneration of their people. They worked in harmony with the Gaelic Society of Inverness and various associations for Highland exiles. But land hunger was the real hunger of the day, and land struggle – almost if not entirely to the exclusion of any other – was their main priority.

The first and oldest pan-Scottish Gaelic association, An Comunn Gaidhealach, from its earliest days attempted to steer so passive and inclusive a course that it was politically neutered. An Comunn's constitution hamstrung itself with a curious requirement that it be both 'non-political' and 'non-sectarian'. This drew an illogical equivalence between politics and religious sectarianism, as though both were regrettable features of general society which An Comunn could somehow circumnavigate, while failing to recognise that whereas sectarian bigotry was an evil in itself, only certain kinds of political activity were and are deplorable and some kind of political activity is inevitable. An Comunn's fastidious rejection of 'politics' hinted at the Tory nostrum that only radical campaigning could be called political, whereas Conservatism represented nothing more or less than God's settled will. An Comunn's purely 'cultural' agenda, whereby titled landlord could supposedly rub tartan shoulders with the schoolteacher son of his tenant and even the tenant himself, attracted ire from politically radical Gaels for a century and more. Erskine of Marr, as we have seen, deplored in 1904 its "'social gatherings" at which tea and gossip (for the most part in English) may be indulged in to the weak heart's unbounded content'.

'I have never been a member of An Comunn Gaidhealach,' said Martin MacDonald 100 years later. 'Nor were many of my generation. They just refused to join.

'There was a vast gap between the academic Gaelic of An Comunn Gaidhealach, which really represented the cities, particularly Glasgow – if you want, the expat Gael – and people like me. They weren't very adventurous politically – you know, they came out of a funny situation. When the Land League broke up, some of the landlords who had actually been fighting with the crofters and the Land League came together on this cultural thing to try and save Gaelic. It gave itself a remit to try and help the Highlands economically as well, in the same sense as the landlords' wives went around doing good things – some of them actually were successful, the Harris Tweed industry was a product of that – finding markets for local produce and that kind of thing.

'But J.D. MacKay, one of the Land League leaders in Skye, actually warned the Gaels about this new funny organisation, An Comunn Gaidhealach, which was a danger to us. And in a sense, whatever it did culturally or whatever it did socially in terms of putting on a Mod once a year, at a time when it was probably very difficult for people to meet, especially the expats, and to encourage Gaelic in a sort of Victorian way – it never tackled the political issue. It became the sort of establishment to which it was very easy for the government to give a grant of £50 and say 'Get on with it', so Gaelic was got out of the political mainstream.

'In a strange way, the revival of consciousness, of awareness that seemed to start around the 1970s might have been a reaction to the fact that An Comunn Gaidhealach for 80 years had done virtually nothing politically. It's difficult to trace all the roots of what happened in the 1970s, I mean, obviously there must have been roots somewhere. Thirty years later, we've still to nail it, to be able to analyse it historically, but I've got a feeling there was an element of reaction to the quietism of An Comunn Gaidhealach – you know, the feeling that they're going nowhere.

'I know that, as young students in Edinburgh, our general feeling at
that time was anti-Comunn Gaidhealach. It was the establishment, and
we were the radicals – or we saw ourselves as radical, that was of
course at a time when Suez was going on, the Hungarian fiasco was
going on, and students did feel at that time a bit radical in Scotland,
maybe some of that brushed off on us Highlanders, I don't know.
Even culturally – An Comunn Gaidhealach type of poetry was very,
very conventional, sort of late-Victorian verse. The supposedly major
poets, those who won prizes from An Comunn Gaidhealach, really
were pretty dead.'

'Not enough capital was made out of the political potential which
Gaelic had at the turn of the [twentieth] century,' wrote the Lewis
author and local historian Frank Thompson in the *West Highland
Free Press* in 1973.

In many European countries, said Thompson, without citing
specifically such disparate examples as Ireland, Greece, Portugal,
Catalonia and the Faeroe Islands, the native language itself:

> had been the basis of political change in favour of that language
> and its culture . . . either the lessons presented by the history
> of linguistic revivals were not taken up, perhaps as being
> irrelevant, or their implications for Gaelic were not fully
> realised. Otherwise we might have had today [1973] a much
> stronger and more vigorous language and culture in Scotland.
>
> As it was, the [late-nineteenth-century] Gaelic revival
> took the emasculated form of reviving the language, its
> literature, and reviving an interest in the history of the Celtic
> peoples, in Celtic music, art, dress and sports. An Comunn
> Gaidhealach was formed expressly for the purpose of
> promoting what might be called the aestheticania of Gaelic,
> leaving the more urgent needs of the Highland people, such
> as socio-economic development, to other bodies.
>
> Had these other bodies come into existence, the state of
> the language, and indeed of the Highlands and Islands
> generally, might well be healthier than it is now, and An
> Comunn would have been justified in continuing its

particular interest in Gaelic music and song. But these bodies did not emerge. And the opportunities for Gaelic and the Highland people, which lay thick on the ground at the turn of this century, were left to rot and fade away.

'It's almost normal and fashionable now to be critical of An Comunn Gaidhealach and to talk about it being geriatric and dinosaur and everything else uncomplimentary,' says Alan Campbell. 'I think that's unfair. An Comunn Gaidhealach was a hugely important and significant organisation in its own time. I think it was overtaken by events; and, also, when development came, An Comunn fought for many years to achieve progress, but it had a clumsy and rather Victorian management board structure which frustrated development. Somebody once said that the Comunn's strength was in its membership and its weakness was in its democracy because, in reality, if one member of its Ard Chomhairle, its governing committee, decided something wasn't going to happen, it didn't happen.

'That was the difficulty with An Comunn, it wasn't aggressive enough. There was too much of the Victorian gentleman and lady about it. It would be quite wrong to say that they weren't important or significant. But, sadly, when we came to the 1970s, An Comunn had lost its way and there were things needing to happen. An Comunn had been trying for many years to make things happen and failing and probably had lost a bit of their nerve as a result.'

The political vacuum would be filled. But as those strangely improved census figures for 1971 emerged, the truth was that recent political initiatives on behalf of Gaelic had been both unambitious and so few as to be practically non-existent. In the early 1960s, the Western Isles Labour Party and its sitting MP Malcolm K. Macmillan had made an unsuccessful attempt to get Gaelic accepted as an examination subject for entry to the Civil Service. In 1964, the Nationalist 'Constitution for Scotland' proposed, with no more success, 'the right of Gaelic speakers to use Gaelic in courts of law and government offices'. In 1969, the Inverness-shire Liberal MP Russell Johnston, who was born in Skye, presented to the House of

Commons a Ten Minute Rule Bill intended to assist all of Scotland's local authorities to subsidise the holding of An Comunn Gaidhealach's National Mod festival in their constituencies.

The well-meaning futility of this last gesture and the astonishing modesty of Gaelic claims are best highlighted by the fact that Russell Johnston's Ten Minute Bill came just two years after the Welsh Language Act passed through Parliament in 1967, giving the Welsh language in Wales some forms of parity with English. Frank Thompson wrote that, following the Welsh success:

> an attempt was made by some individuals to have promoted by a Highland Member a similar Bill for Gaelic . . . this effort has fallen flat on its face . . . It may well be that instead of a Bill giving Gaelic equality of status with English, a mess of potage, in the form of [Russell Johnston's] National Mod Bill, was more acceptable as being compatible with the non-political basis of An Comunn Gaidhealach.

In the 1960s and 1970s, Gaelic was politically isolated not only in Britain as a whole, but even within Scotland. Whereas the Welsh nationalist party, Plaid Cymru, had always a strong base in the Welsh language movement, the Scottish National Party 'hardly acknowledged the existence of the Highlands within its organisation', according to Frank Thompson. The political right was at best condescending towards and suspicious of minority cultural movements, and the internationalist left regarded them as either irrelevant or obstructive to the onward march of the proletariat. There was in the Lowlands of Scotland both a residual hostility to the troublesome Highland host, and in many Protestant quarters an atavistic distaste for anything which smacked of Irishry.

In fact, although it was little known at the time, the 1960s were providing political ammunition for Gaelic and its sister minority languages – ammunition which would in time be effectively deployed in the service of those Gaelic-speaking infants who had for so long been educationally deprived. Luckily, Gaelic was not, as it was increasingly aware, alone in the world.

Early in the twenty-first century, the Canadian writer Mark Abley, who was researching a book called *Spoken Here: Travels Among Threatened Languages*, met a woman in her 70s named Josephine Keith. Josephine had been raised as a native speaker of an old minority language in an advanced, predominantly English-speaking society. But none of her children could hold a conversation in her language: 'They can speak a few words, that's all. I thought it would be hard for them.' Abley says:

> Josephine did what she believed was right. She didn't understand that her kids could have mastered [her language] as well as English; she didn't know that the mind of a pre-school child can absorb languages as effortlessly as a sponge soaks up spilled water. She raised her family in the 1960s, long before anyone . . . heard about the research in Montreal indicating that bilingual children have greater flexibility and form concepts more easily than children who speak a single language. Her kids were grown and gone by the time Hawaiian researchers showed that young children in a bilingual program end up learning English better than their counterparts who get no Hawaiian at school. In the twenty-first century, MRI scans and other brain-imaging tools would prove that bilingualism helps the brain development of small children. But . . . decades ago, Josephine didn't realise that language never had to provoke an either–or decision. She only wanted her kids to do well.

Josephine Keith was not from Lochmaddy or Portree or anywhere else in the Scottish Highlands. She was from rural Oklahoma and her language was the Native American tongue Yuchi. But her experience was identical to that of such parents all over the Western world.

The educational advantages of bilingualism to which Mark Abley refers may not have been scientifically proven by the 1960s. But they were suspected. Murdo MacLeod was dropping serious hints when he cited the school in Harris in the early 1960s in which children who had first been taught to read in Gaelic would by the age of 12 be reading in English material which was more commonly reserved for 15 year olds.

The circumstantial evidence had in fact been present for a century and more, for those with eyes to see. All of the British Empire had encountered the sons – and the daughters – of the Highland croft who had marched forth in legion from their unpromising origins to administer, educate and succour the rest of the world. The educational achievements of Scottish Gaels were legendary. When those achievements were analysed, they were most commonly – and absurdly – ascribed to an anxiety to flee through university and the professions from the sheep fank and the shieling. Gaels, it was suggested, worked harder than anybody else because the price of their failure was a life at home. In fact, bilingual Gaels – which by definition included all of those who had progressed through secondary education – did not have to work harder. They were naturally advantaged over their monoglot English-speaking contemporaries. The very thing which educationalists, politicians and others had insisted for centuries would encumber them, would debar them from academic achievement – their Gaelic language – was in fact a glorious asset all along. They became headmasters, historians, colonial governors, professors, and chaplains to the Queen not despite their native Gaelic, but in large part because of it.

Bilingualism was of course identified by most twentieth-century educationalists as a good thing – but only on the merits of the two learned languages. Bilingualism in such global currencies as English and French or English and German was indisputably helpful to a child's progress in the world.

It was not realised – or, once half-realised, once guessed at, not properly explored – until the last two decades of the twentieth century that bilingualism in any two languages was a cerebral stimulant. Children who had already absorbed a second language found it easier to learn a third and fourth. Children fluent in both Gaelic and English (or, for that matter, Gaelic and Yuchi) displayed notably superior and flexible learning skills across the board of primary and secondary education compared to children who were fluent only in English (or, for that matter, only in Gaelic).

Much of the crucial research took place in such historically bilingual areas of North America as Hawaii and Quebec, and notable work was accomplished by Professor Colin Baker at the University of Wales in Bangor. It represented a sea change in educational philosophy from the orthodoxy established by such authorities as the professor at Cambridge University who in 1890 asserted that 'second language acquisition halved spiritual and intellectual growth'.

In 2000, the American research psychologist Lisa Chipongian wrote that:

> A once-popular theory of second language acquisition depicted the brain as restricted in its capacity to take on more than one language. Using the analogy of a weighing scale, some 'experts' insisted that the more a person learns of one language, the less knowledge he or she can hold of another. Juggling two languages could throw one or both languages 'off-balance'.
>
> Also associated with this theory is the image of two balloons in the mind, one holding an individual's first language, the other containing the second – with no overlap or communication between them. This suggests that the two languages are necessarily isolated from one another and that knowledge acquired in one does not transfer, or generalize, to knowledge in the other. But this model makes little sense. It implies, for instance, that if a child were to learn how to multiply in Spanish, she would have to re-learn multiplication in English or simply confine multiplying to the part of her brain that knows Spanish . . .
>
> Research over the past twenty years has dispelled these myths, demonstrating that positive cognitive gains are associated with learning a second language in childhood . . . Bilingualism has been shown to foster classification skills,

concept formation, analogical reasoning, visual–spatial skills, creativity, and other cognitive gains.

Most of these claims hinge on the condition of fluent bilingualism – in other words, a certain level of competence must be reached in both languages before the positive effects of bilingualism can occur (Baker 1993). According to Virginia Gonzalez, author of *Language and Cognitive Development in Second Language Learning*, the effects of bilingualism on cognition are mediated by the proficiency levels in both languages. Indeed, according to some researchers, 'there may be a threshold level of linguistic competence which a bilingual child must attain both in order to avoid cognitive deficits and allow the potentially beneficial aspects of becoming bilingual to influence her cognitive growth' (Baker 1993). This threshold level is described as the capacity to comprehend the school curriculum and take part in classroom activities in either language.

In his *Foundations of Bilingual Education and Bilingualism*, Baker states that bilingual individuals, by knowing two or more words for one object or idea, may possess an added cognitive flexibility. The following example demonstrates how the knowledge of two words – one in English and one in Welsh – for a single object (a school) could enhance one's concept of 'school': 'in Welsh, the word "ysgol" not only means a school but also a ladder. Thus having the word "ysgol" in Welsh and "school" in English provides the bilingual with an added dimension – the idea of the school as a ladder.'

Bilingual children have also demonstrated superior story-telling skills, perhaps because they are, as Baker suggests, 'less bound by words, more elastic in thinking due to owning two languages'. And in a study comparing monolinguals and bilinguals (four to six years of age), Ianco-Worrall found that bilinguals were two to three years ahead of their monolingual peers in semantic development (Baker 1993).*

* 'The Cognitive Advantages of Balanced Bilingualism', www.brainconnection.com

Professor Colin E. Baker would himself outline those benefits, and their relevance to Scottish Gaelic, at a conference in Glasgow in 2002. 'Bilingual children,' he would point out, 'have two or more words for objects and ideas, so the links between words and concepts are looser, allowing more fluent, flexible and creative thinking.' With specific reference to Gaelic, their other proven advantages included the facts that:

> They can communicate more naturally and expressively, maintaining a finer texture of relationships with parents and grandparents, as well as with the local and wider communities in which they live.
>
> They gain the benefits of two sets of literatures, traditions, ideas, ways of thinking and behaving.
>
> They can act as a bridge between people of different colours, creeds and cultures.
>
> With two languages comes a wider cultural experience, greater tolerance of differences and perhaps less racism.
>
> As barriers to movement between countries are taken down, the earning power of bilinguals rises. In modern Scotland, Gaelic speakers are in great demand – in the media, in education, in local and national government.
>
> Further advantages include raised self-esteem, increased achievement and greater proficiency with other languages.
>
> Through language, a child is cared for, cherished, cultivated and cultured. Within any language is a kaleidoscope of cultures whose full colour and beauty are only revealed to those fluent in the language.

In the bilingual world which over the first two-thirds of the twentieth century had dawned slowly on Scottish Gaelic, those findings and those concepts clearly delineated at least one twenty-first-century future for the language. They would, however, take a desperately long time to sink in.

The language in the early years of the 1970s was battered but unbowed. It existed still in a twilight zone. Its heartland areas, where more than half of the population still spoke Gaelic, had been driven far out to the insular west. On the north-west mainland, a line could be drawn ten or twenty miles inland down the Halladale river in Sutherland, along to Reay Forest and then south to the head of Loch Etive in Argyll. Between this line and the coast, 20 per cent or more of the population might in the early 1970s be native Gaelic speakers. A bare majority of the 7,000 people living in Skye still spoke the language, and a great majority of the 30,000 population of the Western Isles outside Stornoway did so. Thanks to the Gaelic archipelago in the Minch, the county of Ross and Cromarty (with Lewis) was still 35 per cent Gaelic speaking, and 22 per cent of the county of Inverness-shire (with Skye, Harris and the Uists) still used the language. But only 13.7 per cent of Argyllshire was fluent and there were fewer than 2,000 Gaelic speakers left in Sutherland. Throughout those areas, the population was in decline. The crofting system, which for a century had nurtured the Highland rural working class which in its turn had sustained Gaelic as a community language, was losing favour with a younger generation. The Gaelic-speaking Gaidhealtachd was losing its people more quickly than any other region of Britain and more quickly even than were the English-speaking rural areas on the central, southern and eastern mainland.

In the professional arena, in the world of broadcasting and books, Gaelic continued at this time to take half a pace forward for every shuffle back.

As well as the House of Gairm, publishing was enlivened in 1969 by Glasgow University's Celtic Department establishing the Gaelic Books Council and in 1970 by Club Leabhar, the Highland Book Club. An Comunn Gaidhealach published a short-lived magazine entitled *Sruth* (*Current*) which ran for four years until its demise in 1969. Three west coast weekly newspapers – the *Oban Times*, which covered Argyllshire and some of the southern Hebrides, the *Stornoway Gazette*, which sold throughout the Outer Isles, and the new *West Highland Free Press*, which covered Wester Ross, Skye and the islands from Lewis to Vatersay – contained a column or two of regular Gaelic comment. Education through the medium of

Gaelic took place only through the sympathetic offices of a handful of teachers in the first or second years of one or two island primary schools. But in 1972, Gaelic became a subject at O and A levels of the Scottish Certificate of Education. Two teacher-training colleges, one in Glasgow and one in Aberdeen, began instruction in the language. There were Celtic degree courses at the universities of Glasgow, Aberdeen and Edinburgh, and Gaelic could be studied in tertiary education at Oslo, Freiburg, Harvard, St Francis Xavier, Oxford and Dublin. The churches continued their honourable commitment to the language of their congregations, especially the Roman Catholic and Free Church of Scotland in the Islands. As late as 1976, the Welsh philologist Meic Stephens would judge that: 'In numbers and ethos the Free Church is nearer to being a Gaelic institution than any other [in Scotland].'

And the tokens, the small symbols, of Gaelic's modest ambitions continued to emerge. Throughout the summer of 1972, small stickers appeared in the display windows of hotels, shops and other businesses in the north-west of Scotland. Beside a St Andrew's cross they read: 'Tha Gàidhlig air a bruidhinn an seo' (Gaelic spoken here). They were printed and distributed by An Comunn Gaidhealach and represented the organisation's summer push.

In 1969 and into the early 1970s, a curious document began to appear on the walls of student flats and even of some public bars. It was a poster-size sheet of crudely printed paper. It was nothing more or less than the first-ever Gaelic map of Scotland, and it had been prepared in London not by the Ordnance Survey (who would catch up three decades later), but by a young Gaelic learner from Ardrossan in Ayrshire.

'I was in my tiny bedsitter in London at the time,' recalls Roy Pedersen. 'I started learning Gaelic in the City Literary Institute in the winter of 1968, and, being a geographer by profession, I started writing down the Gaelic versions of place names in the books and things that I was learning from – names like Obar Dheathain [Aberdeen] and Glaschu [Glasgow] and Dùn Eideann [Edinburgh]. It started with a piece of paper where I sketched out a map of Scotland, and wrote maybe eight or nine names on it.

'In the next months, I collected more names and the idea occurred to me of doing a proper map and so I did that map. I had moved to a different bedsitter by that time, but the first map I prepared on the table of my bedsitter in Clapham in London, and I found a printer and had him print 250 copies. I only got 250 because that's as many as I could carry on the bus from the printers to my bedsitter!

'My own Gaelic was far from perfect, it still is far from perfect, and nobody had done this before, so I would just do the best I could and I did subsequent redrawings of it, and did more consultation with as many experts as I could to try and get the names as right as possible – the odd thing is how little criticism I've ever had of spellings and suchlike, although maybe people criticise it behind my back, I don't know – not to my face anyway.

'In the first place, I went to the British Museum, night after night, and went through all the books written in Gaelic that I could find and just collected all the names I could find in these books, a lot of them in the nineteenth century, some twentieth-century ones, and the book that I kind of discovered at that time – I still use it as an essential reference for place names – was *Words and Celtic Place Names of Scotland*. It covers a huge amount of ground. I have also to confess to a small number of concoctions.

'Baile nam Frisealach is Fraserburgh and A' Bhruthaich is The Broch but I've now changed that, on my latest map, to Bruthaich nam Frisealach – Broch of the Frasers. That was it, and I printed the first 250. I sold my first 20 round the Gaelic class in the City Literary Institute the day I got it printed – and then I had this article in the *Sunday Post* and I got all sorts of letters asking for copies of it on the back of that.

'I was selling them for six shillings. By the time the printer's bill came in, I had collected in enough money in postal orders and cash and so on to pay the bill. So the Gaelic map has never had any finance of any kind whatsoever right up until the present day – it has always covered its cost, and there have been an awful lot of reprints, an awful lot, and I usually get 3,000 printed at a time. I'm not going to do any more because I'm working on a new map with [the design and publishing enterprise] Stòrlann which will be better. It's in full colour.

'I've sold 30,000 Gaelic maps of Scotland over that 35-year period – there may be the odd other Gaelic publication that has sold more, like the Bible perhaps, but hardly any Gaelic publication has done better. So, that's the story of the Gaelic map. Of course, I did other versions of it, upgraded it gradually, and the most recent map I've just completed is called *Tìr Chaluim Chille*, which is a map of Scotland and Ireland and the Isle of Man all in Scots Gaelic and Irish and Manx, and that is produced by the Columba Initiative, Iomairt Cholm Cille, and that's on sale now.'

In April 1973, Dr Gordon Barr, the chairman of a new young pressure group called Comunn na Cànain Albannaich (the Scottish Language Society), worked his way through the *Radio Times* and calculated that during a typical week there were 2 hours and 35 minutes of Gaelic radio broadcast in Scotland out of a total of 475 broadcast hours. Twenty per cent of this Gaelic radio output was devoted to religion – an emphasis which, if it had been transferred to the mainstream channels, would have resulted in more than twelve hours of English-language religious broadcasts each day.

Worse yet, out of 141 hours of BBC television per week in the spring of 1973, Gaelic received 7.5 minutes – or 30 minutes a month. Even by a proportional headcount of the number of Gaelic speakers in Scotland, Barr deduced, this fell badly short of reasonable provision. The 1971 census had suggested that 1.6 per cent of Scots spoke Gaelic (it did not yet enumerate the more relevant percentage, in broadcasting terms, of those who understood the language but declined to declare themselves fluent speakers; later surveys would indicate that there were at least as many again in this category).

One point six per cent of radio time would have delivered, argued Gordon Barr, seven and a half hours of Gaelic a week – three times the current quota. The same proportion would have lifted the amount of Gaelic TV from its derisory few monthly minutes to two and a half hours a week.

Even the few hours of Gaelic broadcasting then available

occasionally provoked fraction and discord within this small and scattered residual Gaelic world. In October 1972, a letter appeared in the *Scotsman* newspaper which stated that:

> BBC news broadcasts in Gaelic are bereft of Gaelic idiom and frequently the grammar is embarrassing – comparable to saying 'I have gave' or 'they have came' in English. Daily BBC Gaelic announcers display a complete lack of knowledge of the use of the preposition in Gaelic. Singers make similar mistakes, proving that they are singing by rote in a language that they know little or nothing about and never use.

In the same month, the distinguished editor and proprietor of the *Stornoway Gazette*, Mr James Shaw Grant, suggested that the language would be best served by graceful retreat from the modern world into a late-twentieth-century sunset home of peat-fire hearth and heather thatch. Addressing the native speakers at the Rural Choirs Concert at the 1972 National Mod, Shaw Grant insisted that Gaelic was not, could not and never should be a medium of business or commercial exchange. He claimed:

> The value of Gaelic lies precisely in the fact that it is not the language of commerce and technology, it is not the language of the mass media.
>
> It is the language into which one can retire from the hurly-burly of an over-busy world. It offers an escape from canned, pre-packaged entertainment, from the superficiality of instant news and instant comment . . . It is a folk language, in which people still make their own songs and write their own poetry . . . Gaelic has no material value whatsoever and thank God for it. It is not the language of the rat race. That is its supreme value. An Comunn [Gaidhealach] has its priorities right when it puts the emphasis on culture, music, religion and education rather than debasing Gaelic by trying to make it an ordinary workhorse for business and administrative purposes.

This definitively reactionary view of the language as a docile relic of a prelapsarian rural Scotland was unlikely to win friends on the campaigning, radical missionary wing of the late-twentieth-century Gaelic world. It was also about as far as could be imagined from the thinking of a young businessman who had just taken possession of the largest private estate in Skye.

Four

Iain Noble was born in Berlin. His father was a British diplomat and his mother was the daughter of a Norwegian diplomat. They had first met in Brazil and got married in Oslo. Iain Noble himself was christened in Rome and received part of his primary education in Argentina.

But his father's family was an established landowning interest in Argyll, and after all of the vagaries of his consular young life, Noble would settle most comfortably on the north-west coast of Scotland. As a young man fresh from Eton and Oxford University, he went into the insurance sector in London: 'Pretty boring, but I really hadn't decided what I wanted to do at that stage, and my father said he knew somebody who would give me a job. So I just found myself there.'

In the middle of the 1960s, he decided to return to Scotland. 'After four and a half years in London, I wanted to get to Scotland, and I remember thinking how hard it was to imagine living somewhere as remote as Scotland, because all my friends from Oxford were living in London, and I thought it meant cutting oneself off from all those friends, you see, which was a bit daft really, but that's how it felt at the time.' He met in Edinburgh another ambitious young man, named Angus Grossart.

'He said "What's your career ambition?" or something like that.

I told him I was toying with the idea of trying to start a merchant bank because I felt something like that could be very successful up here. I had one or two friends in London whom I was thinking of asking to come up and help me do it because I hadn't the expertise myself. He said that he had the same sort of idea himself and of course he was a qualified accountant and a qualified lawyer, and he'd been working on the corporate side of the legal business so he had a fair knowledge of what went on from almost on the inside and was very interesting. He is extremely bright.

'So we met two days later on the Sunday morning, we sat down and he wrote, I think it was called a summary – nowadays, you'd call it a business plan – it was about six or seven pages, and once he'd done that, he read that CV to investment trusts and said, "What do you think of this?" and they said, "Yes, we like the idea and we'll back it," so it was all done just about in a week or two.'

That was in 1968. Four years later, the relationship between the two founders of Noble Grossart resulted in Noble being bought out. He sought to put his money into a Highland estate.

His intentions were to revive an estate in the Gaidhealtachd, but Iain Noble did not originally consider Skye. Early in 1972, however, he was stuck on the island by a snowstorm and discovered an interesting opportunity.

In 1970, Lord Alexander Macdonald – the lineal descendant of Samuel Johnson's host in 1773 – had died at the age of 60, leaving the extensive Macdonald Estate in Skye to his son, Godfrey. Godfrey, the 8th Lord Macdonald, was a newly qualified chartered accountant. He quickly discovered that his inheritance was effectively one large debt. 'The earliest recorded unpaid bill,' he would later muse, 'was dated about 1804.'

Double death duties and 170 years of accumulated debts and bonds ran into hundreds of thousands of pounds of debit. Godfrey Macdonald put most of his estate up for sale.

Iain Noble was 36 years old when he bought it. A Gaelic learner, his plan for the new form of Highland estate was to resuscitate the economy through the medium of the native language. His model for this was the Faeroe Islands, which he had visited in the late 1960s.

'I found the comparison there with Skye very interesting,' he would tell the *West Highland Free Press* in 1972:

> In 1900 both had the same population – about 15,000. Since then the population of the Faroes has gone up to 40,000 while Skye's has dropped to 7,000. The land area of the Faroes is probably slightly less than that of Skye. In 1900 the Faroes had a complete subsistence economy; the soil was barren and there was absolutely no fishing. Today they have the most modern fleets in the world, fishing off Nova Scotia and selling it throughout the world. That could just as easily be done out of Camus Croise or Portree. At the same time industry has flourished. And there has been an art explosion and literary revival.
>
> Why? When I asked the Faroese, I was amazed when they all replied that things began to happen when they decided to be Faroese and stop being Danish. This sparked the whole thing off. It gave them a sort of self-respect. Danish had been the language of business. Faroese was dying out in families and children were growing up who could hardly speak it.
>
> I am convinced that through the revival of the language there came a pride in identity and all else followed. We mustn't be frightened of being a small community. Instead we must create our own internal binding factors. People here have never believed that things are possible. But there is virtually nothing that could not be achieved in the Highlands.

Iain Noble immediately established an employment policy of positive discrimination in favour of Gaelic speakers on his Skye estate. Those native speakers – from Sleat itself, from elsewhere in the island and from the rest of the Gaidhealtachd – were in their turn instructed to use only Gaelic in all possible business matters, even, especially, when talking to their employer. He published in October 1972 a call to exiled Skye men and women, to:

any young people who have gone away, or who will go away, because of lack of opportunity. I particularly want to meet people with qualifications of some sort. If they have initiative and if they are prepared to take a chance they may be interested in what I am trying to do in Skye.

Alan Campbell was one of those who took the chance. The product of Colbost and Portree High School had progressed to a career in marketing and sales, firstly in England and then in Aberdeen. 'One day, I had a phone call from a guy called Iain Noble, whom I didn't know from Adam,' he recalls. 'He invited me to dinner, and he was talking about Skye, and I actually had been toying with the idea of going back to Skye – I was married and had two kids and I had this thing about "Would I like to go back and try and make a living in Skye?" We spoke in Gaelic and English – Iain was learning his Gaelic then and I remember being very impressed with that, with his commitment. I thought that a lot of what Iain preached then was extremely idealistic, as indeed I do today; I think Iain has not lost that, he and I disagree just as much now as we did then, we're both consistent in that regard. But the upshot was that I went back to Skye to work with Iain, to run his various commercial enterprises, and I took a serious cut in salary and conditions to do that – the only time I've done it in my life.

'Iain had this very strong pro-Gaelic policy and it was a funny thing, it was admired by a lot of people – I think people of my father's generation admired it – but most people thought it was totally idiosyncratic. They admired what the guy was doing but they didn't think it was really going to serve any great purpose, other than to create a few jobs, but good luck to him. Iain himself, people talk about people turning against him, and the reason that is happening is because of overselling, pushing too hard, and I saw lots of that in Iain's approach in my own time there. I think the wider Skye community saw that too, and I would say, this sounds almost unkind, you know, to be criticising, but I suppose what I'm saying here is I think there's a difficulty when you bring a new idea into a community like Iain Noble did, to his great credit, I think what he really needed to do then, at some stage along the way, was to stand back and let somebody else run with it, he had to pass that ball, and I don't think that happened quickly enough or often enough. Part of the reason was that maybe Iain always felt "Well, it's my ball and I don't think anyone can run with it as well as I can," and I think that was part of the trouble.'

Iain Noble was not at first entirely sure of exactly what he had bought from the Macdonald Estate. For many years afterwards, various buildings kept falling out of the property portfolio. One of these turned out to be the big old barn, the *sabhal mòr*, at Ostaig. Sabhal Mòr Ostaig lay actually outside the boundary of the land purchased by Noble. It stood just over the border, in the southern part of Sleat, which had been taken by the Clan Donald Lands Trust. But deeds to the building itself were apparently the property of Fearann Eilean Iarmain, the name Iain Noble had given his new estate headquarters.

'Obviously it was too fine a building to be allowed to tumble into decay,' recalls Iain Noble, 'but what should be done with it?

'We thought about houses, but who would occupy them except incomers or holidaymakers? We talked about using it as an industrial centre, but wouldn't the county council be willing enough to build a factory if one became needed? Someone suggested a centre for piping, as there was nowhere in the Highland area where the pipes were taught on a professional basis except by itinerant teachers, but Boreraig [in north-west Skye, the home of the legendary MacCrimmon piping family] seemed a much more appropriate setting for that.

'One day someone said, "Why not start a Gaelic library, as there is no library today of any significance within the Gaelic-speaking area." All the best collections of Gaelic books were in one or other of the big cities where they were not really accessible to native Gaelic-speaking communities. "Well, that is quite a good idea," I said. "I will certainly keep it in mind along with all the other suggestions." Two or three weeks later, a crate of books arrived from a well-wisher in London saying, "This is to start your Gaelic library," and so, without any definite decision being taken, we were off.

'Ever since then, books accumulated from here and there, from families who had found a volume or two on a dusty shelf, a relic perhaps of a Gaelic-speaking ancestor from long ago. Some larger contributions came as well, and [after a year] there were some 300 Gaelic books in the library, making it probably the largest public collection anywhere in the Hebrides.

'But a library by itself is like mustard without beef. It would have to be open to the public and should become a centre for students. Teachers and an academic ambience were the logical extensions of the new theme.'

Within months, following extensive consultation, the plans had morphed into 'a new Gaelic educational and social centre'. More than one interested party recalls standing with Iain Noble early in 1973 in the courtyard of Sabhal Mòr Ostaig, looking around at the dilapidated, leaking buildings which skirted three sides of the yard like a medieval fortress, and hearing the proprietor muse aloud: 'Wouldn't it be interesting to build a Gaelic college here?' Such a place could become, he said to a visiting young historian and future head of Highlands and Islands Enterprise named Jim Hunter, 'the first Gaelic establishment of further education in Scotland since the Vikings burned down Columba's abbey in Iona'.

Some of those interested parties believed him. Some thought that it was achievable. One of them was the young director of Comunn na Cànain Albannaich who had done that survey of Gaelic broadcasting earlier in the year. Gordon Barr, a Gaelic learner and a lecturer in biochemistry at Dundee University, took a sabbatical from his day job between June 1973 and September 1974 to become the first *fear-stiùiridh*, or director, of Sabhal Mòr Ostaig. His job was to continue with renovating the buildings, with fund-raising, with establishing night classes and summer schools, with developing the library and establishing a shop selling chiefly Gaelic books, records and cassette tapes. He would spend his spare time satisfying his employers at Dundee University by studying the microbiology of peat bogs in the peninsula of Sleat. His three co-trustees would be Iain Noble, the poet Sorley Maclean and the teacher Donald Ruaraidh Macdonald.

The education department of Inverness County Council was initially hostile to the notion of an independent Gaelic-medium college on its turf. The council and Iain Noble had a short but lively history, as we shall see.

Small things as well as large signified the exclusion of Gaelic from the mainstream of Scottish society at the time of Sabhal Mòr Ostaig's establishment. In the early 1970s, only a handful of national institutions recognised the language at all. As well as the churches, bodies such as the Crofters Commission and the Scottish Land Court (which included by statute an obligatory Gaelic-speaking member) accepted and acknowledged its existence. But even the Highlands and Islands Development Board (HIDB), the precursor of today's Highlands and Islands Enterprise (HIE), which had been established in 1964 to steer the region away from economic desuetude, was at best ambivalent and occasionally hostile towards the historical vernacular of its constituents.

That young cartographer who had produced the first Gaelic map while learning the language in London in 1969, Roy Pedersen, joined the HIDB in 1971. 'In those days,' he says, 'Gaelic was perceived by the outside world and by Gaels themselves to have a low status. You know, Gaels very often loved the language but regarded it as not being useful. That was part of the reason why the confidence at entrepreneurship levels was low. In communities where there has been a cultural and linguistic revival – and the classic one that we used was the Faeroe Islands – there was simultaneously an economic revival as well.

'The cause and effect is basically that if the status of the language is raised, so is self-confidence raised, and when self-confidence is raised, entrepreneurship and enterprise are raised – so you get a virtuous circle of rising standards both culturally and economically, as opposed to a vicious circle of decline, economic and cultural decline. So the trick that we tried to pull off was to raise the status of the Gaelic language and, by so doing, hopefully to raise the levels of confidence and entrepreneurship.

'But this was slow to be accepted at the HIDB. I would say the sequence of events was something like this: the HIDB opened its doors in Inverness on 1 November 1965, when Bobby Fasken [chairman of the Highlands and Islands Advisory Panel and first secretary of the HIDB] put the key in the building at Castle Wynd which is now the home of the Crofters Commission, and the first 12 people started. I wasn't there then, but I heard the story. At that time, the chairman was Professor Robert Grieve. He was a planner and a very visionary man and, in a way, what you see in prosperous Inverness today, for example, it almost comes from his vision. At that time, Inverness was a wee market town much like Dingwall, and it is now a city.

'The driving force in those days was really a planning thing. Of course, the Highlands was quite a depressed place in those days, economically, and the concept was that if we got the economy going, then all the social stuff would follow. The Highland Board had, right from the start, a social remit; its object clause in the 1965 Act which brought it into being was to "improve the economic and social conditions of the people of the Highlands and Islands" – a wonderful phrase actually – it was people-orientated, which was quite unique. But the way that was interpreted in those early days was that you get the economy going, get business and get the roads in and all that kind of stuff, then all the social stuff will come in and look after itself, that was more or less the attitude and theory.

'The first change in that approach came relatively soon, within a few years, when Jo Grimond, who was head of the Liberal Party at the time and Member for Orkney and Shetland, asked how many staff the HIDB had to look after its social remit. Of course, the answer was that it didn't have any, and, as a result of that, Bob Storey, who became my mentor later on, was appointed as a consultant to consider how a social remit could be taken forward. And eventually Bob was taken onto the HIDB's staff, but the first task that was done in the social field was to prepare a number of community studies looking at a range of different communities to see what made them tick: research work in communities like, as I recall, Yell in Shetland, and Lismore, I think, Mull and places of that kind.

'The other initiative that was brought in from a relatively early time was things called non-economic grants. In the early days, the rules were relatively non-specific, but it was for things like the village halls, the uniforms for pipe bands and things that didn't fit the stricter economic criteria. Non-economic grants eventually came within Bob Storey's remit, and they became called "social grants" and later on, when I took over, I called them "community action grants" – the first name I thought of was "community in action" and then I realised that of course that could be misconstrued if there was no space between the "n" and the "a"!

'Bob renamed them social grants and tightened up the rules so that the applicants for social grants would have to be properly constituted community bodies with a democratic structure and open membership. A wide range of grants were made available for a whole range of stuff. An odd thing about HIDB assistance is that throughout almost all of the HIDB's existence, clients who got grants and loans were asked if they were prepared to allow their assistance to be publicised and very often they said "no". With the social grants we made it a condition that we publicise the assistance, and, for the first time, in the papers there appeared on a very regular basis a list of all the social grants that were approved. Personally, I think that did more to improve the image of the HIDB than almost any other initiative. People could see that these were things that really were important to communities – even quite small things, playgroups or whatever they might be, a few hundred pounds sometimes made all the difference to getting something off the ground, and some of them were much bigger, many thousands of pounds.

'So there was a gradual growth in the concept that the social side of things was of some value. Then another breakthrough came with the arrival of Ken Alexander onto the board, because he came from a left-wing background and that's really when the community cooperative project started. It was very experimental – the journalist and politician Brian Wilson had seen community cooperatives in Ireland, and he tipped off Ken Alexander that this was a good idea. Ken and Iain MacAskill subsequently went out to Ireland, and then Bob Storey went out and I went out and a whole bunch of folk went out to see how the Irish did it.

'The Western Isles were selected as the test-bed for the thing. That wasn't actually because of local demand, so much as that the Western Isles were a particularly difficult area to stimulate development, so it seemed an appropriate place to try this experiment to see whether doing things on a community basis might actually get development going where entrepreneurs could not be found. I think it was actually proven that was the case. One of the aspects of it was that a number of the people who participated in management committees and suchlike, or community cooperatives, actually learnt a lot of skills through doing that; it was a steep learning process for them and for us, because we were expected to be able to guide them in the process of setting up a community business and had never ourselves done it before. So we had to learn pretty quickly as well! As a result of that, I know I personally learnt an awful lot about business and accountancy and financial control. And the *co-chomuinn*, or community cooperatives, in the late 1970s were possibly the first HIDB initiatives to be given a Gaelic name.

'When the co-op scheme was being pulled together, this scheme to encourage financial assistance and field officers and all that, a manual was created, and for the first time in my knowledge, there was an English and a Gaelic version of it done. It was at that point that the term co-chomunn was coined. The author of the manual was Martin MacDonald, on a freelance basis – he was basically a consultant who was commissioned. I actually did the cartoons in it, as it happens, and did some other minor bits for it, but Martin was the guy who wrote it, with guidance from Bob Storey and others.

'So there was a steady acceptance of the importance of Gaelic within the HIDB's activities. I think it was a combination of Ken Alexander – not that he was a Gael himself, but he had sympathy – and Iain MacAskill perhaps, and it was at this time of growing awareness that these things were important. I would say that Bob Storey, in his own unique style, was probably the person, as much as anyone, who was able to kind of rationalise the thing and demonstrate that it was important.

'I may say that this was against quite a lot of antipathy within the organisation. The Social Development Unit, of which I had now become part under Bob's leadership, had the backing of the chairman, Ken Alexander, and the chief executive of HIDB, so to some extent we were untouchable. On the other hand, the majority of people in the organisation felt that the unit was just a kind of idealistic, impractical proposition, that it would never really work, and it was just being sort of humoured, as it were.

'And there was quite a lot of antipathy towards Gaelic within the HIDB then. It was kind of insidious – even in Inverness there was antipathy to Gaelic among a lot of the populace in general. It was like any prejudice against any racial or other minority who are regarded as having low status; it's a combination of ridicule and a sense that these people are kind of not really up to handling modern concepts, modern life and business. That was the general pervading attitude, and ridicule was commonplace – you know, "teuchters", that type of thing.

'In those days too, now this is interesting, the HIDB had no area offices. It only had one office – just a couple of months before I arrived for my first job there, it was all pulled together into Bridge House; it had been scattered around Inverness previously. Bridge House was the only office that HIDB had, so if a crofter in South Uist wanted a grant, he had either to wait until somebody went out from Inverness or he had to come into Inverness to negotiate it. And that's very intimidating, this kind of fortress, and you don't really know your way around the big bureaucracy with folk sitting in suits with their arms folded in fancy rooms. Then the HIDB people would go out to Uist and they didn't really know anybody and how could they make any contact? So that was a serious flaw in the whole set-up. I remember one occasion when a person came in from, shall we say, the west, and met one of the officials within HIDB who shall be nameless and when he told them his name, the official said, "That's a right teuchter name!" The level of sensitivity was not overly high at that time.

'But that antipathy towards Gaelic occurred throughout the public service. It was either regarded as a total irrelevance or a joke, or even something that was undesirable. But from about the late 1970s, there was a step change in attitude. I think the establishment of Comunn na Gàidhlig, the Gaelic pressure group, Gaelic-medium education, the producing of things on shiny paper, professional-looking stuff, presentations, all these helped. Sabhal Mòr Ostaig, probably as much as anything, has become an icon of modernity for the whole Highlands and Islands – it's one of the most futuristic, exciting hotbeds of energy, and I think that sort of stuff has over a longer period of time absolutely transformed the overall balance of attitude – there are still people who are opposed to the language, but they've got to watch what they say now, whereas in the old days it was Gaelic itself that used to be whispered in corners.

'The important thing about Gaelic development is that a whole lot of things have to happen simultaneously for it to work. It's like: "Which wheel of the clock is most important? It won't work if any of them are missing." Probably one of the key things was, first of all, Gaelic-medium teaching in pre-school. The work that Finlay MacLeod's CNSA [Gaelic Playgroups Council] did, especially in the earlier days, was absolutely vital; without that there would be no transmission of Gaelic. Within families, the transmission of Gaelic from one generation to the next had virtually broken down by 1980 – very few parents were passing Gaelic on to their children by that point.'

The Scottish high street banks, which had a fixed or mobile presence in virtually every Gaidhealtachd community, also pretended in the early 1970s that Gaelic did not exist. Not only was not a word of Gaelic employed on their hoardings or business literature, but they would also refuse to acknowledge a Gaelic signature. It possibly required a well-connected banker to alter that state of affairs. Late in 1972, Iain Noble persuaded the Bank of Scotland to issue him with its first-ever bilingual chequebook. It did not involve much linguistic effort from the bank: 'Bank of Scotland' became 'Banca na h-Alba', the word 'pàigh' was set beside 'pay', and 'no òrdugh' above 'or order'. The bank expressed its reservations but agreed to attempt an 'experimental period' of limited bilingual exchequery which might be continued if there were 'no hitches'. There were presumably none. Three decades later, not only were Gaelic-language chequebooks commonplace, but every Bank of

Scotland in the Highlands and Islands (and quite a number outside) was advertising itself as Banca na h-Alba, in competition with Banca Rìoghail na h-Alba and Banca Dàil Chluaidh.

This was of course a small, token accomplishment, significant only because of the long years of official contempt for the language which had preceded it. Most such gestures – and as the twentieth century drew to its close, many more would be made – represented little more than small good deeds in a wicked world, candles lit in the darkness; and there was one area of public policy in which the rejection of Gaelic had genuine substance.

As we have seen, almost every single place name in the whole of Scotland has either a Gaelic original or a Gaelic rendition of an even earlier form. In some areas, such as the north-west of the country, Gaelic place names – often a Gaelic rendering of a Norse original, neither of which had anything to do with English – were once the norm. But the first surveyors and map-makers to traverse the region identifying the names of hills, glens and townships had overwhelmingly been English speakers. They had recorded place names not in their essential Gaelic orthography, but in a coarsely rendered and usually meaningless phonetic translation.

So it was that in all official transactions and on almost all maps other than the samizdat version produced by Roy Pedersen, the traditional place names of the Highlands and Islands had been scrambled. For a region and a people with so strong a sense of place and identity, this was of more than symbolic importance. The name of the peninsula in which Iain Noble had established his estate headquarters, for instance, was Slèite (pronounced 'Slya-tya'), which in Gaelic means 'hillsides' or 'sloping moorlands' and is a basic description of the topography of the place. On maps and records since before the nineteenth century, however, it had become Sleat (pronounced 'Slate'), which means nothing in either Gaelic or English. The name of the island on which Sabhal Mòr Ostaig stood was An t-Eilean Sgitheanach, which in most people's understanding means – wonderfully and graphically – 'the winged island'. It had been lazily rendered as Skye, which has no particular meaning.

Some phonetics were less acceptable than others. Balgown in

north-west Skye, for instance, has nothing to do with ladies' clothing. Its Gaelic original was Baile a' Ghobhainn, which meant 'township of the blacksmith' – a meaning and purpose which the English name wholly rejected. Baile Ailein in Lewis, which was simply 'Allan's township', was mangled slightly less badly into Balallan. But when the meaning was only half-obscured, the folly of rejecting the full original was only emphasised. When the meaning of a place was fully obscured and replaced by gibberish – usually in stark contradiction of the locals' continuing pronunciation of the traditional name – it represented a form of cultural vandalism. Road signs and place names in English only were disliked especially by the Gaelic educated classes as humiliating symbols of official contempt for their native language, as one of the most blatant and visible indicators of Gaelic's relegation to the edge of invisibility. The earliest cartographers may not have been acting with malice aforethought, but in refusing to amend their mistakes, their late-twentieth-century equivalents were surely doing so.

This denigration of the language had long been recognised and resented. The defacement of English-language road signs in Wales by contemporary Welsh language activists had not gone unnoticed in Scotland. But a comparatively weak and apolitical language movement had found little time or energy to address an issue which was easily discounted as tokenism. Schools, radio programmes, festivals and publications might encourage people to use and explore Gaelic, it was argued, but a bilingual road sign was unlikely to make a single convert.

When pushed, this apparently harmless, symbolic topic achieved significance chiefly through what it revealed about the nature of the opposition. Inverness County Council was in 1973 an unreconstructed bastion of landed power. The islands, especially the Western Isles between Harris and Barra, had taken in the post-war world to sending their own community leaders to represent them, but on the mainland the titled establishment which had steered Inverness-shire through the first half of the twentieth century was still firmly in place, passing on its seats from father to son as part of the inheritance. Education officials such as Murdo

MacLeod may have been able occasionally, after decades of wrangling, to slip through small and inexpensive projects in favour of Gaelic in Hebridean schools. But road signs, as the new landowner in the neighbourhood would shortly discover, were a very different matter. Road signs were apparently of even more totemic importance to anglophone councillors and council officials than they had ever been to Gaelic activists.

Inverness County Council wished to improve the road which entered Portree from the south. In order to do this, they required some of Noble's new land. Noble agreed to give, rather than sell, the council the small amount of turf required if they would in their turn agree to erect three bilingual road signs upon it. One would signify Viewfield Road, another the nearby High School, and the third the town itself, with the Gaelic version, Port Righ, slightly larger than the English Portree.

He was informed that bilingual signs did not accord with council policy. At the full council meeting at Inverness in March 1973 to discuss the matter, two island representatives, one from North Uist and one from Barra, spoke in favour of Iain Noble's suggestion. But the chairman of the Roads Committee was Lord Burton of Dochfour, the proprietor of 11,000 acres by Loch Ness and a large chunk of Glen Shiel, a stalwart of the Scottish landowning community, a fugitive from the pages of a Compton Mackenzie novel who had occupied his seat on the county council since the age of 24 in 1948 and who boasted that his only recreations were 'hunting, shooting and fishing'. Lord Burton insisted upon rejecting even a few 'experimental' bilingual road signs because: 'It does become a matter of principle. If it raises itself in Viewfield Road, it might raise itself throughout the whole of Skye.' Burton's roads surveyor, Keith MacFarlane, dutifully agreed: 'We would have to put them all the way back to Kyleakin. Signs are meant to be confirmatory, not to confuse people.'

Thus began, with a whiff of grapeshot over a tiny scheme on the outskirts of Portree, the great Highland road signs controversy which would run for a further three decades.

Noble refused to relent. Extraordinarily, he persuaded a cross section of the great and the good of Skye to sign a petition supporting bilingual signage on the southern approaches to Portree. The Free Presbyterian minister to Staffin, the Church of Scotland minister to Kilmuir and the Free Church minister to Sleat all joined hands with such dignitaries as the north Skye GP Dr Calum 'Og' MacRae, the procurator-fiscal Donald Macmillan, the Broadford garage-owner and county councillor Angus Sutherland, the headmasters of Portree, Staffin and Dunvegan schools, a selection of local businessmen and the two most celebrated residents of Viewfield Road itself, local businessman Ewan MacKenzie and popular champion of all things Skye Colonel Jock MacDonald.

This coalition of Skye's eminent, educated and professional Gaels wrote to Inverness County Council in April 1973:

> to express our wholehearted support for the proposal that road signs should be in Gaelic or where appropriate bilingual throughout Skye.
>
> So far, no good reasons have been advanced for not doing this. On the contrary, we would regard it as a matter of common courtesy in a Gaelic speaking community. It is based on a principle that has already been accepted by the Government in Wales and it has been adopted in most other parts of the world where there are bilingual communities. Far from causing confusion these signs would add interest for visitors . . . We therefore request the County Council to reconsider their decision.

Not all of Skye, not all even of Skye's native Gaels, supported this or any other of Iain Noble's campaigns. Many were at least hesitant, not because they especially disliked the notion of Gaelic road signs, but because of Iain Noble's social position. He was a landowner, and there was in the twentieth-century Highlands a strong residual mistrust of landowners – especially of landowners who trespassed on the democratic process. 'A lot of Portree people,' recalls Martin MacDonald, 'were dead against him because he was holding back the roads. They were saying to me, "No, we're not against Gaelic,

I'm a Gaelic speaker, we want Gaelic – but we're not having him dictating to us what we'll have and what we won't have." He probably landed in the one part of Skye – Sleat – where, for historical reasons, landlords were almost acceptable, there was a more receptive population. In other parts of Skye, they were highly suspicious of him because he was a landlord. I tend to be antipathic towards landlords myself. I got to know him, and I could see him as a Gaelic militant who would get things moving, which he certainly did, but I had a feeling that he sometimes had a tendency to want to control everything as well. But he also had the guts to do unconventional things in the eyes of other landlords, and I'm sure some of the other private landlords in Skye didn't approve.'

Following the supportive letter about Gaelic road signs, confusion reigned in Inverness County Council. Deputations from the seat of local government were dispatched to Noble's headquarters at Eilean Iarmain in Skye. Compromises were mooted and announced – and promptly denied by both sides. The two landowners, Noble and Burton, communicated by telephone. Iain Noble told the press:

> He said my attitude was holding up the road and that the cost to the county would rise by up to £20,000 as a result. I told him I was surprised he was prepared to consider such a price in order to prevent five words of Gaelic from appearing in public. Lord Burton seemed agitated.

Lord Burton was indeed agitated. The matter of the Portree signs would finally be resolved early in May 1973, just four weeks after it blew up. 'Portree' would be accompanied on the road signs immediately to the south of the village by 'Port Rìgh'. 'Viewfield Road' would also be 'Goirtean na Creige'. Iain Noble temporarily withdrew his request for the school to be labelled as 'an Sgoil', accepting in return a single bilingual sign recognising the south Skye township of Broadford as An t-Ath Leathann.

Just three decades later it would be impossible to travel through the Highland district without being confronted at every corner by

Gaelic and English road signs. But the sudden eruption of these signifiers in the 1990s and 2000s masks the prolonged bitterness of the earlier campaign. Lord Burton and his sympathisers did not intend to lie down quietly. They were correct to assume that the Viewfield Road controversy was for Iain Noble and the Gaelic lobby the thin end of a very large wedge. They had been given an inch, but they wanted a thousand miles. They wanted their place names back.

It is easy to understand the arguments in favour of Gaelic or bilingual road signs in Gaelic-speaking regions. It is more difficult to sympathise with their opponents' case. It appeared to swing from the exigencies of local government expenses to confusion among road users to the notion that the sight of the words 'Port Rìgh' would cause massed pile-ups of tourist caravans throughout July and August.

Lord Burton himself expressed his feelings on the matter in a letter to the *West Highland Free Press* in May 1973:

> The question of whether or not Gaelic signs should be used has been taken as a matter of whether or not people are pro- or anti-Gaelic. This is, of course, by no means the case. I was called an 'isean beag' or a 'donas beag' long before I was called a 'little rascal' or a 'little devil' in English. My family having inherited the Inverness area since about 1400 we have a certain amount of Highland tradition behind us, and no-one enjoys a ceilidh more than myself.
>
> But what are roadsigns for? They are to show someone the way to a place or to warn them of some hazard on the road. The local inhabitants have less need for these signs than have visitors. The majority of visitors to Skye cannot speak Gaelic, and indeed many people whether visitors or residents who can speak Gaelic are unable to write it. Therefore informatory signs should be such that everyone can easily understand them.
>
> If a community wishes the name of their place to be altered, this is a different matter. For instance, Mr Noble

wishes Dunvegan and Sligachan to be spelt differently, and he wants Broadford to be called 'An Ath Leathann' [*sic*]. As far as I can ascertain, the inhabitants of these places have no desire for these alterations. The places are universally known by their existing names. A change would mean alterations to telephone directories, postal addresses and maps. About two years ago I had one digit of my telephone number altered and it caused substantial extra work and inconvenience. To change Dochfour or Dochgarroch back to their Gaelic spellings would cause inordinate delay and confusion which I would feel quite unjustified, but if the people of Broadford wish to have their village name changed to 'An Ath Leathann' I am sure this could be done, but meanwhile the village is called Broadford and should be signposted as Broadford.

Incidentally, it is interesting to note that much of the clamour for Gaelic signs comes from people outwith the islands altogether, or new residents in the islands.

There are other minor considerations in this argument. For instance, the county has for long tried to keep down prolification of signs. At every planning meeting, there are applications for signs rejected. It seems, therefore, to be wrong that there should be more road signs than are necessary. There is also the matter of cost. It appears that £3m is being spent on an experimental trial in Welsh road signs. It is up to the Welsh to choose, but my views are that £3m could be very much better spent on improving our roads than by adopting a tourist gimmick.

Behind this string of misrepresentations (nobody was suggesting changing place names, just spelling them properly, and Iain Noble had hardly invented, as Burton implied, the old Broadford Gaelic name of An t-Ath Leathann), linguistic inadequacies even in English ('informatory' and 'prolification'), attempts at social division ('people outwith the islands') and logical log-jams (tourists to Skye were surely likely to be as unfamiliar with the word Portree as with its Gaelic spelling – and did his last sentence indicate that Lord Burton was not entirely concerned after all with tourist welfare?), there was a slight, forlorn sense of isolation. The letter was the sound of a man being left behind. The old Inverness-shire acreocracy, the titled denizens of the council chambers and the Highland Club, could feel in 1973 the wind of change. Their nursemaid's and New Year's Eve Gaelic, once sufficient to elicit admiring chortles, might no longer be enough. Their old certainties were under threat. And Lord Burton took the Gaelic threat very seriously indeed. Later in 1973, he found himself debating the Local Government (Scotland) Bill in the House of Lords. He took the opportunity to attempt to forestall any use of Gaelic by the new local authorities which would come into being in the following year as a result of reorganisation. One of those authorities would be an all-purpose council serving the Gaidhealtachd islands between Lewis and Vatersay. It would be, argued Burton, 'a waste of public money' if any of the new Scottish authorities followed the Welsh example in promoting their native language. He was persuaded to withdraw his amendment to the Bill.

Even Lord Burton cannot have missed another letter pertinent to his subject, for it appeared in the same column of the same issue of the same newspaper. It was written by an elderly and distinguished Skyeman in response to a proposal from another eminent Skyeman. Far from pouring condescension and scorn on the idea of Gaelic being used on Skye road signs, T.M. Murchison of Kylerhea engaged with the practical problems involved in reapplying Gaelic words which had long been disused and dismissed by the authorities. But T.M. Murchison did not think that the idea was a bad one. Instead, he supported the institution of a Skye Place Names Society to oversee the restoration to the island of its old identity.

Not all of Inverness County Council, therefore, was sympathetic to new ideas issuing from Iain Noble's Skye estate. Under its new fear-stiùiridh Gordon Barr, the Gaelic college at Sabhal Mòr Ostaig would have to take its first steps independent of local authority assistance – and indeed in the face of some hostility from the new

Highland Regional Council. It did so slowly and steadily. The Scottish Arts Council (SAC) was enjoined to subsidise a Gaelic writer in residence, or *filidh*, based at Sabhal Mòr, and the new post was offered to Catriona Montgomery, a 26-year-old poet from Roag near Dunvegan in Skye.

They were cheerful days in the old steading, flying blindly into the unknown. Iain Noble would look fondly back upon the founding months of Sabhal Mòr Ostaig. 'A number of ceilidhs and dances took place in the hall,' he remembers, 'introducing a flicker of life. The stone structure was cold, the draughts penetrated, and the new concrete floor was not the best for dancing, but the atmosphere of the bar was something new and exciting and it became quite a meeting place for younger people from the south of Skye and elsewhere. The ceilidh evenings broke new ground, for they were conducted entirely in Gaelic, quite out of keeping with most public events in Skye, which were organised in English for the supposed benefit of visiting tourists. Actually, we found that most tourists responded with enthusiasm to a genuine Gaelic evening, run for the benefit of local people rather than one obviously put on for incomers.'

In September 1973, An Comunn Gaidhealach chose to run a summer school for Gaelic learners in Sleat. The buildings at Ostaig were still not suitable and a nearby old schoolhouse was deployed instead. But it offered a sign towards the future. 'That was the true beginning of Ostaig's educational story,' says Iain Noble. 'Then there were occasional lectures, a Gaelic playgroup, night classes for Gaelic learners, various discussions and meetings, events for Gaelic-speaking schoolchildren in Skye and Inverness-shire, and two subsequent summer schools lasting a fortnight each during the summer of 1974.'

Duncan MacQuarrie from Mull was by that time a teacher of Gaelic at the Royal Academy in Inverness. 'There was an article in the *Glasgow Herald*,' he recalls, 'about this Gaelic college and library that was being set up in Skye – that was the first I had heard about it. But not the first time I was there. The first time I was there was ten years earlier, in 1964, when we were making our annual family trip to Harris and, for the first time, there was a ferry across at Mallaig and from Uig to Tarbert and we had no option but to travel through Skye because the 24-hour routes round by Barra and Lochboisdale were no more. On the way up through Sleat, my father stopped and we had a picnic just outside Sabhal Mòr, the ruins of the steading. When I took my father back in later years to about see what we had done at Ostaig, he reminded me about that visit.

'Anyway, at the academy we were in the habit of taking the post-Higher Gaelic pupils on an expedition, on a field trip somewhere – I had been to Barra with them, and my colleague Lachie Dick had been to Uist and Harris, and so, this time, we decided that Sabhal Mòr would be a good venue. This would have been June 1974. I knew very little of Skye, and I took a dozen or so children, and we slept on mattresses, boys separate from girls obviously, up in the loft and there was still straw and things there.

'A little had been done: the big room was there and there was some kind of primitive kitchen. We were there a fortnight, and I had the school minibus, and I took them to Raasay for a day to see the iron mines and various other things. I took them up to the north end of Skye, and we did a range of activities. Gordon Barr was there at that time and we had a ceilidh or two and I think we even ran a dance. The year before, we ran a dance at Castlebay in Barra with my squad, to help pay for the trip!

'On our last night at Sabhal Mòr, it was a lovely night, and we decided that to use up all the remaining food and what not, we would have a barbecue down on the shore just below the entrance to the Tarskavaig road, and the children were with me, and Gordon Barr was there and various other people. We got the barbecue going, and this chap walked along the shore quite diffidently and shyly. Gordon Barr welcomed him and introduced him to me, and that was my first-ever meeting with Iain Noble. As it so happened, that summer I was still single, and they needed a teacher for the summer schools so they invited me to do it and I did. I went back for a fortnight or something like that and taught.

'So, they invited me back, and I came and I taught there in 1974 and I taught in 1975 and I taught in 1976, and by that time, they had got round to making a constitution and getting trustees and suchlike, and they invited me to join the trustees in 1977, I can't recall the precise date, which I did do, and then, at a meeting of the trustees, they decided they would need a chairman so they put Iain Noble in the chair, and he was chair from 1977 to 1978. The trustees then asked me to become chair in 1978, which I did do, and the roller-coaster started then.'

Not all first encounters were quite so rosy. 'My own first experience of Sabhal Mòr Ostaig,' says Alan Campbell, 'was when I went back to Skye from Aberdeen to work for Iain Noble's estate and, within a matter of weeks of being back there, I was at the filling station in Ardvasar. There were only two local people in and one man asked me if I'd been to Sabhal Mòr. I said, "No, but I must go – what's it like?" He said, "Ach, it's just a dump, it's just a ramshackle building and people go there for these courses from all over the world, absolute crackpots, Americans and people who are just not on the same planet as us."

'Now, putting aside the slight exaggeration that I'd heard there, there was a general feeling that Sabhal Mòr was a little bit like a Martian settlement that had been dropped onto Sleat, and the local community, particularly the Gaelic-speaking community, didn't really take to it at first; they felt suspicious about it, they felt that there was something phoney about it, something slightly crazy. It struggled to achieve identity and to be accepted in the community. There was another problem as well, I suppose, and that was that a lot of the trustees who were giving of their own time, endless Saturdays and nights and God knows, for meetings, weren't people who lived in Sleat. I mean, I lived in Sleat for ten of the years that I was involved in various ways with Sabhal Mòr, but it's true to say that a lot of the other people were not of the immediate area. So it struggled to be accepted, and clearly it was vitally important that it was accepted.'

In November 1974, following the return of Gordon Barr to Dundee University, the charitable trust the Gulbenkian Foundation offered Sabhal Mòr Ostaig a three-year grant towards the cost of a full-time director. Farquhar MacLennan, a teacher from the small neighbouring island of Raasay who was currently headmaster at Balivanich School in Benbecula in the Western Isles, was offered and accepted the post in the spring of 1975. MacLennan had the virtue of being not only an educationalist, but also a native Gaelic speaker and – as a Ratharsach – the nearest possible thing to a Skyeman.

At about this time, in January 1975, Iain Noble prepared a kind of loose mission statement for Sabhal Mòr Ostaig. It would prove to be wonderfully percipient:

> What will Ostaig do? At this stage no plans are definite, but three functions seem to be evolving as the natural role of the new College. The first of these is to provide a course for Gaelic learners during the summer months, to meet the tremendous demands from people throughout Scotland and indeed from all over the world, who would like to learn Scotland's ancient language. In theory, it should become possible for a keen learner to become moderately fluent during a single summer period of say three months.
>
> The second idea is to start a course which would last either one or two years with some kind of award or diploma at the end. These courses would be in Gaelic, and would be intended either as an addition to or a substitute for a University degree. Students would be taught about the flourishing literature of the Gaels, local history and environmental subjects of every kind including geology and biology. There might be scope for certain practical subjects as an optional extra, such as agriculture, trawling and other trades, and the theme could be to educate people for life in a rural community, rather than to train them for professions in the cities. An exciting prospect indeed!
>
> The third function of Ostaig, and some might say its most important, could be to act as a teachers' laboratory, producing new teaching materials and visual aids, carrying out comparative studies with what is happening in Ireland, Wales and elsewhere, and acting as a publishing centre for new text books.

Within 20 years, all of that vision and quite a lot more would be realised.

Throughout the late 1970s, Sabhal Mòr Ostaig steadily found its feet. It did not do so in complete isolation. An itinerant Gaelic theatre company named Fir Chlis (Northern Lights) would regularly stop by to refresh itself at Iain Noble's Eilean Iarmain bar in Sleat before embarking on another odyssey around the schools and village halls of the Gaidhealtachd. 'They sowed seeds,' says Alan Campbell. 'Fir Chlis came and went like the name says, the Aurora Borealis, they flashed and lit up the Gaidhealtachd in the 1970s with humour and drama and laughter. Some of the people involved are still around – Sìm MacKenzie, Mairead Ross, Rhino Morrison. They sowed a seed. They showed that there was a real demand for what Gaelic-language theatre could offer the community. It was as a result of Fir Chlis that the youth drama thing developed with Pròiseact nan Ealan [the Gaelic Arts Agency] – Rhino was loosely involved in that. That has led to the Gaelic theatre group Tosg, and we now have Meanbh-chuileag as well – the puppet show within the schools. All those skills were developed along the road from Fir Chlis, fed by superb work by people like John Murray and Finlay MacLeod writing for them – without these writers, it wouldn't have happened either. So these things exploded into the quality soaps and drama which have appeared on Gaelic television, like *Machair* . . . all these things have grown out of these initiatives that were taken and all these little chemical processes that were happening 25 and 30 years ago – it's just wonderful.'

Gaelic publishing continued its stuttering revival with the introduction of magazines such as *Crùisgean* and concerns such as the Stornoway company Acair. 'We rightly aspired to a Gaelic newspaper,' says Campbell. 'But we have to recognise that if there is one sector of consumerism which is totally dependent on the marketplace, then it is a newspaper. If people don't like what you're writing, they don't buy it. If they don't like what it looks like, they don't buy it. And at the end of the day, from your perspective as a producer, they have to buy it, because you have to spend real money to get that damn thing out there, and you cannot sell advertising unless it's going out there, so the whole thing is a vicious circle. The reality of our Gaelic community, sadly still, is that it is a very small market. Even if you were to write half of it in English, it is still a small marketplace. You're struggling for credibility with a readership which is prepared to pay real money for this thing and credibility with advertisers who have to put their money on it. *Crùisgean* suffered from that, it was too small a market.'

In 1976, BBC Radio Highland was established in Inverness with a specific Gaelic-friendly remit, and when in 1979 it was joined by Radio nan Eilean, Scotland had its first Gaelic radio station, which was based in the Western Isles, and its first Gaelic morning news magazine programme, *Aithris na Maidne*. For possibly the first time, broadcast journalists began to be hired by the BBC for their ability to research, prepare and transmit items purely in and through Gaelic, rather than merely translate English news copy. A new category of Gaelic professional was consequently created.

Meanwhile, the reorganisation of British local government which was initiated by the Conservative government of 1970 to 1974 had resulted in a substantial change to the Scottish Gaidhealtachd. The inhabited Western Isles from Lewis in the north to Vatersay in the south, which had previously been divided between Inverness-shire and Ross-shire county councils, were re-formed into a single, all-purpose local authority, Comhairle nan Eilean, the Western Isles Islands Council.

The implications were substantial. The crofters of the Outer Hebrides had, since the wider enfranchisement created by the Third Reform Act in 1884, consistently registered a radical vote. Following their formation into a single Western Isles parliamentary constituency in 1919, the Islands had returned a succession of idiosyncratic and latterly socialist or nationalist MPs. While the council chambers of Inverness and Dingwall continued into the second half of the twentieth century to be dominated by mainland aristocrats and landowners, usually returned unopposed, the few island councillors offered a leavening of more genuinely popular representation. They could have too little impact on the mainland polity, but once given an authority of their own, the prospects seemed promising.

One of those island councillors was Father Calum MacLellan. Born into an Eriskay family in 1926, Calum MacLellan was raised in that independent, virtually monoglot community. 'It was an island of 500 people,' he remembers, 'very self-contained. The island had its own life; we never thought even of going to Uist for the day – it wasn't easy to do. The only time we went to Uist was to go to the cattle sale and then walk miles with the little steer and come back holding four pounds or something, if you were lucky. Then we would sail to Lochboisdale to go to the shops there on a wee sailing boat. Sometimes we would go to Barra, that was easy – there were shops in Barra. Apart from that, we never went off the island, really. We had two shops and the school, there were over one hundred children at the school, and the church was very much the centre of the life on the island. It was hard work. My father was away at sea a lot, or he would be fishing, and there were eight of us so my mother had quite a lot of hard work to do. She had to bake every day because there was no bread available except what you made yourself, and your life was tied up with working the croft, getting peat together, getting the harvest in or planting it. You can't plough in Eriskay, everything had to be done by spade, so it was hard work.

'It was a monoglot Gaelic-speaking community. Not much English, except my first two teachers had no Gaelic at all! I was talking once to somebody who used to sit beside me in school and I said to her, "We were the same age," and she said, "No, I'm a year older, you skipped the infants because you could read English when you went to school." I still remember that. There was a book – "The cat sat on the mat" – I remember particularly. So, I could read, but then you weren't allowed to speak Gaelic in school, you couldn't address your teacher in Gaelic or any of these things – the language of the playground was all Gaelic, but eventually, if you were sending a note, you had to do it in English because you weren't taught to do it through Gaelic.

'Eventually there was an attempt made there [to promote the use of Gaelic] – the headmaster we had at the time was Donald

Campbell who was a very good musician, a nice singer, and we used to sing Gaelic songs. I think I used to sing a sort of alto. There were Gaelic books around at school, but really I learned the Gaelic that I loved by reading the New Testament. I learned the literature, how to read Gaelic, how to write Gaelic myself, without having to go to school. The Church languages were Latin and Gaelic – it made life very simple!

'One of the teachers was quite progressive and she used to produce a pantomime every year. I remember her giving me a test to see whether I could dance, and she dismissed me out of hand, so I didn't get a part in the thing. It was just a school, I didn't dislike the school but, with so many children – we only had three teachers and there were one hundred kids – it was mainly learning by memory work, there was very little individual teaching. They would help you along, so if you had a good memory you were all right. Then there were some other teachers – "All those who don't know, come out to the floor" – bang! – some of the children would be terrified because what little they knew would have disappeared. I was saved all of that because I had a good memory. I wouldn't necessarily say that I was highly intelligent, but I had a good memory, and it was mainly memory work.'

When he left Eriskay School at the age of fourteen, Calum MacLellan decided to enter the priesthood. After five years at Blairs College in Aberdeen and a spell in the army, he studied for six years in Rome before returning to the Diocese of Argyll and the Isles. After an extended period on the mainland at Oban and Dunoon, he was able in 1962 to return to the Islands, to St Peter's at Daliburgh in South Uist. In the late 1960s, he was posted to Northbay in Barra. At that time, remarkably, both of the Barra representatives on Inverness County Council were men with island connections who actually lived on the mainland.

'One of them, Iain MacFadyen, came to me and he said, "Will you go on the council?" I said, "I'm not interested in these things," and he said, "Well, I don't think it's fair that both councillors should be on the mainland." So I went onto the Inverness Council and that's how it started. I went to Inverness and the refrain was:

Sir Iain Noble
welcomes HRH Prince
Charles to Sabhal Mòr
Ostaig in 2004.
(courtesy of SMO)

Sorley Maclean, the great
Gaelic poet who was one of
the first trustees of the
college. (© Cailean Maclean)

Alan Campbell: 'There used to be a cynical perception that this was the crazy notion of an Edinburgh merchant banker.' (courtesy of SMO)

Part of the present library at Ostaig, which started life as a book repository. (courtesy of SMO)

Revd Jack MacArthur. 'If you had a problem you felt you couldn't deal with yourself, Jack was always there.' – Norman Gillies (courtesy of SMO)

The politician and journalist Brian Wilson, who worked tirelessly for Gaelic all across the country. (courtesy of SMO)

Farquhar MacIntosh: 'The exclusion of Gaelic from schools by the 1872 Education Act was probably the most serious blow it has suffered.' (courtesy of SMO)

Donnie Munro: 'There was in the 1970s almost no opportunity for young people to experience any contemporary expression of Gaelic.' (courtesy of SMO)

Roy Pedersen: 'Thirty years ago, Gaelic had a low status both in the eyes of the outside world and of its own speakers.' (courtesy of SMO)

Seán O Drisceoil: 'Our brief was to establish the first college of tertiary education to be run through the medium of Gaelic anywhere in the world.' (courtesy of SMO)

Duncan MacQuarrie, the man from Mull who 'made the college a reality'. (courtesy of Duncan MacQuarrie)

Jim Hunter: 'Something which most other societies take for granted – that young people should have the right to be educated in their own language – still seems to us to be in the nature of a novel and daring experiment.' (courtesy of SMO)

The growth of Gaelic-medium primary education and pre-school playgroups came just in time to arrest a chronic decline in the numbers of young speakers. (courtesy of SMO)

John Norman MacLeod: 'The world is changing and Gaelic has moved on.' (courtesy of SMO)

Norman Gillies: 'If you think that this college is here only because of Gaels, or even people who speak Gaelic, you're very wrong.' (courtesy of SMO)

President Mary Robinson speaking in Skye: 'Perhaps we can create an island space for ourselves to celebrate what Scotland and Ireland share.' (courtesy of SMO)

First Minister Donald Dewar: 'There are [in the Highlands] people in good heart, proud of their inheritance, determined to build a future in which they will flourish.' (courtesy of SMO)

Chancellor Gordon Brown: 'What a bland and uniform place this Britain of ours would be if Britishness meant we all spoke the same way, sang, danced and celebrated the same way.' (courtesy of SMO)

"We've solved the education problem everywhere except the Western Isles; we've solved the housing problem, except in the Western Isles." It was a bit frustrating, but eventually I quite enjoyed it. I wasn't a wilting lily.

'Nearly all the chairmen were county types. They met and put their policies together in the Highland Club and the rest of us went to a pub. So when the idea of decentralising local government was first mooted, we knew that Shetland and Orkney would be promoted to an all-purpose island authority, and I felt there was an opportunity for us too. All I got was discouragement from Lord Macdonald, who was convener. James MacKay was the deputy convener, and he said, "There's no one in the Western Isles who can run such a council. I only know one suitable person and he's in London"! Actually, some of the old councillors from the Islands weren't all that keen – they didn't want things to change all that much, and they were suspicious of Lewis for some reason. I asked the Skye people if they would come in, and they were also suspicious of Lewis, funnily enough. I sent word down to Tiree and these places as well – I had a vision of a little Gaelic empire!

'But it really annoyed me that the mainland Establishment were saying, "You can't do anything for yourselves" – that's precisely what it was about. I had public meetings in Barra and it wasn't easy to convince everyone; they wanted to stay with whatever was there. Then I decided that I would get all the local councillors together, from North Uist and so on, and we had a meeting in Creagorry in Benbecula. Well, local community leaders heard about all this in Stornoway, so I went up to meet them. That was a breath of fresh air, to meet the young people there. The businessman and politician Sandy Matheson and a number of others . . . They were so positive. They found out that we in the Southern Isles were quite serious about the whole thing.

'Then there was a conference to discuss the proposal in Inverness, and this nice man from Glasgow said, "It's not possible, it just won't work – the Sabbath observance thing in the northern islands, you know, it's not applied in the south," and he tried to imply that we wouldn't be able to work together because there were planes flying into Barra on a Sunday, and he put in a few other objections. It was not plain sailing.

'But then, the whole thing, the Western Isles Islands Council, Comhairle nan Eilean, started to take shape. It was exciting, and hard work because you had to start from zero and you had to start employing people. What was so great about it was the young people coming back. Actually, because one of the attractions of having your own local authority was that you could create jobs, many jobs of various kinds, I proposed at one stage that they should put a department in Tarbert, one in Lochmaddy, one in Daliburgh, one in Barra, and they said, "You can't do that, they're too far apart," and I said, "Multinational companies communicate over the telephone." Anyway, I lost that one.

'I had to do most of the interviewing, and it was chaotic. We would be interviewing until two o'clock in the morning because they were coming on boats and going away in the morning, and you were getting bad tempered, and they would be queuing up for hours and so on.

'I can't say that the language, the fact that almost everyone involved was a Gaelic speaker and that we would be dealing with a constituency almost entirely composed of Gaelic speakers featured much in the early discussions. I just had this thing in me about "Why do we have to go to the mainland for everything?" After we got established, or began to get established, it was then that the bilingual thing came on.'

Perhaps the most influential of the 1970s Gaelic revivalists was a distinctly non-governmental initiative. In 1973, a group calling itself the Run-Rig Dance Band performed for the first time at Glasgow's Kelvin Hall. It was a three-piece unit consisting of two brothers of North Uist extraction who had been brought up in Skye – guitarist Rory Macdonald and drummer Calum Macdonald – and a Skye accordion player named Blair Douglas.

The following year, an art student named Donnie Munro, who had attended school at Portree in Skye with Calum Macdonald, joined the band as vocalist. He was followed shortly afterwards by another old Skye schoolfriend, Robert Macdonald, who replaced Blair Douglas.

For a number of years Runrig – the name derives from a traditionally communal Highland form of field tillage – operated as a younger, hipper version of the part-time ceilidh bands which routinely traversed the north of Scotland. But they developed a unique sound and style. They wrote many of their songs themselves, adapted traditional airs to a folk-rock format, and, most crucially, they wrote and performed in Gaelic.

They became the sound of a generation of young Gaels. Their first two albums, *Play Gaelic* and *The Highland Connection*, achieved saturation coverage in the north of Scotland in the late 1970s. They were attractive, clever, accomplished and local. They were sensationally accessible and easy on the ear. They were the Beatles, or the U2, or the Boyzone of the Scottish Gaidhealtachd. Runrig may have done more to legitimise the Gaelic language among teenagers than any other project of the second half of the twentieth century. When in Skye, they occasionally performed at Sabhal Mòr Ostaig. It was the beginning of a lengthy symbiosis, perhaps most fully realised when lead singer Donnie Munro became development officer at the Gaelic college in the late 1990s.

'It is important to recognise the poverty of opportunity, at that time, in the early 1970s,' Donnie Munro recalls, 'for young [Gaelic] people to experience any contemporary expression of their language and culture. Strangely enough, the major musical influences at the time emerged from outwith Scotland, namely through Alan Stivell in Brittany, Fairport Convention in England and Horslips in Ireland.

'What had basically happened by that point, in common with so many other minority language communities throughout the world, was an almost complete rejection of the language and culture by young people, the result of their alienation from their own social history, and of the unspoken conspiracy of Establishment elites who had systematically dismantled the status of the language.

'One of the significant turning points in the lives of many young Gaels at that time occurred at the point of displacement where they found themselves in the large city universities, where distance and separation created the opportunity for reappraisal. At that time

Runrig had begun to perform this new form of Gaelic and Gaelic-influenced music around the Scottish university circuit. There was a sense of pride and identity emerging from young Gaels in the cities, and they in turn were a major influence on their non-Gaelic friends.

'However, it took this form of almost external validation to allow young people in the Gaidhealtachd itself to feel comfortable with a band which was performing through a language and from a cultural root which they themselves had so recently rejected.

'I always remember the negative response which the band encountered when we played our first all-Gaelic set in our home village of Portree, and our being hurt and dismayed by this rejection. In retrospect, it is easy to see why these young people, on that night, waiting to see a band that had become popular on the basis of playing current rock and pop covers, were so negative. In a sense we were the mirror image of all that they had rejected. Things changed dramatically when success was achieved outwith the Gaidhealtachd and through the impact of the external validation of mainstream pop and rock music culture.

'Runrig were aware of the role of SMO [Sabhal Mòr Ostaig] at that time, indeed playing on a number of occasions the Talla Mòr [Great Hall] at the Arainn Ostaig campus. Both Rory and I had had some links with the college, with Rory having designed the original logo, and I myself illustrated their first promotional brochure.

'However, despite there being no official links between SMO and Runrig, in tandem with all the other key influences at that time, the political vacuum filled by the *West Highland Free Press*, the historical work of Dr James Hunter, the Gaelic development agencies etc., there was an emerging sense of a critical mass of activity, a sort of groundswell of support for the language.

'In Runrig's case, I believe this was to achieve a national context, with many young Scottish people looking for an authentic icon of Scottish identity which culturally distanced them as far as possible from Margaret Thatcher's Britain.'

There was no official focus for all of those initiatives and reforms, but if there was a social one, it would be found in Sleat. The renovated public bar at Tigh Osda Eilean Iarmain, the fine old hotel around the corner from Iain Noble's estate headquarters, became something of a Gaelic clearing house. The landowner's continuing insistence on employing mainly Gaelic-speaking staff attracted employees from as far afield as Lismore in Argyllshire and Port of Ness in Lewis. Noble's open-armed approach to everybody and anybody who was professionally involved – or even just interested – in Gaelic resulted in many of them regarding this bar as a local far from home. Summer-school students from Sabhal Mòr would naturally gravitate there, and many people from Sleat had long regarded the bar at Eilean Iarmain as their native hostel. The result was a lively and intriguing social centre, whose first language more often than not was Gaelic.

Three miles down the road at Ostaig, Farquhar MacLennan's Sabhal Mòr was progressing cautiously. Catriona Montgomery was succeeded as filidh by the pre-eminent Gaelic writer of the twentieth century, MacLennan's fellow Ratharsach Sorley Maclean. Maclean himself gave way to a brilliant young poet and future Scottish Writer of the Year, Aonghas MacNeacail from Uig in north Skye. Còmhlan Phìobairean Shlèite, the new Sleat Pipe Band, found a congenial home there among the summer piping classes. A grant from the Catherine MacCaig Trust assisted the library, and friendly links with the University of Stirling aided MacLennan in his development of courses.

In July 1978, the trustees of Sabhal Mòr Ostaig established a committee to look into the prospects of delivering a two-year full-time diploma course through the medium of Gaelic. Two years later, the committee reported that:

> If the social and cultural progress of the last few years is to be turned into a secure long-term economic revival, it is essential to harness local talent for the service of the area.
>
> Courses should be made available which offer training in business and administrative skills, and which relate this training to the problems, way of life and potential of the area; these should include a long-term course, and short specialist

courses using the same materials and teacher skills. It is
desirable that these courses be made available within the
area, thus not being of themselves a means of separating the
students from their home environment; and for the same
reason teaching should be for the most part in Gaelic, as the
indigenous language for the area . . .

The course should be . . . practically rather than
theoretically oriented, and should introduce the student to
the principles of a wide range of disciplines. The present rate
of technological and economic change underlines the
importance of flexibility and an ability to supply well-
understood principles of analysis to new problems. Students
should also have some opportunity to study in detail the
management and operation of Highland industries.

Students should be awakened to an understanding of
Highland society, its history, its problems, and its potential;
this implies a study of other comparable societies, their
similarities, differences, successes and failures. The
indigenous culture of the Highlands should be studied both
in its own right and as an expression of the lives, hopes and
difficulties of the inhabitants of the area.

Improved relations with most local authorities, the increased
number of Gaels from within the educational establishment who
were connected with Sabhal Mòr Ostaig and consequent
connections within the Scottish Education Department made these
aims appear suddenly feasible. The October of 1983 was suggested
as the most realistic date upon which such a course might
commence.

The chairman of the trustees, Duncan MacQuarrie, recalls the
process: 'Farquhar MacLennan was there and he was the
administrator/college secretary. He had come from being a head
teacher in Benbecula. I think Aonghas Dubh MacNeacail was the
writer in residence at that time. By this time Iain Noble and I had
become firm friends, and I had gathered round me another group
of, I felt, powerful people who were not afraid to challenge for

things, and I thought it very important to have people who were not afraid to challenge ideas. It sounds very vainglorious to say it, but I had been reading a book about Churchill, and the reason for his success was that he had got the most powerful people in the land round about him in his Cabinet, and I thought that was a good idea.

'So I approached Donald John MacKay, who was then chief executive of Harris Tweed, previously head of personnel for British Alcan. I approached Lachie Dick, who had become depute director of education in the Western Isles, and I approached Alan Campbell, who was working for Iain Noble at Fearann Eilean Iarmain in Sleat. Then I took them on as a kind of executive group and I gave them each distinct roles. I wanted Lachie Dick to support me in driving forward education, and I wanted Alan Campbell to take on the role of making sure the buildings were fit for their purpose, insofar as we could, and Donald John I took on to ensure the administration side of things was looked after.

'They were an exceptionally loyal group of people who gave unsparingly of their time. We used to start our meetings at 11 a.m. on a Saturday, and they would finish at 5 p.m. on a Saturday, long meetings because we were breaking new ground the whole time, and we could not foresee, in many respects, what the consequences of what we were doing were. That was, broadly speaking, the group of people that determined the role that the college would take in the 1980s and beyond.

'There were wheels within wheels . . . Iain Noble and I were asked to give a talk at a series of talks that Inverness Museum was holding at that time on the place of Gaelic in today's society, so Iain came to stay with me in Inverness and we spoke at this lunchtime talk. Willie Morrison, the reporter, was with the *Aberdeen Press and Journal* at the time and we got front-page headlines with our theme of 'Gaelic can make a difference – Gaelic as an economic tool', and this arose out of a discussion we'd had, probably the previous summer.

'There was a good ferment of ideas going already, even though it was still only the late 1970s. We managed to get some money from the Anglo-German Foundation for the Study of Industrial Society to employ Neil Mitchison as a researcher to work on a feasibility study for a course in business studies that would encompass entrepreneurship and so on. I had been briefing the trustees at every meeting as to what was happening and also briefing them on the telephone, and they were all signed up to the idea. A lot of people in the Gaelic world were not signed up to the idea, but we nonetheless got some crucial support. We got support from Ronald MacDonald at the Highland Regional Council in Inverness and we got very clear and sharp support from Neil Galbraith at the Western Isles Council.

'I was going to Skye probably once every two or three weeks and holding a series of meetings and holding meetings out in Inverness and what not . . . it was like having another job. But it was really exciting and we were, at the same time, negotiating with the Highlands and Islands Development Board, and they, of course, had to be taken aboard as key players. That wonderful man Bob Storey was our main link there, and once we had convinced Bob, and once Bob had convinced Iain MacAskill and Ken Alexander, things began to move. To give them their due, both of those people saw merit in what we were proposing.

'There were one or two flashes of inspiration – there was a great hullabaloo at that time about the economics of the Pacific Rim in Japan and Korea and suchlike, and I said, "What about the economics of the Atlantic Rim?" and that has, over the years, developed into the Honours degree in North Atlantic studies. Also, a component of it all was visits to the Faeroes and to Ireland, particularly Donegal, to see what work was going on in cooperatives. We had, as I said, quite a ferment of ideas flying around. So, with the help of a variety of people and the help of the Job Creation Programme, we started getting the building repaired, and key to getting the roof put on was the money raised by the Fiddlers' Rallies which Marion Whyte ran in various parts of Scotland. It was for the college's benefit that she ran them and, you know, she was taking in say £3,000 at a time or something like that, and that put on a big chunk of roof and windows and what not.

'As part and parcel of this, Iain and I decided that we would try and raise some money in London – by that time I was married so it must have been post-1979. We had arranged a number of meetings with organisations such as Gulbenkian and Total Oil and so on, and we had a presentation ready for them. We made presentations to a range of people, to The Pilgrim Trust and to the Anglo-German people again, and, in that one day, between pledges and promises and actual cheques in the post, and this would be spread over about five years, we raised about £90,000 – it was quite amazing.

'In parallel with that, we approached the Scottish Office in 1981 with our ideas, with our feasibility study, and made an application to have this course recognised as a Higher National Diploma. The reason we went for that route was that people coming to do an HND would get grants which were fixed amounts, and there was more money in them for students than there was in going for further education courses which would only attract local authority bursaries which seemed, at any rate, to be awarded in a more arbitrary fashion – that was one principal reason. The other reason was that an HND had status.

'And we were of course working with Stirling University at the time, with the late Robert Innes there, and we were looking for somebody to give us verification or to accredit these courses. We tried CNAA [the Council for National Academic Awards], as it was then, we tried Stirling University, and we approached the Scottish Office, who sent up some inspectors to see us. The lead inspector was convinced that what we were proposing was not viable and that the students we talked about would be better off going to Lews Castle College in Stornoway, and whatever we did, we could not assure them that there was no rivalry between SMO and Lews Castle College and that it was a different clientele altogether. There were statements of objection quoting things like small numbers, remoteness, the usual very centralist approach, and so the first application was knocked back.

'We went away and revamped our application and came back about a year later, and this time they had put in charge a different gentleman of a more senior rank, and he listened to our arguments, and along with him were another two gentlemen, one was from

Kintyre and one was from the Islands, and our arguments won favour. They agreed to give us recognition, surrounded by a number of caveats for the first three years, and we would have to reapply after three years for revalidation. One of the caveats was that SCOTBEC would award the HND and that Robert Gordon's University would work with Sabhal Mòr to develop the courses. That happened, and we opened for business in 1983 with the first tranche of students and with our first principal, Seán O Drisceoil.'

'In the early days,' says Alan Campbell, 'however much people might have lauded the concept of what Sabhal Mòr Ostaig was all about, there was nonetheless a rather cynical perception that this was a rather crazy notion that had come from an eccentric merchant banker, Iain Noble. The perception that he was playing in Skye, playing at creating colleges, and some people said, I think quite wrongly, playing at creating a name for himself.

'I remember very clearly when we struggled to develop the first course and to get validation for it. I was working for the BBC, and I remember, the day the validating committee finally met at Sabhal Mòr Ostaig, I was in Stornoway and came back to Inverness that evening. I had arranged to get a day off the next day – I was living in Skye then – and I headed hell for leather from Inverness Airport to Skye and straight to Sabhal Mòr, where Professor Ralph Hart, who was the chair of the validating committee had been through the whole validating exercise earlier in the day.

'They were now coming to assess the building itself, which was my responsibility at the time. Now the difficulty I had with the building was that a lot of the money – looking at it today it was chicken feed, we're talking about £120,000–130,000, but it was a huge amount of money then – a lot of the money which I'd actually been promised was validation dependent. So we couldn't actually trigger the money until we got validation, and we couldn't issue a contract to do any work until we had money. We were now in April, as I recall, and we were due to have the doors open at the end of August for an intake of students. We had the summer holidays. One of the blessings at the time was that the new primary school in Sleat, Bun-sgoil Shlèite, was being built. I was actually the school board representative and very much involved in getting that school. The fact that we had contractors on that site made it possible for us to do some of the most complicated bits like the fire stairs at Sabhal Mòr, and the contractor John D. MacGregor did that for us at a very good price. That was the kind of thing that wouldn't have been possible had these guys not been "on site", so we had luck running with us.

'I remember Ralph Hart saying to me that evening at Sabhal Mòr that things had gone quite well, and he said, "What about the building? We've looked round, it's OK, but there's a lot to be done." I said to him, "Well, what do you want from me?" and he said, "There's only one question: can you deliver the building?" I said, "Yes, I believe I can, but I can't promise it will be painted." He said, "That's all right, as long as there are doors and windows and heating and plumbing before winter."

'And that's my memory of that day, and it was pretty fraught from then on to get that building finished, but we got there. This was the conversion of the old building. There were signs to say not to walk underneath here because a slate might come down and kill you – there was what they call 'nail fatigue', so when we had ceilidhs in the old hall the slates used to fall off.

'I've often thought about the people who were involved at that time in Sabhal Mòr, people like Sorley Maclean and D.R. Macdonald, Iain Noble, Donald John MacKay, Duncan MacQuarrie, the minister and wonderfully effective local politician Jack MacArthur – so many of those champions are gone. I remember it was one of Jack's aspirations when we were making the case for the hall and trying to get funding for the college itself, that we should make the case that we were creating a community facility. It was vitally important that the community would see Sabhal Mòr as a resource. I remember Jack saying, "I would like to think that we could use it as a facility for practising church singing, precenting and so on." I don't know if we ever achieved that.'

But before all these worthy things had the slightest chance of achieving fruition, the anarchic, activist early years of Sabhal Mòr Ostaig enjoyed a last, short fling.

Five

I t blew up – perhaps inevitably – over road signs. English-language road signs were still there. They had never gone away as a symbol of callous authority. Iain Noble had enjoyed a further little spat with Inverness County Council when – in the wake of his Viewfield Road dispute with them – he chose one of the loneliest and least-travelled lanes on his estate to erect a cattle-grid warning sign. The sign, just outside Ord on a single track which runs around the west coast of Sleat, was as triangular and neat as any other cattle-grid warning sign. Beneath the words 'Cattle Grid' it announced 'Cliath Chruidh'. Dutifully playing its part in the roundelay, Inverness County Council ordered him to take it down.

Iain Taylor was a Gaelic learner from Elgin in Morayshire on the north-east coast who had spent his summers in the mid-1970s working behind bars in Portree and at Eilean Iarmain. Holidaying while a boy with a grandmother in Stratherrick had given him a rudimentary understanding of Gaelic, and later, 'in Elgin Academy, we were lucky because there were two Gaelic speakers who were prepared to teach the Gaelic O grade syllabus. But it had to be done informally. There were six of us in my class, five native speakers and me. It was funny, you wouldn't normally get that in Elgin but it just happened. The other pupils were all from Lewis families, apart from one who was from north-west Sutherland, and they'd all moved into Elgin. So I think six of us would have done Gaelic that year, and that would have been us leaving school in 1972. But the headmaster was from Inverness town and very anti-Gaelic, so he wouldn't let us sit the O grade as school pupils – we had to go as external county candidates because as far as he was concerned Gaelic just wasn't spoken in Morayshire!'

Taylor progressed to the Gaelic course at Aberdeen University, working every summer throughout the middle of the 1970s in Skye, did a 'hellish' stint with the Department of Health and Social Security in Barnet, Hertfordshire, returned to Aberdeen to work for Occidental Oil, and late in 1979, he saw an advertisement in *The Scotsman* for fear-stiùiridh of Sabhal Mòr Ostaig. 'It was basically to keep the place ticking over, to keep the short-courses programme going and to try to develop more things associated with it – fund-raising was a major part, and I was crap at that.

'Anyway, I replied to that advert and was interviewed here in the college and there was Duncan MacQuarrie, Iain Noble, I think Ailean Beag MacDonald, the headmaster from Staffin who was extremely active in Gaelic issues, and Sorley Maclean. That's right, I think there was the four of them. And the others who were in for it. I remember that Neil Mitchison, who you hear regularly on the BBC, was in for it, but I don't think he wanted it particularly because he was on the point of going to the BBC. I got the job; I think that must have been December or November in 1979, and I started just after the New Year of 1980.'

He moved into an old shepherd's cottage adjacent to the college buildings, which had earlier been home to Gordon Barr and which served as rough-and-ready tied accommodation. Along with the renowned Gaelic singer Christine Primrose from Lewis, who worked in a part-time secretarial capacity, Taylor settled into his new position. 'The job was trying to raise money. Our pay was safe because that came from a grant from, I think, the Scottish Education Department at the time, so it was to raise money to buy books to extend the library and to increase the numbers of members of Caidreamh an t-Sabhail [Friends of the College] and to just try to kind of make the place tick along.

'We had three teachers at the summer schools: Jean MacLeay, who teaches at Lìonacleit in Benbecula; Donnie Murray from Lewis, who died; Tommy Ross who was a Gaelic teacher in a Glasgow school, Woodside, I think. There were also classes at other times of the year, like piping – Davy Garrett, Evan MacRae and Andy Ventors were the tutors there – and there would also be school trips. Iain MacIllechiar who works over in Inverness College, he was the Gaelic teacher at Pitlochry at the time, he would bring pupils, Duncan MacQuarrie would bring pupils and they would just kind of rough it.

'We would get manuscripts from people, and it was before there were computers, so we would get manuscripts of plays and stuff like that from the theatre group Fir Chlis, because Mairead Ross was in charge of that and we were quite friendly. So Mairead would send us any scripts that she got, and we would type them up and try to make them look as nice as you can on a typewriter for publication; but the plays never got published at all. Groups of students from Aberdeen or Edinburgh or Glasgow would come – you know, the Celtic societies, that sort of thing – just for glorified piss-ups really, but also to visit the Highlands and Islands. You would get isolated individual researchers – I remember there was a French girl who stayed in Eigg, Camille Dressler [now a fellow of the Centre for Human Ecology there and the author of *Eigg: The Story of an Island*], and she was over here a few times using the library. Even then, it was a very good library, it wasn't bad at all. There was herself and people doing different research projects, because things were just starting in Gaelic then, and Ken MacKinnon was doing a lot of work at Hatfield College, so he would get research students doing particular projects, and they would just come and live at the college and use the library, or use it as a base.'

In the summer of 1980, Iain Taylor was given willing assistance at Sabhal Mòr Ostaig by two more young people, Stephen Maceachern and Anne Martin. Stephen was a Gaelic learner from Pitlochry: 'Gaelic had skipped his mum's generation and so he was wanting to do a thing on Perthshire and eastern dialects, but we never had the money to do anything, there wasn't even a tape recorder that worked. Stephen would have come at the start of the summer of 1980 and remained for the year before going back to Junior Honours in Aberdeen. It actually meant having an extra pair of hands, and I think that we held more short courses the second summer, because it meant that he could do things in the office and I could teach a class at the same time.' Anne Martin was a native speaker from Kilmuir in Skye who would stand in for Christine Primrose as college secretary and would later establish herself as a Gaelic singer of great range and ability. She had always, she says, seen Gaelic as 'an asset and a positive part of my inheritance'.

'And then,' remembers Iain Taylor, 'all of the things happened with Donald Stewart's Bill in Parliament.'

Donald Stewart had been the Scottish National Party MP for the Western Isles since 1970. In 1981, he was one of the winners of the annual lottery to introduce a Private Member's Bill to the House of Commons. Following some consultation with An Comunn Gaidhealach and the Gaelic Society of London, of which he was chief, Stewart decided to introduce a Gaelic language Bill.

Retrospectively, in purely political terms, it was the wrong Bill at the wrong time. Stewart insisted upon a range of far-reaching reforms. In his own words, he demanded: 'increased choice to pupils to choose Gaelic as a school language; to give the language equal status to the level of Welsh in Wales; [and] some improvement in the time allowed for broadcasting in Gaelic.'

This was both vague (what constituted 'increased choice' and 'some improvement'?) and over-ambitious. Parity for Gaelic with Welsh was clearly a legitimate aim, but was unlikely to be rushed through any parliament in one fell swoop, let alone a parliament dominated by the triumphant foot-soldiers of Margaret Thatcher's first Conservative administration.

In his autobiography, *A Scot at Westminster*, Donald Stewart would recall:

> To my surprise, [the Bill] ran into violent opposition, mainly
> from Tory members, although Albert McQuarrie (Tory,

Aberdeen East) was a staunch supporter. Opponents of the Bill were John MacKay (Tory, Argyle), Bill Walker (Tory, Perth), Iain Sproat (Tory, Aberdeen South) and even the English Tory Douglas Hogg, a son of Lord Hailsham.

Some of the speeches by these Tories showed ignorant prejudice against Gaelic. Bill Walker's objection seemed to be based on his claim that the Black Watch found little use for it. On the day of the debate, the Bill was late in coming up, due to filibustering to delay a Bill on compulsory wearing of seatbelts and a Bill to help the disabled which had the support of no less than 260 Members.

As the 2.30 deadline approached, the closure vote was moved to end discussion and secure a vote on the Bill. This requires 100 Members in favour to be successful and as it was Friday and with only 71 Scottish Members of Parliament, most of whom were in Scotland on that day, the closure vote fell, although a number of English colleagues who were in the precincts came in to vote for closure.

There was anger in Gaelic circles at the failure of the Bill, and particularly at the volume of hostility expressed by the Members mentioned above. An Comunn Gaidhealach quickly issued a statement dissociating their organisation from any defects in the Bill, although I had taken the entire responsibility throughout. One unexpected development was that within a few weeks, Bill Walker MP presented and spoke to a Ten Minute Rule Bill for the assistance of Gaelic! I can only assume that he had been under some pressure for his stance on my Bill. But I was so disgusted at this turn-about that I walked out of the Chamber in front of Walker holding my nose.

Meanwhile, up in Skye, 'We knew it was going to fail,' says Iain Taylor, 'because we'd written to every Scottish MP asking them what they were going to do. Those who replied, which was actually a fair few, wrote back and said, apart from a few bizarre exceptions, that they were not going to support it at all and that they probably wouldn't be there anyway. One of the least supportive was running NATO until recently: George Robertson. He wrote a fairly damning letter back. So we knew this was going to happen.

'We went down to London. Mairead Ross organised that we would get the Fir Chlis minibus, and we rounded up students from the different universities to be in Parliament just to witness the event.

'We bought the paint before we left, because we knew what was going to happen.

'Poor old Comunn Gaidhealach, they're so decent, they were there and, after the Parliament thing, Donald Stewart's secretary organised that we would get a room where everything could be discussed, and here was this nice guy from An Comunn, Ruairidh MacKay was his name, and somebody else from the Comunn Gaidhealach, who were genuinely hurt and surprised, but we weren't. They said, "Well, we've written to these people and they assured us of their good will."

'"What kind of questions were you asking them? You know you were asking the wrong questions, you're just being silly."

'It was then, actually in Westminster, that Ceartas [Justice] was founded. At that meeting was myself, Stephen – I don't think Anne Martin was there but she was there very shortly afterwards – so me, Stephen and Anne, and students from Glasgow, Edinburgh and Aberdeen, and that was it. Then Kay Matheson [one of the Home Rule campaigners who stole the Stone of Destiny from Westmister Abbey in 1950] joined later, and the MacDonalds [the well-known piping brothers] from Glenuig.

'We left London on the Friday night and drove up, dropped the students off in various places, stayed over at Stephen's parents' place in Pitlochry on the Saturday night. We had left the paint in Pitlochry in Stephen's mother's shed on our way down, so we just picked it up on the way back, then we started beside Bruar and went up the A9 from Bruar to Laggan up over Dalwhinnie.

'The first road sign that we ever changed in Scotland was Pitagowan beside Bruar in Perthshire. We didn't actually alter any at that time, we just painted the name with white paint, we didn't know what we were doing, we were writing slogans on the road – '*Ceartas airson na Gàidhlig*' ('Justice for Gaelic') and things like that – and then we would drive through the paint leaving a perfect set of tyre marks. How the cops never got us at that time, I do not know, we were so amateurish, it was laughable.

'We did all of them, starting at Pitagowan, then Bruar, up to Dalwhinnie, Laggan, Spean Bridge, and then, of course, we ran out of paint and couldn't do any more. We made our way back to Skye, and then we sent off a load of letters to newspapers and to different organisations outlining why it was being done and that sort of thing, but we weren't quite sure, we really were very amateurish and really didn't know what we were doing. I remember hearing somebody on the radio saying that this document that we had issued anonymously was obviously written up by a very sharp legal mind, because it absolved any individual of legal responsibility. Myself and Stephen and maybe Anne Martin drew it up in the living room in Christine Primrose's house.

'It was quite exciting, but, I tell you, it was scary, because I had never been in trouble in my life. By nature, I am very law-abiding. I really believe in the rule of law and in law and order, because it always protects the weakest in society, and if you don't have that, you just have anarchy, and the weakest will always lose. So it took an awful lot for me to do something illegal because it would never have entered my head to do anything bad before; I was very conformist and still would be.

'We did the airport sign at Ashaig in Skye, which attracted a lot of attention at the time because it was bigger news. Then we did the Scullamus junction. And then there was a big conference being held on the future of Gaelic down here at the college, and we'd gotten away with so much that we thought, "We're just going to paint, we'll just do Sleat." We did a complete frenzy in Sleat, giving hints to the police, because another thing that we wanted to do was to get arrested to get a trial. Because you would be able to say in court, "There is nothing to prevent us, Gaelic is a perfectly legal language, there is no restriction on its use." Then, for a final clue, we got red

paint and painted an arrow at the Achnacloich sign right outside
Sabhal Mòr Ostaig to try to get the bloody police to arrest us. After
that, they couldn't avoid paying us a visit.

'I don't know if they arrived during this fancy conference or
immediately after it, but they did arrive searching for paint. But the
only thing they could find was emulsion, and not even a fool would
use emulsion outdoors on road signs. They went away with a lot of
different shades of buttermilk and magnolia and things like that.
They were very ham-fisted. They had this guy with a very strong
Lewis accent pretending that he couldn't speak Gaelic, which really
must have taken some doing, because the poor lad could barely
speak English. But, no, they didn't arrest us at all, and they didn't
fingerprint us for anything, they were just taking statements. I think
they came when Kay Matheson and [the Scottish National Party's
Highlands and Islands Member of the European Parliament]
Winnie Ewing were here – poor cops, their timing was rather shit –
and we were never taken into the cells and fingerprinted until they
got us for doing the sign at Moll, Sconser, and they couldn't avoid
it.

'But I was the only one taken to court, because they got a
fingerprint of mine from the airport sign and they matched it up
with the Moll sign. So I had to go to court in Portree but the other
three got off. They weren't charged with anything, so I was charged
with doing the airport sign or the Moll sign, I can't actually
remember.

'I was really worried because I had never been in court before, I'd
never even been inside one, and I didn't know what happened in
them or anything like that at all. I went from being scared to being
just absolutely furious, absolutely enraged, not at the fact that I was
being taken to court or anything, because I'd broken the law, which
is fair enough, but at the fact that the court hearing couldn't get
done through Gaelic.

'That was utterly outrageous. I can't really particularly remember
when it hit me, but I think it was when two guys from the Welsh
Language Society came up to give a talk here at the college, and the
way that they spoke regarding Welsh was that by that stage they

took it for granted that being a Welsh speaker meant that, to a pretty large extent, the state didn't interfere with you. They had gone through all of that problem before, from not being allowed to use Welsh to just accepting that they could use Welsh because they are Welsh and living in Wales. I suddenly thought, "Why the hell can't it be the same here?"

'Just because you want to do something through Gaelic, doesn't mean that it's anti-English. We're so lucky that there's more than just Gaelic and more than just English in this country, and, instead of seeing these things as a problem, you know, they are such a benefit. It's the same with people who have come to live in Scotland, particularly from India; it's such an enhancement for a country to get new people. I can just about remember Scotland in the late 1950s, when I was very wee, and it was a completely boring dump before we got large numbers of people moving in. It was really just a question of variety and diversity – I thought it was necessary to encourage that sort of thing.

'My lawyer was Donald Ferguson, the Gaelic-speaking lawyer from North Uist practising in Portree. Donald asked what I wanted to do, and he explained that if I insisted on speaking Gaelic, I would probably be put down to the cells until I changed my mind.

'I said that the whole purpose of the thing was to highlight the position of Gaelic in law. There had been a lot of rubbish spoken by MPs saying that of course Gaelic had equal validity with English and there was no need for legislation, there was no need for any change. So it had to be pointed out that, yes, Gaelic was viewed as completely inferior at that time, and I think it is still the case today; speaking Gaelic was the equivalent of remaining mute, and that was just so utterly insulting, you know. It's so demeaning that the state can use its power against its own citizens, because we are the state, and what right does the state have to just make pronouncements like that and to automatically denigrate a section of the community because of its language. Any educationalist would tell you that the best way to attack a child in primary school is to attack the way they speak, to attack their language.

'So we decided between ourselves, me and Donald Ferguson, that

I would try to speak as much Gaelic as possible and that he would put me into the dock so that I would have to speak Gaelic. And then I would have to be put down to the cells, right? That was what we had hoped, anyway. And that they would then presumably bring me up again after I had changed my mind. Then I would speak Gaelic and be put back down again, and this yo-yo business would go on hopefully for a very long time, and it would highlight the ludicrousness of the situation.

'As it happened, when I had to identify myself in court, I did it in Gaelic, but the judge didn't put me down to the cells. It had to go through the procurator-fiscal's office first. Now, during that process, one of my witnesses was forbidden from speaking Gaelic in court. That was very good: they were forbidden from speaking Gaelic while giving evidence, and that was excellent because it proved that politicians and legal advisers had been lying when they said that Gaelic speakers are allowed to speak Gaelic in court. They'd always previously got away with this one by saying, oh, if someone was a native speaker, they would be allowed to speak Gaelic. But these witnesses were forbidden from doing it, and that was great.

'To cut a long story short, the police evidence was tainted before I got a chance to go into the dock, so I didn't get a chance to speak Gaelic and I didn't get a chance to be put into the cells. Fortunately, Donald Ferguson made an appeal to the High Court in Edinburgh, which was heard by three of the big judges, but they came down on the side of a ruling based on something called the MacRae case from the 1890s. In that, some sheriff had decided that only if someone who could speak Gaelic could not speak English could they be allowed to use Gaelic in a court. And that is still, as far as I understand it, Gaelic's legal basis in the courts. So it is far from satisfactory, and there's never been an attempt to improve the second-class status of Gaelic speakers at all.'

Later in 1981, Iain Taylor left Skye and Sabhal Mòr Ostaig to pursue a teacher-training course at Jordanhill College in Glasgow. He was not altogether sorry to go: 'I actually used to hate coming to

Skye. I virtually hated everything west of Inverness, I just thought it was a hellhole. I couldn't understand why people allowed themselves to be governed in such a colonial way. Visiting home was almost a relief: to get to Inverness, to head east and go to Elgin. Can you believe that Elgin actually seemed like a progressive place in comparison with the likes of Inverness-shire? I just found it very, very depressing, deeply depressing, and I didn't see that there was any particular grounds for optimism at all.'

After qualifying from Jordanhill in 1982, he was offered a post as teacher of Gaelic at Daliburgh School in South Uist. 'I'd never been in Uist and I didn't want the job. Before I ever went to work in Uist, I presumed it would be just like a remote version of Skye, and I didn't really look forward to going there at all. But I went, and it was a complete eye-opener. I was just dreading going because I thought, "Oh God, this is another place that's going to be dying on its bloody feet. It's just going to be a horrible version of Skye."

'And it just wasn't. I'll never forget this: the second night I was there, I walked in to Lochboisdale to phone home, and there were two kids playing. There were brambles growing in a ditch, and these two kids – and I know who they are now, two brothers – they were eating the brambles and speaking Gaelic to one another.

'At that time, they would have been seven and eight years old, I think, and I had never heard children voluntarily speaking Gaelic. There wasn't an adult there, you know, to force them, and they were doing it voluntarily. I was just flabbergasted. And then the other thing, especially after having come from Sleat, was just how many young people are in Uist. I remember the first time I went to the public bar at the Borrodale Hotel in Daliburgh. It was Hallowe'en and Hallowe'en is massive in South Uist. I actually presumed that all of these young people, in their late teens and 20s, were home for Hallowe'en. It never dawned on me that they actually lived there all the time, because in Sleat there were only – I remember we tried to count up one time – I think there were about a dozen people between 16 and 30 that we knew of. It was hellish, absolutely awful, and Uist was just utterly different. They were perfectly normal people doing perfectly normal things that we would do in a perfectly normal place like Elgin but doing it through Gaelic. You know, I was utterly flabbergasted that people my age and younger would voluntarily speak Gaelic. Because they wouldn't do it here in Sleat, in Skye.'

Six

The Ceartas arrests and trial achieved national publicity. It was not, however, the kind of publicity which many of Iain Taylor's employers wished to be associated with the Gaelic movement as a whole, let alone with Sabhal Mòr Ostaig.

'When Ceartas first declared themselves,' says Alan Campbell, 'and the media grasped it, it was a Saturday, and of course the Sunday papers were full of it. Duncan MacQuarrie was then chairman of the trustees, and he phoned me on the Monday morning saying that he'd had a call before nine o'clock from a major oil company saying that they were withdrawing their sponsorship.

'Duncan asked them, "Why would you do that? It's not the trustees who are declaring themselves to be involved in a public or civil disobedience over the language." I think Duncan, in fairness to him, said that many of the trustees would support the aspirations of Ceartas in terms of the language, but that that might not be how they'd do it, and this guy said, "Well, I'm very sympathetic to your argument and to your position, but you've got to remember that we can only award our charitable contributions to completely non-controversial issues, and yours is not a non-controversial issue any more. Therefore, I'm sorry, but we're not going to give you any more money."

'That was a real kick in the guts for us. We lost a bit of money then, and the important point was that that money and the support of these companies were a hugely important lever to us when we went to public bodies as well. We could say that we had the support of the private sector and that gave us credibility.

'The episode had a humorous side to it. I remember a press commentator said at this time that the whole Gaelic community was like a shrivelled and dried up something or other, and I remember Duncan and I talking to a lawyer in town who said very jovially, "I don't think you trustees have anything to worry about, but I reckon if I were Ruairidh MacKay, [president of An Comunn Gaidhealach], I'd be seriously thinking about taking action against this." I said, "Why?" and he said, "Do you not know, he's got a young wife and a couple of kids – he could actually go to court and prove that he is neither shrivelled nor dried up."

'But there was a general awareness that we had to be careful. If we were to achieve the objectives of the college, we had to be careful that the college wasn't seen to be synonymous with, shall we say, almost a student-type campaign for the language. Because we were trying to set up something that was going to have credibility within the education sector, something that would attract public and private money, and clearly we weren't going to achieve that if we allowed ourselves to become known as, and known only as, a hotbed of civil disobedience.

'So, yes, there was a preoccupation with that, and I think it's fair to say that some of the trustees, maybe the older ones, the ones who were the age I am today, they were probably, shall we say, less sympathetic to the whole Ceartas approach than others.'

Iain Taylor left for Jordanhill College in the middle of 1981. As the trustees of Sabhal Mòr Ostaig steeled themselves to locate a replacement, the Gaelic movement as a whole found itself with other concerns.

The 1981 census revealed, predictably, a further fall in Gaelic speakers. But it was an oddly ambiguous result. There were in that year apparently 79,307 Gaelic speakers in Scotland. This was a fall of around 10,000 from the 1971 figures. But as the 1971 figures had been widely accepted as flawed, it was perhaps better to compare the 1981 numbers with 1961. And they were almost identical.

If there were, give or take a thousand, as many Gaelic speakers in Scotland in 1981 as there had been in 1961, a couple of useful points were indicated. The first is that the numbers for 1971 probably had been artificially inflated by confusing questions on the census form. And the second is that the 150-year decline might not have been reversed, or even finally halted, but it had slowed down in the second half of the twentieth century by a remarkable degree. In 1961, Gaelic speakers represented 1.6 per cent of Scottish society. Twenty years later in 1981, they still comprised 1.6 per cent of the Scottish population.

There was one other noticeable trend between 1961 and 1981. It lay in the proportion of Gaelic speakers who lived in the Highlands and in the Lowlands. In 1961, 71 per cent of Gaels lived in the Highlands. By 1981, that percentage had fallen to 60. Those 20 years had been a period of considerable emigration from the Highlands and Islands, of unemployment and depopulation across the North-west. The sensible conclusion appeared to be that, despite everything, Gaelic-speaking families in the 1960s and 1970s had not given up on their language. Children born and bred in the Islands and western mainland were, right into the middle of the 1970s at least, still learning Gaelic from their parents. They were certainly not getting it from many other sources.

In 'A Century on the Census: Gaelic in Twentieth Century Focus' the distinguished Gaelic scholar and analyst Professor Ken MacKinnon wrote that, of the 79,307 speakers of Gaelic counted in the 1981 census:

> only 20,345 resided in local neighbourhoods (census enumeration districts) in which 75% or more of the inhabitants spoke Gaelic. (Almost all these areas were in Skye and the Western Isles, but also included the Isle of Canna, western and north-western enumeration districts in Tiree, the Kilninian enumeration district in Mull, and the Tormisdale enumeration district in Islay.)

Thus only 25.65%, or just over one in four of Scotland's Gaelic speakers could have been said to live in a truly Gaelic local environment. A further 7,471 Gaelic speakers lived in enumeration districts which were between 50–75% Gaelic-speaking. These areas were chiefly in remaining areas of Skye and the Western Isles, but also included the rest of Tiree, four enumeration districts in Islay and one in Mull. So in total there were only 27,816 Gaelic speakers normally resident in predominantly Gaelic-speaking neighbourhoods. This represented 34.92% or just over one in three of all Gaelic speakers at the time of the 1981 census.

In 1981, virtually every parish in the traditional Gaidhealtachd still had a proportion of Gaelic speakers greater than the national average and within this area, comprising the Western Isles, Highland Region (less Caithness District), Argyll and Bute District, and the Highland area of Perthshire, there were 46,410 Gaelic speakers or 58.52% of Scotland's total. In 1981 there were thus 32,897 Gaelic speakers, or 41.48% of the national total, normally resident in areas which could not be described in any sense as Gaelic in either present-day or recent historic character. It cannot really therefore be said, as it sometimes is, that Scotland's Gaelic speakers are to be found mainly in the Hebrides and northwest coastal fringes. Today, the majority are in fact to be found elsewhere in Scotland. Their numbers are sufficient to liken them to a Gaelic Archipelago more populous than the Hebrides – but set in a Lowland 'sea'.

There were, by the early 1980s, some indications that both public and private sectors might be about to offer some aid to those parents who had sustained the language. A steady increase was taking place of Gaelic broadcasting on both the BBC and independent television channels and on BBC radio. The bilingual policy of Comhairle nan Eilean in the Western Isles, which had begun to come on track in the late 1970s, was making its presence felt. Gradually, between Lewis and Vatersay, phonetic road signs were giving way to properly spelt Gaelic place names with, in many cases, no translation.

A good many of the developments of this time came from within Gaelic communities – one of the most striking and influential from one of the smallest of Hebridean islands. Early in 1981, an Englishman who had recently been appointed development director of the Scottish Arts Council (SAC) in Edinburgh received representation from a group of people who wanted to hold a festival of Gaelic arts on Barra, an island of just over 1,000 people, one of the most southerly links of the Outer Hebridean chain. In an interview with *The Scotsman*, John Murphy recalled:

> I took my wife and our three children camping on the island, to check out the scene, and it was simply wonderful. It was quite clear that they were onto something, because there was so much community enthusiasm to keep the traditional arts alive.

Fèis Bharraigh was duly sponsored and went ahead (with Murphy obliged to act as honorary accountant). It was an extraordinary success. Within a very few years *fèisean* (festivals) were being held in localities throughout the Highlands and Islands. In 1988, Fèisean nan Gàidheal was established to serve as an independent umbrella organisation, and by the early years of the twenty-first century, some 37 fèisean were involving 3,500 young people across Scotland in week-long festivals of Gaelic music, song, dance and drama. In Edinburgh, John Murphy had appointed a Gaelic arts development officer at the SAC. When he retired in 1998, Murphy (who never personally learned more than '600 words' of Gaelic) announced that becoming involved in – and subsequently helping to spread – the Gaelic youth festivals which had originated in Barra in 1981 was his proudest achievement in 20 years at the Scottish Arts Council.

In 1982, a driven young Lewisman named Finlay MacLeod established Comhairle nan Sgoiltean Àraich (CNSA), the Gaelic pre-schools movement. Noting the decline since his own childhood in the numbers of toddlers speaking Gaelic and the fact that no established pre-school or nursery group in Scotland conducted its business in the language, MacLeod formed four Gaelic playgroups. Within 20 years, CNSA was helping to administer no fewer than 120 pre-school groups across the whole of Scotland, catering for over 2,000 infants.

In 1984, the Scottish Office founded a new body to coordinate the various new strands of Gaelic development. Comunn na Gàidhlig (CnaG) would be based in Inverness. The organisation has charitable status. Its corporate policy evolved from national conference discussions at which all organisations involved with Gaelic development were represented. The first of those conferences took place in 1985 at Sabhal Mòr Ostaig in Skye. Since 1985, CnaG has organised an annual Còmhdhail (Congress) to discuss and develop national policies for Gaelic. CnaG's policies would be guided by its board, which originally consisted of representatives of its corporate sponsors – the Highland Council, Comhairle nan Eilean, Strathclyde Regional Council, HIDB and An Comunn Gaidhealach – plus seven co-optees from the Gaelic community.

It was a time of unmistakable change. 'When the HIDB think tank recommended the creation of a Gaelic language board, it took a number of years to materialise, and Comunn na Gàidhlig was a hybrid,' remembers Alan Campbell who was working for Highland Regional Council at the time, setting up a development office in Skye and Lochalsh. 'Maybe concurrent with the HIDB group starting the work, there was yet another report done on An Comunn Gaidhealach, and it was done by a company in Dublin called Trident Management Consultants. I think it's fair to say that that report just disappeared onto a very low shelf somewhere.

'But it raised a hugely controversial and very fundamental, challenging question for an organisation, a membership body, because if An Comunn Gaidhealach was to be true to its mission, then, in the view of Trident, all full members of An Comunn had to be Gaelic speaking and all the non-Gaelic-speaking members, if they must have such, should be associate members. In reality, this was, at that time, going to mean that the vast majority of An Comunn's members would have been associate members. And a lot of people felt that an associate member was a second-class being, and I think that was where the real challenge was and what presented all the difficulties.

'There was also at that time, or around that time, back in the early 1980s, a move from within An Comunn itself that their meetings should be held in Gaelic, and this was an initiative that was run by the Young Turks of the day. They moved such a motion, a surprise motion, at an AGM, and they carried it, and this caused some consternation because it was maybe seen as a step along the way towards the Trident recommendations. There was subsequently an Emergency General Meeting of An Comunn called very shortly afterwards to reverse this. The Young Turks who had led the motion for Gaelic were present, of course, and when they lost, which they did, because the thing had been arranged that way, they walked out – with the press of course anticipating that move – and they immediately set up a splinter group for which they used the Gaelic name Sgealb, which means splinter. Of course, Sgealb didn't exist for very long afterwards, but they posed a bit of a problem for me. I was on a very short secondment – in fact I was seconded from a secondment – to HIDB to try and find a way through the difficulties that were imposed by the Scottish Office response to the HIDB report on setting up a Gaelic language board, to try and rescue something out of it.

'One of the problems was that the Scottish Office required the HIDB working group to get agreement or consensus among the Gaelic groups before they would allow the creation of this Comunn na Gàidhlig. That meant I had to sell the idea to a whole variety of groups, and Sgealb was one of these groups. So I had to sell the idea of CnaG to these Young Turks – one of them was actually a bit older than I, Aonghas Dubh MacNeacail (who now by trades description should change his name because he's not *dubh* [black] any more, he's getting grey like the rest of us), and Roddy John MacLeod, a distinguished sheriff of the parish nowadays, and Matthew MacIver [now secretary-general of the General Teaching Council] and Boyd

Robertson [now head of Gaelic at Jordanhill Campus, Strathclyde University]. These are pillars of today's Establishment but they had a life once, they were there fighting the cause.'

The first director of CnaG was a young Lewisman named John Angus MacKay, who had been a trustee of Sabhal Mòr Ostaig. MacKay was a product of Stornoway's Nicolson Institute, Aberdeen University and Jordanhill College of Education who had worked in the 1970s as a salesman for the Dundee publishing group DC Thomson and as a teacher in Glasgow before joining the HIDB as a development officer in 1977.

MacKay took up his position at the newly created CnaG in 1984 at a time of rapid and heartening expansion in the BBC's Gaelic radio output. The Broadcasting Council for Scotland had established a Gaelic Study Group. In 1982, the group reported that 'the overwhelming view [of its respondents was] that there was an urgent need for increased hours of broadcasting on radio and television to create a service of Gaelic broadcasting'. The BBC promptly backed this report and set itself to double Gaelic broadcasting to 30 hours a week by 1988. The target was met, chiefly through the creation in 1985 of a Gaelic radio service, Radio nan Gàidheal, and by the expansion of studio facilities in Inverness and Stornoway. John Angus MacKay set himself and CnaG the task of creating a similar improvement in Gaelic television.

'CnaG was, in its day, crucial,' says another member of that HIDB working group, Roy Pedersen. 'It still has a very important role in trying to pull a lot of diverse elements together and stimulate their development and win people round. The key thing that CnaG did was to win government support for Gaelic in things like broadcasting. Without CnaG, I'm sure there would be no Gaelic television, and that is because of the work of CnaG's first director, John Angus MacKay; he is one of the most wonderful men that I know in terms of what he has been able to achieve, a very courageous man. It was not at all easy for him. Maybe I saw, more than most, because we are good friends, what he had to go through to achieve all these things.'

At the same period, after 110 years of state neglect, primary school children in the Western Isles were about to be offered an education through the medium of Gaelic. The Gaelic-medium unit (GMU) in primary education had been pioneered in Glasgow by Strathclyde Regional Council in the 1985–86 school year. The first GMU in the Gaidhealtachd heartland – at Breasclete School at Callanish on the west side of Lewis in the Outer Hebrides – would not open until the start of the 1986–87 school year, and it would have no more than 4 pupils out of a total of 3,010 island schoolchildren. But within 10 years that number had risen to 660. It was still only 25 per cent of the total school roll in the Western Isles, and would remain at that level into the twenty-first century. But it was another kind of fresh start.

According to the census, there were in the early 1980s roughly 10,000 teenage Gaelic speakers in Scotland. The trustees of Sabhal Mòr Ostaig perceived their job as providing tertiary education for those young men and women. Duncan MacQuarrie in particular was inspired by a memory from Mull. 'My grandfather,' he recalls, 'who was also Duncan MacQuarrie, went to Salen School in Mull with a fellow, and they became apprentice stonemasons together. Now, this other chap was called Fletcher and he inherited money. They set up a building firm between the two of them, started in about 1885, building schools, and there were loads of schools to build after the Compulsory Education Act. They then started building churches, and their biggest contract was to do part or most of the work on Kinloch Castle in Rhum. They then got a contract, at the turn of the century, to build Glenborrodale Castle in Ardnamurchan and they were involved in work of that kind right up to the First World War.

'My grandfather died of pneumonia in 1920 and the firm folded in the late '20s or thereabouts, at the time of the Depression. What they had then was a firm which operated virtually 100 per cent in Gaelic, and they employed, between all the different tradesmen, between 400 and 500 people, all based in Tobermory.

'I interviewed some of the survivors in the late 1960s, some of whom had come back from America and some who had stayed on in Scotland, and each and every one of them – joiners, masons, blacksmiths and so on – could all discuss in Gaelic the tools they used, the processes they used and the way they went about things. Because that was the language that they learned and that they used at work. My father reminded me of this and that was one of the other things that underpinned my conviction that something like this could be done in Highland business and industry in the late twentieth century. I knew it was possible.

'We were incurably optimistic in believing that what we were doing would help, over time, to revitalise the age profile of the Gaelic-speaking areas of the Highlands and Islands and that we would return the leadership to the Highlands and Islands which we felt had been leeched out by umpteen careers masters.

'We believed that Gaelic was not simply a language but also an economic tool, it was something for people to use to give them identity and self-confidence so that they could set up any kind of business they liked, which would root them in the communities. We were on the same wavelength as the people who were setting up cooperatives in the Outer Isles and in Acharacle, and on the same wavelength as those who were setting up *comuinn eachdraidh*, the local history societies. And also, if you look at the sequence of events, we started off with our first tranche of students in 1983; 1985 and 1986 saw the first beginnings of Gaelic-medium education in primary schools; 1984 saw the launch of Comunn na Gàidhlig. Comhairle nan Eilean was established and was driving things forward, but there were other movements as well. Things were obviously on the move – there was a groundswell of activity.

'I think that probably our motivation was, certainly mine was that I had seen Gaelic disappear in my own island and I wanted some kind of mechanism whereby I could try to reverse that tide.

'We set out to try to give people tools with which they could either earn their living or they could set up businesses. And we monitored very closely where people went; I don't know what the figures are today, but for the first ten years or so, if I recall correctly, there was a very high percentage of Sabhal Mòr Ostaig graduates, round about 90 per cent, who were actually staying what you might call north of the Highland Line.

'We struck lucky in the early 1980s as well because we were shouting about entrepreneurship and it was the height of the Thatcher era. It was a theme that struck a chord with broad policy development. I think that because we could argue our case on economic grounds and the need for economic regeneration, rather than on simply "saving the language", that was probably one of the major factors in opening doors.

'First of all, we tried to analyse what gave businessmen sufficient confidence to go and open up new businesses. How they went about it and what their motivations were besides making cash. We tried to present the argument in those terms. We came to the conclusion that one prerequisite for success was a security and a confidence in your own culture – that your people and language could deliver the goods. We were drawing what lessons we could from what used to be called the old-boy network, in that we felt that that was based on the participants being secure and confident in themselves and that we had to find a means to give the Gaelic world a way of actually developing that same security and confidence, so that people were prepared to take up the baton and run with it.

'There was also our hope and belief that native Gaels would see opportunities which we might not see, and be confident enough to try to exploit those opportunities. These were the arguments which we tended to use, and we sometimes came at it, as well as from a socio-economic point of view, from a more academic, cultural point of view, and this is where we had the benefit of Bob Storey's learning and his work on similar minority cultures in Sweden. And of course we could point to examples of where the folk high schools which taught local dialect and culture in Norway and in Denmark had actually been influential in developing this confidence. And we had concrete examples too from the Faeroes and Iceland.

'At all costs, we tried to avoid the whinge that nobody was doing enough for Gaelic. We would hope to say: "We're looking at propping up Gaelic, but we're coming at it from a different angle, not demanding that the heavens change overnight, and this is the way we think and this is a sector of Gaeldom that is making its voice heard."

'There was a strong recognition that the job was a long, long one and a big, big one. One of the things that was most difficult to counter was the cynicism within the Gaelic community or certain people in the Gaelic community. The ordinary people in the street, as it were, in Harris and in the Uists and what not – and I was keyed into them because of my family connections and suchlike, and because they were relations – they had no hesitation in telling me I was talking nonsense! We knew that the girl pushing the pram down the road, the young woman – or the young man – appreciated what we were talking about, but some of those in what one might call "promoted posts" or other posts of influence were quite cynical. They felt that it would not work, that the route out and the route to success was still to the south.

'I have to say that a great number of them have changed their minds, and a great number of them have said so to me. Some interesting things happened. When Fraser Morrison took over as chairman of HIE/HIDB (his family was from Easter Ross and his grandparents were Gaelic speakers), he initially rejected our thesis that Gaelic could bring economic regeneration. But he then thought about it a bit more and actually stood up at the CnaG conference in Aviemore, this was in the early 1990s, and said to the whole world that he was wrong, he had changed his mind.

'When we were getting established in the early 1980s, there was a group of people who were very concerned and who still are, there were elected representatives who went out of their way to make sure that initiatives happened. But there were others who did not bother because they said, "Och, they'll have Gaelic anyway," and that was one of the things that drove us to try and change things back in the late '70s and early '80s.

'Because learning and speaking, teaching and listening in Gaelic in the pub or on the Carbost omnibus doesn't give you the skills of reading and writing, and it's through reading and writing that you actually raise language registers and that people begin to have professional discussions in Gaelic instead of lapsing into English, that they actually unconsciously use Gaelic vocabulary.

'That tendency to lapse into English was a big worry to me, it's still a worry to me, and that, I think, has improved quite considerably, particularly amongst those who are using Gaelic in a professional or a business or an economic capacity from day to day. It's also been a feature of education through the medium of Gaelic that it has also reduced that phenomenon. One of the things that is discernible amongst the graduates of Sabhal Mòr is the confidence that they have and the certainty that they have that they can use Gaelic in any context whatsoever. And that was a principal aim that we had originally, but it was not the one which we broadcast to the world, if you know what I mean! We didn't use it as a selling point.'

Having achieved in 1982–83 a licence to teach – in association with SCOTBEC and Robert Gordon's University – to HND level through the medium of Gaelic, the trustees of Sabhal Mòr Ostaig set out to find a college principal for their first full-time courses. The job was crucial. If Sabhal Mòr Ostaig was now on the verge of actually becoming, in Iain Noble's words, the first Gaelic college of tertiary education in Scotland since St Columba established himself in Iona, then presumably little less than a secular saint would suffice. They found one, most fittingly, in Ireland.

Seán O Drisceoil was a chemistry and mathematics graduate from Kilkenny. Not a native speaker of Irish Gaeilge, he achieved fluency through the Irish educational system. 'An excellent scheme was introduced into the schools here in the late 1950s,' he explains. 'I had the usual schooling that everybody got in Irish – everybody had a certain capability, but not necessarily fluency. But this scheme offered Gaeilge students the opportunity to go to a Gaeilge home for three months during normal school term, not during the summer. So you became one of the family. It was limited to one student per household, so you literally became part of the family.

'I went to Connemara. At that stage, in linguistic terms, it was like going to France. The people in the house I stayed in during the early 1960s – in 1960, in fact, in the year Kennedy became president – had no English. The father and mother were monoglot Irish speakers; the daughter had only broken English. So I went from school Irish to fluency within a month; but I wouldn't have achieved fluency without the school Irish. That was the most important step: if you came in there at the deep end, you'd have floundered. Now, that has convinced me of one thing: that, although it's often criticised, the language teaching that people get at school is absolutely essential. It's a first step, and it gives you a choice, the choice to go on and get fluency.

'I went to University College Dublin, and I was living in Dublin during my college days, and my first job was there in a chemical company where I went as far as quality control manager. I wanted to get out of Dublin at that stage, and I also wanted to make, if possible, a horizontal move; certainly the life in the lab wasn't the life I wanted. An opportunity came up to go to Tipperary as training and recruitment manager in another chemical company – you could make the horizontal move within the industry, so I did. I went there and got the professional experience I needed to move to the Gaeltacht, which was my ultimate aim.

'I was three years in Tipperary, getting excellent experience in management development and training recruitment, and having that meant I could move out of the chemical industry. Udarás na Gaeltachta, the Gaeltacht authority which started up in 1980, were doing a lot of recruiting at that stage. I spotted the ads and applied, and was taken on by Udarás as a training and recruitment executive in Galway. Their headquarters are about ten miles west of the city, in the Gaeltacht, so that was the main aim achieved: I was involved in the language.'

The Gaeltacht areas within Ireland were defined in 1925, early in the life of the Irish Free State, as 'those areas of Ireland in which the Irish language (Gaeilge) is still spoken as a community language, and its culture and traditions are very much alive and thriving'. In such places, determined the state, lay the future of the language. It was a device to protect and sustain Gaeilge in the precious few districts where it had defied clearance, famine and official neglect to survive. By 2004, the Gaeltacht areas were chiefly on the seaboard of the four western counties of Donegal, Mayo, Galway and Kerry, and in the southern and eastern counties of Cork, Waterford and Meath. By the twenty-first century, Gaeltacht areas varied from those with a minority of Gaeilge speakers, such as Kerry, to those such as the

Aran Islands and large parts of Donegal which retained Gaeilge as the pre-eminent vernacular. Connemara, where Seán O Drisceoil did his Gaeilge immersion course in 1960, was and remains a crucial Gaeltacht area. The function and definition of such districts included the availability of primary and secondary education through the medium of Irish Gaeilge (*Gaelscoileanna* and *Gaelcholaiste*, of which there were at the start of the twenty-first century almost 200, educating 30,000 schoolchildren across Ireland), encouragement of sympathetic development and Irish-speaking workforces, and the assertion of Gaeilge on most signage. Not only place names but also 'Stop', 'Go Slow' and 'No Overtaking' road markings are inscribed in many Irish Gaeltacht areas only in Gaeilge. According to the Irish census of 2002, there were a total of 90,000 people resident in these scattered and diffuse areas.

Not all of the 90,000, however, were speakers of Gaeilge. In 2001, a commission of the Department of Community, Rural and Gaeltacht Affairs reported that:

> If the criterion for defining Gaeltacht boundaries was that 80% of the community must be Irish speakers, as was initially set down by Coimisiun na Gaeltachta in 1926, then according to the 1996 census only 14 district electoral divisions of the 154 would qualify for Gaeltacht status.

But neither the threshold nor much else from the 1920s any longer applied. In stark contrast to Scottish Gaelic, Irish had become a national language once more – albeit a minority national language – with many more speakers outside than within the Gaeltacht districts. 'It's estimated,' says Seán O Drisceoil, 'that probably you could now take about 10,000 off the supposed Gaeltacht population of 90,000, and reduce it to 80,000. Then another 10,000 is urban overspill into the Gaeltachts, which is undoubtedly weakening the language. So I would estimate, in terms of fluency, of that remaining 70,000, about 50,000 would be native speakers.

'Across the whole country, I think 1,500,000 people now term

themselves as Irish speakers. In the last two censuses this question
has been further specified and the figure of fluency and actual usage
looks likely to be about 350,000. There will be in that 350,000 a very
fluent what you might call 'interim population' – schoolkids all over
the country between the ages of 10 and 15 have high levels of usage
and fluency. Now, they, unlike me and many others like me, may go
on to lose it in time. But again, they won't. They won't really lose
it.'

In the 1970s, Seán O Drisceoil took two holidays in Skye. 'I
visited the island in 1975 and again in 1977. The first trip, I was
actually going out with a girl from Wales at the time so we started
off in Wales – a long trip up. We went as far as Kyle of Lochalsh, we
went across to Kyleakin, and, of course, we saw the *West Highland
Free Press* at its first offices at the quay then. On that 1975 holiday,
it was Kyleakin only, we went onto Skye and back across again on
the ferry. So the second time, two years later, I went with my
brother Ciarán, and we went up and stayed near Uig and went right
through the backbone of the island. My brother and I stayed in
Earlish before heading off to the southern Western Isles, to the
Uists.

'Oddly enough, the first bit of Gaelic that I heard on that first trip
in 1975 was actually on the mainland, in the hotel at Dornie, where
we were introduced to some old people who spoke Gaelic. We went
into Dornie for a few pints and there was an enthusiastic and heated
discussion about the language. We certainly heard the language
being used around there, but outside the village itself, in Ardelve.
Even at the time I started at Sabhal Mòr Ostaig in 1983, I still came
across Gaelic speakers in Ardelve. On the second visit, when we
stayed in a B&B in Earlish, there was Gaelic no problem – so we
could see there was Gaelic on Skye. Of course, we then went out to
the Western Isles and discovered how much of the language there
was out there.

'On one of those two holidays, I placed a subscription for the
Free Press. The *Free Press* came every week, and it was through that
that I first became aware of the position at Sabhal Mòr Ostaig. I
would never otherwise have become aware of it because, at that

stage, there weren't the same contacts between the two Gaeltachts as there are now, no radio links, so it was just through that accident that I became aware of the principal's job at Sabhal Mòr Ostaig early in 1983.'

'Donald John MacKay and Duncan MacQuarrie and I were the panel who interviewed the first applicants for full-time principal of Sabhal Mòr Ostaig,' recalls Alan Campbell. 'One of the applicants was Seán O Drisceoil. The interviews took place in the offices of the Manpower Services Commission on Academy Street in Inverness. Donald John MacKay was on the board there, and I think he borrowed a room. We were sitting in these extraordinary foam sideless and armless chairs, the three of us and Seán, who was probably quite nervous. Donald John MacKay was something of a human resources expert. He was full of management techniques and theories and strategies. One of his techniques that he liked to use was attempting to throw the interviewee by asking a question completely at odds with everything else.

'So here we were talking to Seán, and suddenly Donald John said, "Do you have any brothers and sisters?" Seán was a bit thrown, and he said, "Yes, there are 12 of us," or however many. And Donald John said, "Where do you come in?" Seán said, "Sort of halfway. I have a twin sister." And Donald John said, "Identical?" and Seán put his finger to his lips and said, "No, she's a girl." Duncan MacQuarrie and I literally fell off our chairs laughing.'

'The first interview in Inverness,' says Seán O Drisceoil, 'was, as usual at that level, a fairly long and probing interview. They had checked with people back here in Ireland. The first interview was on the Good Friday of 1983, and then I had to go down to Skye to meet Jack MacArthur, who was taking over the chair of the trustees from Duncan. The Inverness interview started off in Gaelic, but we very quickly established that with Irish Gaelic and Scottish Gaelic you can go only so far. At a social level, you may be able to get further, but at that type of interview level, it's difficult. Ears need to get attuned.

'But we clicked very well, and the next thing was, apart from providing details of my qualifications and experience, I went on to

169

Sleat, met Jack, and we clicked easily, so there was little doubt in my mind that there would be an offer made after the interview. I saw Jack MacArthur at Sabhal Mòr, and that was the first I'd seen of the building itself. Half of it was shocking and the other half was hopeful; one "L" of the rectangle was functional and the other "L" was . . . well, the lorries were there and the diggers were there, and I could see that it had potential.

'I started on 1 July 1983. I actually came over for a number of meetings before the start of the contract; there were crucial discussions being held with the Department of Education at the time and the principal had to be at the meetings. There was initially still a question mark over the starting date, the whole thing might have had to wait another year, which would have caused financial problems, and there were enough financial problems anyway. So, the brief from 1 July was to get SMO up and running and launch the first diploma course in business and Gaidhealtachd studies by 1 October 1983. Starting from 1 July we had to recruit staff, recruit students and get the finance sorted out. That was a fairly hectic three months. I arrived and stayed initially in the Ardvasar Hotel for the first month while looking for accommodation.

'I got on with the job. I quickly discovered that recruiting staff was fairly conventional: get the advertisements in and then interview the potentials. We identified and got acceptances from John Norman MacLeod – he would have been the senior lecturer at the time – and then Alan MacDonald and Alan Ainsley.'

John Norman MacLeod had progressed from Digg Primary School and Portree High via Jordanhill College to teach history at Plockton High School in south-west Ross. 'I'd been in Plockton, teaching mainly history, for five or six years when the advert appeared for Sabhal Mòr in 1983,' he says. 'They were advertising for lecturers – they basically just outlined the subject areas, and I sent away for an application form and was sent a prospectus. I must say I was very interested, because this was my own history, if you like, whereas in Plockton I taught the usual school syllabus of the recent period of 'official' history. I spent my time teaching history from First Year right through to Higher and so on. History was always something I'd been interested in, but I was particularly interested in local history, and there was very little opportunity to teach that sort of thing.

'It's changed now in the schools, I think, because there are more local studies and there's more emphasis on things like the Highland Clearances, and pupils can do various studies. But like a lot of people, I think our history back then came through the poetry. I did Sixth Year Studies in Gaelic, and I remember doing one of the Gaelic poets – I think it was Iain Lom – and you get an awful lot of history through studying such poetry. But in 1983, I was very much taken with the Sabhal Mòr Ostaig syllabus – it wasn't only that it was looking at our own history, it was very much looking out as well, and I think this has continued to be a feature of the courses and the education that's offered and all of the opportunities that are offered at Sabhal Mòr.'

'Basically,' says Seán O Drisceoil, 'our brief was to establish the first college of tertiary education to be run through the medium of Gaelic in the world. It didn't exist in Ireland, so we were the first. The nearest precedent you could draw upon at the time would have been University College Galway. They had a brief from the government to be the institution for courses through the medium of Irish, and they did that in terms of using streaming. You could choose to do science through Irish or English, you could choose to do the arts through Irish, and most people were happy enough with that until the Irish content became diluted. Oddly enough, in the early 1970s when it began to seriously weaken, we, on an inter-department linked committee, actually asked Galway, "How many of your courses are available through the medium of Irish now?" We didn't get an answer. They knew that things had pretty well gone. The old weakness of a stream: it wasn't a dedicated institution and had weakened badly. But they'd done a lot of good in their time, and they were the only real precedent for Sabhal Mòr Ostaig.

'I came to the college on a secondment from Udarás, and I'm grateful to them and the college is grateful to them. They were very generous, they agreed a three-year secondment, but they did make it clear that it was to be no more than three years. I think that the financial dimension was significant; but the other thing that was significant, at that stage, in 1983, was that people were saying that Sabhal Mòr Ostaig would last a year or two years, and people were holding back their commitment. So we can all be grateful to Udarás that they provided the secondment option, because the college was a risky venture and the secondment meant that I could go without risk to Skye, because I knew I could go back to Ireland and Udarás.

'In Skye that summer, I started ordering furniture. We had to work on the basis that the cash flow would be all right; I just got on with it. We needed computers, we certainly wanted to be up to date with everything, so we got computers from the Highlands and Islands Development Board. We had four lecture rooms and An Talla Mòr (the Great Hall), and we got them equipped. We took the main lecture room and equipped it in a management-type style, the classic oval table – the whole idea was that students would run companies. So we got the furniture in and we got the computers in.

'The first thing I attempted to do was a cash-flow projection for the coming year of 1983–84 and, more critically, the first six months, and I discovered that we were going to run out of cash at the beginning of October. That would have been precisely the time that the first students were coming in, and once you run out of cash, you run out rapidly. We had an overdraft of £15,000 at the Bank of Scotland in Broadford at the time, with a very strict manager, Ronnie Morrison from Harris. I would get called to the phone even if we were £100 over the £15,000. I dreaded being called, it was not very nice.

'So we had a meeting of the trustees in Fort Augustus, around the end of August 1983, and I put the projections on the table and said, "We're going to run out of money in five or six weeks' time. That's precisely the time that the course will have started. I know we'll have lots of publicity then, but two weeks later it'll all be gone.

'"I seriously propose that we put the course back a year. It's got to wait until the extra funding has come." And of course the answer came from the governors, the trustees: "No way, no – we're going ahead!" So we carried on. And exactly a month later, myself and Tormod Dòmhnallach, Norman MacDonald, the college secretary at the time – he was a tremendous administrator, and I relied so much on him – were summoned to Inverness. Duncan MacQuarrie, who was still chairman of the trustees at the time, said, "We're going to run out of money in the next week; you've got to give redundancy notices to all the staff." It was exactly as had been predicted in the cash-flow projection. The extra money hadn't come in the mean time. Norman and I looked at each other. A month earlier we'd asked John Norman MacLeod to leave Plockton High School, and I was saying, "How can I ask this man to leave a permanent pensionable job and take on this – should I tell him the real situation?" Norman and I said to each other, "How can we do this?" We argued with Duncan and said, "Look, it's not that easy." At the end of the day, Duncan said, "There's one last chance: get a loan from somewhere to fund it."

'I'm not quite sure who made the call, but in the end, there was only one possibility, and that was Iain Noble. So we got on to Iain Noble, and he came up with the goods. He managed a £50,000 loan. Looking back, that was the critical moment, because we then got a European Social Fund grant and loads of other funding. But that period was critical.

'Now the funny side of the story was, up at the Bank of Scotland in Broadford, Ronnie Morrison was used to keeping an eye on the figures. Once you went over the £15,000 overdraft limit you got this terrifying phone call. I would tell Christine Primrose, "Don't put it through!" So Iain got the £50,000 loan we needed, and it disappeared into the college's current account, where most of it was rapidly eaten up, but we were left with about £17,000 in credit. I was in my office, and the phone rang, and Christine said Ronnie Morrison was on the phone. "Hello, Ronnie, how are you?" And there was no "How are you?" back, it was: "What are you going to do about this? You're at £17,000, and I never authorised you to go over the approved limit." He was so used to seeing DR there on Sabhal Mòr's statement, he never checked to see there was no DR there! And with the greatest pleasure of my life, I said, "Ronnie, is that DR or CR?" A silence at the other end of the line, and then spluttering apologies!

'So the first batch of seven students were able to start. In that first cohort, I think they were all native speakers, all from the Western Isles, literally from Barra up to Lewis, and all the main islands were represented: South Uist, North Uist, Harris and Lewis. It was a two-year course in business and Gaidhealtachd studies, so there was a combination of business and management along with regional development. Those were the core areas of study at first at Sabhal Mòr.

'I think now that the most significant things about that course were: firstly, we had to ensure that, coming to an area like Sleat, the students were not turned off. Coming from even the Western Isles to a quiet rural area like Sleat at that time, they could quickly have become dissatisfied. Nothing much was happening. So great efforts were made in the field of social activity. We were very lucky with the hotels and bars at Ardvasar, Armadale, and, of course, Eilean Iarmain and Torvaig that we were able to get social events going there.

'The other crucial thing was our approach to learning. Business studies and management in particular are usually taught to postgraduates, to give them some vocational experience. The way we got over that with undergraduates was to make the thing real. We ensured that companies were established; the students had to run companies. We made sure that the course was interesting through the use of real companies. We started off in week one saying, "Look, we're in Sleat," so the whole idea would be to work from Sleat outwards. "However you learn accounting, business, regional geography, you've got to deal with Sleat first, and you'll apply the course to Sleat. You've always to relate it to there, and then you can work out."

'During the first week, we took a boat trip out from Armadale onto Loch Slapin. The idea was to show the students the environment that they were now in, the local environment, because they were all from the Western Isles and they didn't know the local area. We showed them the deserted villages – I think one of them may have been Boreraig over in Loch Eishort. That was an example of the type of thing that we could do. It did the trick. It meant that accounting became real; I won't say that economics became real, but certainly accounting and computing did. Sociology was also very important, and a lot of thanks go to John Norman MacLeod and Alan MacDonald, who was another early tutor; they really took on a great burden during that first year. A lot of people said to me, "Only seven students!", but it doesn't matter whether you have one student in the class or thirty, you've got to prepare the same course, and, in fact, the less you have in a class the harder it can be, although, at the same time, seven is a nice number.

'Another interesting thing about that first year is that of the seven students six were female, and another mini-crisis developed around that gender imbalance in February 1984 when the one male student threatened to leave. He felt that the course wasn't for him. That became a real crisis because, even though none of the girls were going out with him or anything, it became very clear to us that they would feel isolated if they were a totally female class. It was a very interesting situation. We recognised that there was a problem, and we managed to persuade Donal Saunders to stay, and we're forever grateful to him for changing his mind.

'There was in that first year's intake a definite sense of pioneering. I think that was crucial in keeping the motivation right up. One thing that brought the pioneering spirit out was the amount of television attention. I think we had every main channel in the UK there, and this went on for about six months. We had Welsh television come up too, in time, because of the interest of the Scottish channels, BBC and ITV, then in time it filtered down to the others. So in the end, over a six-month period, it was not uncommon to have television companies on site. They would say, "Would you mind if the students came and did this or that?" and that all helped to foster the pioneering spirit, which was critical.

'And fairly early on in 1984, we had to start touting for the next intake of students. That meant, for the Western Isles, getting the attention of the Nicolson Institute, the high school in Stornoway. The first thing we got arranged was that we would get in on the Nicolson tour. It was quite clear that the principals and major influences on the market like Eddie Young, the rector of the

Nicolson, and Jim Rodger, the headteacher at Portree High School, were at that stage sceptical about Sabhal Mòr Ostaig; they were very sceptical. It was hair-raising, because I realised how vital their support was.

'Somebody – one of the trustees, I think – wangled an invite for me to go along on the tour that Eddie Young did of the Islands every year. So I would go out to North Uist and we'd stay in Lochmaddy, and we'd do South Uist, we'd do Benbecula, and we'd go to Barra separately. Eddie Young and I got on very well, but I realised that I was there on tolerance. He was sceptical but very pleasant and polite. I found it nerve-racking because I literally had to be on my very best behaviour all the time. It was morning, lunch and dinner. We'd have dinner and we'd have a few drinks at night and talk about the fishing and the brown trout; but in a situation like that, the only time you're on your own is when you fall into bed. And Eddie would typically have with him somebody from the University of Aberdeen, which would have been his students' main destination at the time . . . it was stressful!

'And it didn't pay immediate dividends. We didn't find there was a rush of students coming from the Nicolson, so, come the summer of '84, Norman Gillies – who had come to SMO in December as college secretary – and I sat down and said, "Applications are low again, what are we going to do?" So we embarked on our own tour of the Western Isles. We advertised in the *West Highland Free Press* and the *Stornoway Gazette*, and we had meetings in Stornoway, Barvas, Carloway, Tarbert, Lochmaddy and Benbecula.

'They were very well attended in Stornoway and in the main areas, maybe less than we had hoped in places like Barvas on the west side of Lewis and Tarbert in Harris. But then, I think we were doing something new there by advertising and saying, "You can come to us in Barvas." We were at that time specifically looking for native Gaelic speakers. The students had to feel capable of doing a course through the medium of Gaelic. We weren't going to insist on them having the Gaelic Higher certificate; a lot of potential students, even native speakers, may not have had a Higher in Gaelic. The same applies in the Irish Gaeltacht.

'We ended up at the start of the second academic year with exactly the same number of students as in the first year: another seven. Angus MacDonald went on to another job at the end of the first year, so we were looking for somebody on the accounting side of things, and we were very lucky to get Ruaraidh MacPhee from South Uist to come along and do that.'

The appointment of Norman Gillies as college secretary at the end of 1983 was arguably the most important in the story of Sabhal Mòr Ostaig, and therefore one of the most crucial in the modern history of the Scottish Gaidhealtachd. Like so many of his generation, he had left the north-west of Scotland: 'If you were being educated, there was the assumption that you weren't going to get what you wanted on the island.

'It worked both ways. I'm quite sure that John who was in Digg Primary School with me failed his 11-plus deliberately because he didn't want to go to Portree High School. He was very happy with mechanical things – he was driving before he was out of primary school, he was into stripping engines and a whole variety of other practical things – and he didn't want anything else, so I think he just made sure that he didn't go to Portree. I think also that there was always an assumption that you would move on, that there was nothing here for you, being brought up on a croft. I wouldn't have made a very good crofter anyway, but I don't think I would have got that opportunity; there was always a push on me to do something "better". I suppose it was the usual parental thing that "You have to do better than we've done." I didn't have any clear vision as to what I wanted to do after school. I remember toying briefly with things like the Hong Kong police, or India and places like that, which seemed dreadfully romantic; the colonial stuff was still there at that stage, so there were always those opportunities.

'Farquhar MacIntosh was headmaster in my later days at Portree High School, and Farquhar made me school captain – whether I was a good one or not is debatable. I remember a boy who was a bit of a lad wrote in one of the school magazines: "Norman Gillies is a good prefect because he doesn't throw you out of the toilets for smoking." But I wasn't quite sure what I wanted to do when I left school. The careers service was not brilliant at that stage. I ended up doing hotel management at Strathclyde at the Scottish Hotel School, and that, in retrospect, was good for me but was not, I think, where my heart was. I was just talking about that last week: if you were going back to university right now, in the twenty-first century, what would you do? I would do English literature or something like that. But back in the middle of the twentieth century I did management. Management is what I have been involved in ever since, and management is what I still do here.

'Before coming to Sabhal Mòr in 1983, I had done eight years in the hotel and catering industry and eight years in the building industry. I worked in hotels in Glasgow, in Blackpool, I was here, there and everywhere. I then came back home for a while to the Flodigarry Hotel which was owned by a Miss Kelly in those days. I spent a couple of years there, and that's where I met my wife, Jean, who arrived as a student along with a friend of hers to spend the summer working in Flodigarry. (They thought that because it said in the advert "Flodigarry, by Portree", they were actually going to Portree. They came to Portree by bus, they were met by Miss Kelly's Jaguar car with driver, and then they were still on the road an hour later, and totally confused. When they came to No. 1 Flodigarry, all they could see was this one little house and nothing else, and then another three-quarters of a mile without anything, and then they finally found themselves at Flodigarry Hotel.)

'Anyway, to cut a long story short, I met my wife there so, when she left to start work at Strathclyde Social Services, I followed her to Glasgow, and that's where I went into the building industry, working in administration. Then the company that I was with moved out to Lanarkshire, where Jean comes from, and so we moved house to Lanarkshire. I was in the building industry for eight years.

'There's always the hankering that it would be quite nice to go back home, but I never thought that I would be able to until I retired. But there was always that wish there, and in about 1980, I saw an advert for a job with the Highlands and Islands Development Board, and I got speaking to Bob Storey. Bob was a great guy who did a great deal of good for the Highlands in terms of his approach to social development with the HIDB, and he said, "The salary in the job we are offering at the moment is not very good; you would probably be better elsewhere, but if I come across anything, I'll let you know." This job they were advertising was a development officer or something like that, I'm not quite sure. Then Iain Noble had an advert in the paper so I met him in Edinburgh. Iain and I had a chat, and he seemed quite interesting, and I was interested in what he was doing.

'Things were all right where I was in Lanarkshire. I got on very well with the guy who owned the company. But then about 1983, I got a chance to go down to London. I wasn't too opposed to that; to be quite honest, I would have been happy to think about it. But Jean was not so happy, and, in retrospect, she was totally right. We had had our first child by that stage, and she wanted to stay in Scotland if possible. I didn't have any contacts at that stage who were actively involved in Gaelic development. The little that I knew was all gleaned from the *West Highland Free Press*. I was consequently aware that there were pro-Gaelic initiatives taking place in Skye, but my awareness of Iain Noble and what he was doing was just through the *Free Press*. When the job of college secretary at Sabhal Mòr Ostaig came up here, I think Iain mentioned my name to Jack MacArthur. I got a phone call from Jack and he mentioned Alan Campbell. I had been at Portree High School with Alan – he's a year younger than me. This was in October 1983, and after that it happened very quickly.'

Revd Jack MacArthur played a key role in Gaelic and educational development in at least three Highland counties. A native of Lochs in south-east Lewis, he had become interested in politics while at Glasgow University, where he was a contemporary of the future Labour Party luminaries John Smith and Donald Dewar. In 1966, he accepted a call to the Church of Scotland ministry at Kinlochbervie in Sutherland, where he became chairman of the local Education Committee before moving to Carloway in Lewis in 1971.

MacArthur was well placed to become a driving founding force in the new Western Isles Council, Comhairle nan Eilean, when it was established in 1974. As chairman of the new council's Education Committee, he was 'very forward-looking and able', says Father Calum MacLellan, 'with a certain charisma as well'. Another colleague from those early days of the Stornoway assembly, Sandy Matheson, would add: 'Jack very quickly proved himself to be a highly articulate and strategic thinker, with strong ideas on how communities should be developed. That was the case not only here, but also in other areas where he continued to give sterling service for years after leaving here.

'He was here at a very vulnerable time for the Western Isles, when many people in the Central Belt and in the Scottish Office questioned whether the Islands had the talent to be successful as a local authority. In that sense, Jack was a most capable ambassador for us.'

In 1979, MacArthur moved on again, to the congregation at Broadford in Skye – and was promptly elected to the Highland Council as well as the board of Sabhal Mòr Ostaig.

'I first met Jack when he came as minister to the Church of Scotland in Broadford,' says Alan Campbell. 'I was living in Sleat then and I didn't know him well but I got to know him better when I came to work for the BBC and he was a Highland councillor. Over a period of years, I'm very proud to say, Jack and I became very good friends and, like so many people, I really mourn his passing in 2002. His was the kind of wisdom and talent that we need. If there was ever somebody who shouldn't have retired until he was at least 100 years old, it was Jack MacArthur. Jack had a vision and he achieved that vision; it was our vision also, but maybe his greatest skill of all was in actually selling it. I remember the late Councillor Duncan Grant saying once, when I was manager of the BBC in Inverness and we were talking about the never-ending saga of the Skye Bridge, something like: "We were in committee and there was this absolutely bloody ridiculous suggestion. I was sitting there trying to block it, to put a motion together in my head, when up popped Jack MacArthur with a motion so convoluted you could have hidden it behind a corkscrew. While I was still trying to work out what it meant, they'd approved it!" Duncan said that in admiration, and Duncan was a master of convoluted motions himself.

'When Jack came to Sabhal Mòr, he brought to the trustees a huge experience of education at local authority level from Sutherland, Western Isles and Highland councils. He brought a huge experience of local government finance and protocol – the kind of vital skills which you need to obtain credibility with the public sector. And he also brought something which is not always found in people with these skills: he brought vision and commitment to developing, to reaching beyond where we were and to always keeping going.

'On one occasion – and this is typical of the sort of thing Jack would do – we'd got a modest extra contribution from the Scottish Office; not what we'd asked for, needless to say, but we got something nevertheless. At the trustees' meeting, instead of saying, "Well, we got something we didn't expect," everyone said, "We asked them for that and they only gave us this"; it was a case of whinge, whinge, whinge.

'Jack listened. Jack was always very skilful at this; he let other people say their piece and he seemed to know just the right time at which to come in. He had a unique talent for that, it was interesting watching him in committee, he would sit for half an hour and say nothing, and when all the yahs had had their say, he would then come in and pull the threads together. He would massage all the egos. He said that day at Ostaig, "You know what I think we should do? I think we should write a letter to Edinburgh and thank them for what they gave us. It is not natural for the Gael to be impolite or inappreciative, and yet that's the image we're creating for ourselves. It is quite understandable, because we're never getting what we should be getting; that's absolutely true, and because of that, we've fallen into the habit of always moaning.

'"The guy sitting at a desk down there, who might have done a lot of work to get this few thousand pounds for us, what's he hearing? He is hearing us complaining. How's that guy going to react to that? He's going to say, 'Away with them!' On the other hand, we could drop him a couple of lines saying, 'Thank you very much for what you've done for us here.' He'll remember that too." That was the kind of practical wisdom and humanity that Jack brought. He had great humour. I remember Duncan MacQuarrie at a meeting once, when Jack was chairing, and Duncan was very ill at ease. Duncan kept popping in and out and in and out, and eventually he felt the need to explain to Jack: "I'm sorry, Chairman, but I need to get in touch with Raigmore Hospital because we're expecting another addition to the family." Jack said, "Oh, congratulations, how many's that?" Duncan said, "The third." Jack said deadpan, "That's the thing with people who are late in getting started, you can't stop them!"'

At the end of 1983, Norman Gillies received that auspicious phone call from Jack MacArthur. 'It was during the week, asking me if I could come up for an interview on Saturday. Up I came, and I met with Alan and Jack, and that was it. The job was college secretary, in charge of administration. Now, the college in those days didn't consist of very much, they were just getting staffed up; Tormod Calum Dòmhnallach [Norman MacDonald] and Christine Primrose were the people who were actually looking after things. Of course, everyone painted a very rosy picture. Jack was very good with words and very optimistic, and Alan Campbell was also very articulate, so I got sold this fantastic story. I don't think they were quite open as to what the finances were like: they were a bit ropey to say the least. Sabhal Mòr Ostaig always has been a bit of a wing and a prayer, but in the early days there was a lot of prayer and very little wing.

'I got offered the job after that interview. I was here within a month. I came up before I started work and spent a week with Tormod Calum to find out what the systems were like, and I had a great time with Seán, John Norman and a whole variety of other people. It was a fantastic experiment, and it was brilliant that it worked.

'I never thought that the college might be doomed or short-lived. I had been totally convinced by Jack and Alan, otherwise I would have thought more deeply about taking the job, because by that stage I had two kids – Emma and Christopher, who was only nine months when we moved. We uprooted two kids from a safe environment, and I gave up a safe job to come here; I must have been convinced that I could make a go of it before leaving the house and everything else in the south and coming here to live in temporary accommodation for a while. I was convinced.

'My academic interest is not in the language per se, because I have very little formal grounding in that aspect; what was interesting to me here was that people were doing business and management through the language. I could understand that, and I could see myself fitting in with what people were trying to do. That was important.

'I got to know the people who were actively involved here, like Duncan MacQuarrie, and I remember meeting Sorley Maclean at my first meeting with the trustees. That was totally brilliant, coming across these guys, so I was in for the long term. But, having said that, I didn't know how scary the finances were. If I had thought I was coming back to a quieter pace of life, those hopes were pretty thoroughly and quickly dashed. I've probably found myself working harder for the last 20 years than I've ever done before – Gaelic development is not an easy life!

'The finances were shaky back then for a variety of reasons. But when you think of what had been achieved with very little back-up in 1983, when they were still working on the building – they had managed to get accreditation through SCOTBEC, they had managed to convince the Scottish Office that this was a viable proposition, there was all that sort of thing. And then they had found the necessary finance to kick-start the thing, and I think they were right doing it on a wing and a prayer because, if they had waited until the circumstances were totally right and they knew their cash flow was secure, that point would never have come. You had to take that leap of faith and say, "Look, we know this is a wee bit ropey, but we're actually going to do it," hoping that the money would follow through. And that's what happened.

'I take my hat off to the guys who were involved in those early days. It was a fantastic achievement to convince people that this could be done. The student numbers were disappointing because people were projecting an annual intake of 20. When you are putting forward a business plan, it's always the same: you have to over-egg it to make sure that somebody buys in, and then you have the problem of how you sort it out afterwards. I think there was a bit of over-optimism. If something of this scale is based on twenty students and you get seven or eight, there's plainly a shortfall there, and it has to be made up, the place has to be justified in other ways.

'And we were lucky to have Seán. As well as being a very nice guy he was quite an inspired appointment, because it cut out all the crap in terms of baggage. If they had appointed someone from within the Scottish Gaelic community, from within the Highlands and Islands, that person would obviously have come with a whole pile of baggage which could have meant that other organisations might not necessarily have been supportive. Being from Ireland, Seán took all that out. I think there's also a strength in naivety. I believe that it can be better not knowing too much about the situation you're going into, I think it's better not to know some of the internal and external politics. Seán was a very good guy, a very friendly guy and obviously a very bright guy who had the capacity to get along with people. He steered the college well in the early days. I think he was probably more optimistic about it than somebody would have been who knew more of the background in the Highlands and Islands in particular and Scotland in general. Seán wasn't deterred by any of that.

'And his Scots Gaelic came on remarkably well! Sometimes you would find Seán speaking three languages at once: Gaeilge, English and Gaelic! Going back to 1983 and the start-up, somebody like Seán was vital to the mix, because he wasn't interested in a 'them and us' relationship between the students and the administration. If it had been like that, I don't think we would have been here very long. Seán encouraged cooperation – mixing in and learning together – which was essential because this had never been done before, and the lecturer was learning at the same pace as or just a wee bit ahead of the students. The process had to be open and informal with such a very small group, and Seán was totally right for that.

184

'Jack MacArthur was a strategist. I had a great regard for Jack. He was somebody who wasn't terribly interested in detail. One of Jack's strengths was that he would allow people to do what they felt was right. He was good at delegating. He didn't want to know all the problems because he expected you to sort them out. But if you did have a problem that you felt that you couldn't overcome yourself, Jack was always there. He had the contacts as well, he was a political operator. That was his strength, he felt: "That's your job, that's what you should be doing, do it, and if you ever get stuck, give me a call." If you were writing a press release or something like that, Jack would never give you a statement, he would say, "Well, you know what I would say."

'And the whole thing wouldn't have worked without Duncan MacQuarrie. I don't know how Duncan did it, really. My memory of being here in the first four years is that Duncan was always there at the end of a phone. He was always there to check up on things. He was the guy with all the knowledge; he was the guy who had built the thing up and put it together and sold it. That's not doing anybody else who was there a disservice, it's just that Duncan certainly was the guy who knew how it should all be done. Again, if you had a query, Duncan was the guy to phone up. It was quite amazing to think that this guy was holding a full-time job elsewhere and he was actually doing this as well. Not only that, but he was writing a lot of things at that stage. Fantastic! You can't take Sabhal Mòr Ostaig away from Iain Noble, it was Iain's idea; but the guy who made it a reality was Duncan MacQuarrie.

'As well as that, people within the HIDB like Ken Alexander and Bob Storey, and Highland Council and Comhairle nan Eilean, were extremely supportive, and went to lengths they needn't have gone to to make sure that we survived in the first few years. Once, most starkly, we didn't have enough money to pay the salaries at the end of the month, and somebody within Highland Council made a decision that a cheque could be released in time to meet the demand. I also remember a bank manager granting us an overdraft at a critical time, which put him out on a limb. It's very humbling when you think back on these things. And people still make an effort to help Sabhal Mòr, because when people believe in something and believe it should be happening, they want to play their part in it.

'In the early years, the support of Strathclyde Council was also critical. Remember, Strathclyde had started the first Gaelic-medium unit in 1985. Again, it was an act of faith on behalf of Strathclyde Council: why should they be supporting a Gaelic college in the south end of Skye when they had plenty to do, thank you very much, in their own patch? But they did. I think Brian Wilson, who was always so active politically on Gaelic's behalf both in the Lowlands and the Highlands, had been in there doing the ground work, so when we went to call, it was that much easier. Strathclyde were instrumental in helping us at specific and important times.'

And so it came about that during a very few years in the middle of the 1980s, Scotland – which for over a century had been denied almost any form of education in its oldest, its original national language – rediscovered Gaelic-medium teaching at pre-school, primary, secondary and tertiary levels. It was a form of renaissance, and it may have arrived only just in time to rescue the language, for the evidence was that just as officialdom, politicians, schools and colleges were accepting Gaelic, its 1,000-year hearthside transmission from parent to child might be coming to an end.

This sea change would be recognised by Alan Campbell in his later role as director of Comunn na Gàidhlig. Writing a dawn-of-the-new-millennium address in the year 2001, Campbell stated:

> For Gaelic, as has been the case with so many other languages (languages that are now classed as 'lesser-used' or 'minority' languages), it was the breakdown of the intergenerational transference of the language that was the beginning of this crisis. To put it quite simply, parents stopped speaking to their children in their native language. They most probably thought they were doing what was best for their children – or at least that they were not depriving them of anything really useful – but in truth they were denying them of a part of their natural, and national, heritage and culture, and part of their

birthright! . . . Why did a people who have a natural pride in their identity desert their linguistic heritage in this way? There can be no doubt that one key cause was the constant negative messaging from a state education system, over generations, where Gaelic-speaking children were taught that their language had no real value and as a consequence they were not even taught to read it or write it!

The first few intakes of students at Sabhal Mòr Ostaig were largely comprised of native speakers. They – and the Gaelic-speaking professional men and women who established their alma mater – were by the 1980s and 1990s part of a dwindling body. The hope given to Gaelic at the end of the twentieth century was the legacy to their mother tongue of the last generations of Scottish Gaels who had been born and bred in monoglot Gaelic homes and communities. The merits and undoubted advantages of bilingualism would henceforth be Gaelic's last, best hope. Gaelic's position now was such that it was unlikely to realise that hope – of a sustainable future as a lesser-used but still vital language – without government help.

Throughout the 1980s and for the first half of the 1990s, the Conservative Party was in power in Britain. The condition of the Gaelic language itself had ceased to be a party-political issue with the expiry of the land reform movement of the late nineteenth century, and the end of the first, late-Victorian Gaelic renaissance. It could be argued that thereafter all political parties were equally indifferent to it. But of all the late-twentieth-century political groupings, the Conservatives seemed at face value to promise least to the vernacular of a small group of Scottish Highlanders who rarely if ever returned a Tory MP to Westminster.

Between 1979, when she was first elected to government, and 1986, Prime Minister Margaret Thatcher's Conservative Secretary of State for Scotland was an MP named George Younger. The scion of a major Scottish brewing family, Younger had been the Conservative MP for Ayr since 1964. Even from that unlikely stance, he offered occasional clues to the future.

'George Younger was very supportive of Gaelic,' recalls Duncan MacQuarrie. 'He never explained it, but I know broadly why. In 1972, George Younger gave a keynote speech at the evening concert at the Mod in Ayr, and he committed himself there and then, as MP for Ayr, as he was at the time, to supporting Gaelic in all its manifestations. Prior to that, he and his family used to go on holiday to Mull. By some strange coincidence, when my grandmother was widowed in the 1930s, she took summer lodgers in our house at Tobermory and the Youngers had been there at some point. I didn't know this until one day in Mull in 1969 or 1970. My father had just retired and we were building a garage. It was the summer holidays and I was with him, and this car drew up and a fellow came out and introduced himself as George Younger. At the time I hadn't a clue who that was, but it was him.

'There had obviously been some kind of influence on him, because as Scottish Secretary he was always very staunch in his support. It was under Younger that the scheme for specific grants for Gaelic was introduced, and a variety of other improvements as well. These chaps would be very supportive when we sometimes met hurdles with officialdom and the Civil Service. When you explained and explained and explained again what you were about, they suddenly discovered that their great-great-great-granny was from Skye, and doors began to open.'

In 1985, the newly established Comunn na Gàidhlig organised a conference at Sabhal Mòr Ostaig, which it billed as 'Towards a National Policy for Gaelic'. Secretary of State George Younger agreed to give the main address. He said:

> Central government efforts cannot save the Gaelic language unless Gaelic speaking communities act out their own convictions and commitment to their mother tongue . . . That is why it is so important that this conference should encourage voluntary initiatives involving the community at large and young people in particular. We are prepared to do our part . . . working in partnership with local authorities,

> voluntary organisations and individuals who wish to build
> on the foundations already laid in support of Gaelic.

This statement of intent – that if the Gaelic community itself took
the initiative, Younger's government would follow up with hard
cash – was properly seen at the time as being of great significance.
'Ah,' says Alan Campbell, 'the day George Younger came to talk to
the troops! The road to Damascus! He said in effect: "The Gaelic
language will not survive because the government legislates, but the
Gaelic language will survive because the Gaelic people will it to
survive. So if you act out your beliefs in the language, then the
government must respond."

'I have quoted that back to them many, many times and I have to
say that the government has responded, and here we are 20 years on
with a government body called Bòrd na Gàidhlig. For many years
we had that Conservative government, and we had people saying
that the greatest things that ever happened for Gaelic happened
under the Tories. Well, there was something slightly odd about that,
because we and they didn't seem automatically to fit as natural
partners. But in fairness to George Younger, he took the view that
here was an argument he was convinced of, and he therefore
supported it. And so did Malcolm Rifkind, the Scottish Secretary
after him, and then Michael Forsyth.'

In 1990, Norman Gillies would tell *The Scotsman*:

> The Thatcher years. Well, they've been good to us. I don't
> know why. It might be in their interest to try and swing a
> pocket of Tory votes. It could be a feeling among some of the
> older Tories for the language of the ghillies, a feeling that we
> must do something for the poor Highlanders – whatever the
> reason, it has to be said that we have had great support from
> the Conservative Government.
>
> The incident that has probably struck me most over the
> past ten years happened one Saturday morning. I was sitting
> at home and the television had been left on. It was showing
> a report from the Conservative Party Conference in

Aberdeen, and there was a Scottish Tory MP standing before a great audience of Scottish Tories, welcoming Margaret Thatcher to the conference – and he was doing it in Gaelic!

For an important 18 years between 1979 and 1997, the Conservative government was the only government available to the Gaelic community. Luckily, in many important respects, it was as good as George Younger's words – not least in the realm of television.

Seven

There had been, by the late 1980s, Gaelic television of some kind for several decades. Not until the early 1960s, however, had a Gaelic programme which was not filmed at the National Mod gone out on BBC Scotland – and then it was, inevitably, half an hour of Gaelic song, introduced in English by the editor of the *Stornoway Gazette*, James Shaw Grant.

Commercial television in Scotland is divided between three institutions: Grampian, which holds the northern franchise; Scottish, which provides for the south and west; and Border, which transmits to the eponymous marches with England. Both Scottish and Grampian managed effectively to ignore the language of their western and north-western constituencies throughout the 1960s and 1970s. A System Three poll of 350 'educated and committed' Gaels as late as 1989 indicated that only 1 per cent thought that television served them well; 80 per cent thought that TV used Gaelic 'not very well' or 'not at all well'. But 78 per cent of those people agreed that 'I make a point of watching Gaelic television programmes whenever I can', and an unsurprising 87 per cent agreed that 'Gaelic programmes play an important part in keeping Gaelic culture and language alive'.

A broadcasting White Paper issued by the Labour government in 1978 insisted for the first time that television 'has an important role to play in the preservation of Gaelic and Welsh as living tongues and in sustaining the distinctive cultures based upon them'.

The Broadcasting Act that followed in 1981, which expanded the UK commercial sector, instructed the Independent Broadcasting Authority (IBA) to ensure that when 'another language as well as English is in common use' a 'suitable proportion of matter in that language' was broadcast. As a result of this instruction, the IBA's Scottish Advisory Committee asked both Grampian Television and Scottish Television to put 30 minutes a week of Gaelic material on the airwaves.

It was apparent to John Angus MacKay and his colleagues at Comunn na Gàidhlig that any significant increase in the quality and quantity of Gaelic television, particularly in the commercial sector, was unlikely to be provided voluntarily. The TV stations would need to be bribed. And the amount of money needed to bribe them could only feasibly come from one source: central government.

By the middle of the 1980s there was within the UK one remarkable – and to some Scottish eyes, galling – comparison to be made. Following a long and bitter campaign in Wales, language activists had eventually succeeded in forcing the new Conservative government to abide by an earlier promise and give the Principality a dedicated television channel in Welsh. The same 1981 Broadcasting Act which had resulted in Grampian Television broadcasting half an hour of Gaelic a week had in Wales established S4C, or Sianel Pedwar Cymru (Channel 4 Wales). From November 1982 onwards, all Welsh-language TV programmes from whatever source were transmitted on S4C.

On average since its inception, S4C has managed to broadcast some thirty-two hours a week of Welsh television, ten of them provided by the BBC under the corporation's public service remit in the 1981 Broadcasting Act, and the rest from independent producers and the Welsh commercial channel, HTV. Prior to S4C, the company says, 'the limited number of Welsh programmes produced were scattered throughout BBC1 and ITV schedules'. Much the same, in other words, as continued to be the case with Gaelic in Scotland.

Malcolm Rifkind, the Edinburgh MP who had succeeded George

Younger as Scottish Secretary in 1986, was another Scottish Conservative patrician. He was equally well disposed towards Gaelic. Like a good many other British Tories, Rifkind was fond of shooting excursions in the Highlands. It may be significant that this recreation led Rifkind to hunting weekends on the Skye estate of Iain Noble, as a guest of the landowner.

Although there was discussion in certain circles in the mid- to late '80s about the idea of a devoted Gaelic TV channel in Scotland on the pattern of S4C in Wales, it was not pursued for long as a real possibility. John Angus MacKay and his colleagues were persuaded that the best and quickest answer in the short term was to increase the paltry amount of Gaelic broadcast on the two main commercial channels while supporting and bulking out the BBC's public service produce. In the words of one extremely interested party, Scottish Television's then controller of features and director of programmes Alistair Moffat:

> MacKay and Comunn na Gàidhlig conceived the neat idea of using television to get Gaelic back beside the hearth, and set about campaigning. He approached one of the reddest in tooth and claw Thatcherite economists, Cento Veljanowski, brought him up to Lewis, showed him the blackhouse at Arnol . . . and promptly hired him as a consultant to help press the case for more Gaelic television.

The first public hint that MacKay's and CnaG's lobbying was having an effect came in June 1989 when Scottish Secretary Rifkind told the House of Commons:

> Earlier this year, I met the chief executives of Scottish Television, Grampian Television and Border Television to discuss their views on the White Paper 'Broadcasting in the '90s: Competition, Choice and Quality' and on the possible future arrangements for broadcasting in Scotland, including the future of Gaelic broadcasting. My officials had similar discussions with staff of BBC Scotland and last December I

discussed Gaelic broadcasting with BBC representatives at
the offices of Radio Nan Eilean in Stornoway.

In April this year, I met representatives of Comunn na
Gàidhlig specifically to hear their views on the future of
Gaelic broadcasting. As my right honourable friend the
Home Secretary said during his statement on 13 June, we will
make announcements before long on our proposals for
Gaelic broadcasting.

Alistair Moffat would suggest in a lecture at Sabhal Mòr Ostaig that:

All of this enterprise might have met with the usual
indifference if it had not been for one piece of huge good
luck. I cannot say who this person is, but right inside the
engine of government, one of the key cogs happened to be a
Gael. At a critical time, lobbying from Comunn na Gàidhlig
on the outside was matched by lobbying on the inside. My
source told me that he hoped for perhaps a million pounds to
be given for dubbing and sub-titling. When a minister asked
him how many people in Scotland spoke Gaelic, he replied:
'80,000, I think.' 'Fine,' said the minister involved in
compiling the [1990] Broadcasting Bill, '500,000 Welsh
speakers get £50 million, that means pro rata that Gaelic
should get £8 million.'

On 18 December 1989, Malcolm Rifkind declared that the 1990
Broadcasting Act would establish a Gaelic Television Committee,
Comataidh Telebhisein Gàidhlig (CTG). The CTG would be given
an initial annual grant of £8,000,000 and thereafter 'an annual,
though variable, sum as determined by the Secretary of State'.

The £8,000,000 would chiefly be used to fund new Gaelic TV
programmes. In the late 1980s, there were approximately a hundred
hours of Gaelic television broadcast on the four terrestrial channels
each year. Channel 4 effectively ignored the language. Grampian and
Scottish put out their statutory twenty-six hours each twelvemonth,
and the BBC was responsible for the rest.

MacKay, as consultant on behalf of CnaG, and Rifkind planned that the £8,000,000 administered and issued by the CTG would triple this output from 100 hours to 300 hours a year, or around 6 hours a week on the terrestrial stations. That would still be a long way behind S4C's 32 hours a week (or 1,660 hours a year) of Welsh television. But it would be a start. And significantly for such an institution as Sabhal Mòr Ostaig, the 1990 Broadcasting Act gave the CTG the ability to provide funding not only for original programmes, but also for 'training, research and for related purposes such as support materials'. There was clearly going to be an increased demand for Gaelic reporters, broadcasters, presenters, technicians and producers. A whole new industry might be born, uniquely accessible to Gaelic speakers.

There was only one real candidate for the job of first director of Comataidh Telebhisein Gàidhlig. John Angus MacKay, the former chairman of the trustees of the Gaelic college at Ostaig, left Comunn na Gàidhlig to take up the new post in October 1991.

To John Norman MacLeod, who watched these developments with an interested eye from Sabhal Mòr Ostaig, they were indicative of a change in approach. 'There was more professionalism. I suppose we all make the argument that we don't get sufficient support at executive level, and particularly in education we have always needed more recognition. There is maybe the argument that too much money went to broadcasting as opposed to other initiatives. But the money that CTG got was only a drop in the ocean in television terms. And it was achieved professionally.

'John Angus MacKay's lobby for [Gaelic-language] television in the Broadcasting Act and the setting up of the Gaelic Television Fund was a good case of making and winning arguments. Not in the sense of: "We're worthy of it" and "We should have this and that", but demonstrating the difference that investment could make and the economic case in its favour.'

Changes had been made at Sabhal Mòr Ostaig during the late 1980s. Seán O Drisceoil returned to Ireland after three years in 1986. He was briefly replaced by the Lewisman Colin MacLeod, who was convinced that the peripheral location of Sabhal Mòr

195

Ostaig worked to its detriment. There followed a period of uncertainty, following which Norman Gillies and John Norman MacLeod were appointed jointly to govern Sabhal Mòr Ostaig. They would prove to be inspired and lasting appointments.

'We had Colin MacLeod as principal after Seán,' says Norman Gillies, 'who never sort of settled here and who didn't think that the college could, on this site, produce what was needed. Colin was only here for a year. In 1987, the trustees decided that rather than advertising for another principal, they would have a change of tack, so they offered me the post of director and they offered John Norman the post of head of studies.'

'Dr Colin MacLeod came between 1986 and 1987,' says Farquhar MacIntosh, who would become chairman of the trustees in the reshuffle. 'It wasn't a happy time. It was only subsequently that I came to realise how unhappy it was. He considered that the college was in too isolated a position. He wanted to move to a more central location like Portree, or even to the mainland. I think at one point he toyed with the idea of buying the disused catering college building at Duncraig Castle by Plockton in Ross-shire, which I was dead against, because it would have sunk us, I'm sure.

'Anyway, he departed for one reason or another, and Norman was appointed, and that was really the great turning point. It wasn't that Colin MacLeod wasn't an able chap, but he didn't seem to me to be so committed to the college or to have a grasp of what we were trying to do through the medium of Gaelic – the philosophy behind the college – whereas Norman did, having been secretary at Sabhal Mòr for a number of years. He was an inspired choice really. That was the start of the growth and development of the college which we have witnessed since Norman took over. Soon after that, in 1989 or thereabouts, John Angus MacKay who was then the Comunn na Gàidhlig director, was the chairman of the trustees and he had to give up that position under the terms of his contract with CTG. I was approached by the trustees and asked would I take over the chair. I was very happy to take over the chair but didn't foresee that I would have to do 13 years in the chair – and counting! In fact, I didn't think at the time I would give it so long because my father and his father before him had died at the age of 60, and I was reckoning that if I got the allotted span, I would be doing quite well. But here I am.'

'I don't know about the word "promotion" to describe what happened to me in 1987,' says Norman Gillies. 'It depends how you interpret the role. If you think in terms of management, the job didn't change very much, because I was still the person responsible for administration. I think it probably meant that I could move into other areas of interest. It was an interesting time. I learned in that period that there were a lot of people out there who were willing to help, and I think that's been true about Sabhal Mòr since its inception, there have always been supporters. Life can be difficult at times but you will always find somebody who is willing to go that extra mile to help out. That helped me a lot in 1987.'

Despite both originating in the same few square miles of north-western Skye, Norman Gillies and John Norman MacLeod had never previously met before their paths joined at Sabhal Mòr Ostaig. 'I would have known of him,' says Gillies. 'I knew his folks, but he would have been too young then. I would have seen him, I suppose, on a bus or somewhere, and I was aware also of his sister; but, no, I didn't know John Norman until I arrived here. We struck up a good working relationship. I think it's like a lot of things in this place, it's a question of trust. It's not about glory-seeking, it's a team effort and it's as simple as that. You can trust people to do things; we've been very fortunate in that regard at Sabhal Mòr because, at key times, we've had the necessary strong individuals to take it forward.'

In 1987, the college added a second course to its curriculum. Business studies with information technology was an early acknowledgement of the importance of the new information and communications technology, even – or especially – to a language which had been spoken by the first monks on Iona. Student numbers had risen slightly and reached a modest plateau of roughly ten to each annual intake, or twenty at any given time. It was a living, but only just. That television initiative of Sabhal Mòr's former chairman John Angus MacKay would provide the economic kick-start.

As the Glasgow University lecturer Donald MacLean would later explain in 'Sunshine and Storms on the Isle of Skye', a case study of the Gaelic college:

> In the early 1990s, by which time Sabhal Mòr Ostaig had established itself as a small further education establishment, with a handful of staff delivering its two courses to around twenty students, another development was to occur which would have a major influence over the college in years to come. Television broadcast franchises were coming up for renewal in Scotland at a time when there was increasing political pressure to provide Gaelic broadcasting on a larger scale than ever before. There was thus a real pressure on TV companies to prove that they were taking Gaelic seriously. To SMO, this constituted a timely opportunity.
>
> Keen to upgrade and enlarge the campus in order to facilitate growth, staff at SMO identified a clear opportunity in the development and provision of a Gaelic Broadcast training course. Such a course would strengthen the college's links with the media whilst allowing TV companies to demonstrate commitment to Gaelic. In practical terms, if SMO was to increase the flow of a critical and limited resource – skilled Gaelic-speaking personnel for TV companies – the companies in turn might invest in the development of such a resource.
>
> In 1991, Scottish Television and Grampian Television donated £300,000 and £100,000 respectively to SMO with no formal strings attached, but on the understanding that the college would use the money to progress its aspirations in relation to Gaelic broadcasting (a placement-based course was launched in 1991). By 1993, the money had been used to leverage access to other funds and in 1993, the college campus was upgraded to include more teaching and admin space, new student accommodation and an (as yet unequipped) TV studio. The studio was equipped later that year on the closure of the BBC studio in Aberdeen, at which point SMO became a provider of in-house Gaelic broadcast

training, for which it has subsequently developed a very strong reputation.

The findings of the 1991 census trickled out in 1992 and 1993. Its results were by now predictable. The total number of Gaelic speakers in Scotland had fallen by just over the standard 10 per cent to 65,987. In some previously reliable heartland areas such as Skye and Lochalsh, where the total population had risen dramatically in the previous decade, the proportion of Gaelic speakers had fallen to below 50 per cent.

The census figures seemed to run against a flow of optimism and activity. If the word 'renaissance' meant anything, it surely defined the level of resurgent energy which washed over Gaelic in the 1980s and 1990s. One of Sabhal Mòr Ostaig's former *sgrìobhadairean* (the term which came to replce filidh as the title of SMO's writer in residence), the writer Aonghas Dubh MacNeacail, who had previously harboured explosively pessimistic views about the future of the language he had grown up with, would say in 1988: 'The infrastructure has been created which makes it possible for the language to survive. I am much more confident now than I would have been 15 years ago.'

As the 1980s drew to a close, Iain Noble looked around him and commented: 'I thought I knew almost everything that was happening in the Gaelic world in terms of new ideas and projects; today there are so many that I don't even begin to keep up with them. There is now a recognition of the problems and a pride in the language which did not really exist before.'

In recognition of what he and others had done in Britain to preserve their mother tongue, Revd Jack MacArthur was in 1987 made president of the European Bureau for Lesser-Used Languages. From Friesland to Sardinia, it seemed, minority language movements were casting respectful glances at the Scottish Highlands. From his office at Sabhal Mòr Ostaig, the level-headed Norman Gillies was tempted in 1990 to predict that the census results might display an unpredicted increase in Gaelic users. He observed (correctly) to *The Scotsman*:

> I might be proved totally wrong, but I think a lot of people now are more willing to identify themselves as Gaelic speakers than before. It has a different kind of image now. People are beginning to realise that we have got something which is not to be hidden but to be expressed, and I think that should probably make a difference [to the census total].

Norman Gillies's optimism was more reflective of the mood than the cold reality. Gaelic had perhaps never been more sympathetically regarded, its public profile never higher; but its old people – the generations which came from huge families of eight, ten, twelve Gaelic-speaking siblings – were dying. The traditional crofting system which had sustained the communities which in their turn had sustained the language was in retreat. The reason was not hard to find.

In 1988, at the height of the economic boom in London and the South-east, a survey of 50 random crofts by the North of Scotland College of Agriculture revealed that the average annual net profit was £729. In the Western Isles, the average hourly return on a crofter's agricultural labour was 28 pence. Their croft did not – could not – alone sustain most crofting families, of course. But with all ancillary incomes, all part-time jobs and occasional hires and bed-and-breakfast cash factored in, the average Western Isles crofting family earned in 1988 a total of £6,788, or £130 a week, before tax. Little wonder that their children left, and took their Gaelic with them.

Even the 'educated and committed' Gaels who had been polled by System Three about Gaelic television in 1989 (82 per cent of whom could read as well as speak the language – an unusually high proportion) admitted that fully half of their children could not or did not speak Gaelic.

What consolation there was – and it did exist – was to be found by determined searchers in the barely visible small print of the 2001 census, amid extrapolations too arcane by far to concern the man on the Colbost omnibus. The consolation was this: in every adult age range throughout Scotland, the number of Gaelic speakers had fallen. But within the age range between three and fifteen years, the decrease had slowed down almost to a halt. For the first time in perhaps half a century, the collapse in the number of children able to speak Gaelic looked capable of being stemmed.

This was not the result of more infants growing up in Gaelic-speaking households. Quite the contrary. By the early 1990s, it was generally accepted, a number of factors such as the dissolution of the traditional Highland rural working class and a growing number of marriages and shared parenthoods where one partner – wherever he or she came from – was monoglot in English had led to an increased decline of Gaelic as a hearthside language.

If this steadying of the numbers of Gaelic-speaking under-15s was not merely a temporary blip, it had only one cause: improved educational provision. Professor Kenneth MacKinnon summarised in the early 1990s:

> In the late 1970s, a more thoroughgoing bilingual primary project got under way in the Western Isles, which was extended to all schools in the early 1980s, and similar provisions were made in Skye by Highland Region.
>
> In 1981, a voluntary Gaelic playgroups organisation commenced, and by the late '80s had established over 30 'cròileagain' or Gaelic-medium playgroups, about half in Gaelic areas, and half in urban centres elsewhere. The success of this movement attracted grant moneys and enabled full-time and part-time paid staff to be appointed.
>
> This in turn stimulated the inception in 1985 of the first Gaelic-medium primary units in Inverness and Glasgow. By 1986/87, 68 pupils were being educated through Gaelic as a teaching medium at four schools: in Inverness, Glasgow, Skye and Lewis. In 1987/88 two further such schools commenced in Skye, and in the following session two others in Edinburgh and South Uist.
>
> Unfortunately, in 1979 when Comhairle nan Eilean was contemplating an extension of its bilingual policy to the secondary sector, which would have been supported by the

then Labour-controlled Scottish Education Department, its nerve failed. The ensuing delay and a change of government wrecked what might have been the best chance for the survival of Gaelic in the Western Isles. The incoming Conservative government insisted on a two-year feasibility study, which eventually reported in 1987, testifying to the effectiveness of the bilingual primary education policy.

Meanwhile some minor advances in bilingual education have occurred in Western Isles secondary schools. A new six-year secondary for the southern isles opened in Benbecula in August 1988, and was heralded as an opportunity for a new start. A pilot bilingual secondary scheme had commenced at Lionel some two years earlier, with some useful curriculum development. In 1988, the pupils proceeding from the Glasgow Gaelic-Medium Unit were to receive some form of bilingual secondary education at the neighbourhood comprehensive at Hillpark. Prior to these developments the paradoxical situation was that the Scottish system had developed bilingual education at primary and tertiary levels – but had omitted a linking secondary stage.

In 1985, there had been just twenty-four children attending two Gaelic-medium primary classes in the whole of Scotland. By 1991, there were 614 pupils at 31 units. Their impact would be substantial – not least on the confidence of those adults who strove to sustain the language. Angus Peter Campbell, an acclaimed novelist and broadcaster, and one of Sabhal Mòr Ostaig's many distinguished sgrìobhadairean, said in 1990 following a visit to the Gaelic-medium class in Sleat:

> You see all of those children being educated in Gaelic from the age of five, and you think: it will be there, in their bones now. They will never lose it. I watch something like that and I become confident, perfectly confident, that the language will not die.

Over the next ten years those 614 GMU pupils and 31 Gaelic-medium units would respectively treble and double. They were never, from first inception, dominated by the children of Gaelic-speaking households. More than half of the children who passed through Gaelic-medium units in Scotland had either one or both parents who could not themselves speak the language. They were, therefore, restocking the language bank from an entirely new source.

Much of the above-mentioned tertiary level of Gaelic-medium education was of course delivered at Sabhal Mòr Ostaig in Skye. But there a demographic change was under way – a change made necessary by the so-called 'missing generation' of Gaidhealtachd teenagers who had missed out on learning Gaelic at school or in the home in the 1970s. The days had passed within less than a decade when an ambitious Gaelic college could recruit all of its annual intake, however small that intake, from a ready supply of Hebridean native speakers. From the 1990s onwards, Sabhal Mòr Ostaig made a determined effort to embrace not only those who had learned Gaelic, but also those who were learning Gaelic. As often as not, such students would arrive from without the Gaidhealtachd – indeed, from without Scotland, and from without the United Kingdom.

In the early 1990s, Sabhal Mòr Ostaig was enrolling ten or eleven full-time students a year, and was arguably not in a position to deal with many more. In November 1990, Norman Gillies was quoted in *The Scotsman* as saying:

> We have not attracted the number of students that the initial
> feasibility report into the college indicated. I am afraid that
> in a lot of ways the prediction of the authors of that report,
> of an annual intake of 20 students, hangs around our necks.
> It was an over-optimistic number, which has been enshrined
> in tablets of stone. The legacy of it has been that if we don't
> reach 20 a year we're supposed to have failed.
>
> In fact, if we'd started in 1983 with 20 students, rising to
> 40 in the following year, I think that this college could have
> collapsed quite dramatically, because there had to be a

terrific learning process. In teaching a business studies course in Gaelic we were doing something entirely new, and that required a rapport between students and staff which was possibly only going to happen with small numbers.

This current year, 1990, we have an intake of 11 students. That is not great, but at the same time it's not bad. We're talking still about the business studies core, despite the other courses and options that we can now offer, and our number of students is probably comparable to the numbers that they would have on a similar English medium course at Lews Castle College, or in Thurso, or in Inverness.

As the 1990s progressed, student numbers at Sabhal Mòr Ostaig improved dramatically. They also reflected what could best be described as a sea change in the Gaelic constituency. Andrew Adam Gossen was a graduate of Harvard University who attended Sabhal Mòr Ostaig in the late 1990s, and later wrote a PhD anthropology thesis – 'Agents of a Modern Gaelic Scotland: Curriculum, Change, and Challenge at Sabhal Mòr Ostaig, the Gaelic College of Scotland' – on the college and its context. For the academic year beginning in September 1998, Gossen noted, thirty-five new students enrolled at the college. Ten of them came from the Highlands and Islands. Nine came from other parts of Scotland. Five originated in England and Wales, and four in Ireland. Two came from the continent of Europe, two from Canada, two from the USA and one from Asia.

The great majority of the class of '98 was therefore from without the immediate geographical constituency of the college, as it had originally been conceived. Almost half of them were from outside Scotland. The number of students from within the historical Gaidhealtachd had therefore remained constant, at around ten a year. But the increase in student enrolment was due to a marked surge in interest from the rest of the world. By offering an immersion course to enable non-fluent Gaelic learners rapidly to achieve proper comprehension of the language, Sabhal Mòr Ostaig had both encouraged and catered for this trend. (A trend which also, incidentally, would not largely show up in the census figures. The British National Census only enumerates speakers of Scottish Gaelic resident in Scotland; not in England, Wales or any part of Ireland.)

'The original notion,' says John Norman MacLeod, 'was that young people from the Islands and west Highlands would arrive at Sabhal Mòr Ostaig and then receive business training courses in their native language which would enable them to go back and, say, start a haulage company in Lochboisdale.

'We found that that philosophy was overtaken by events. The philosophy was that people would go and set up their own business. Very few of our graduates have actually set up a business; it takes a lot of confidence. In business studies they were taught through the medium of Gaelic, so we were looking for fluent Gaelic speakers first and foremost, and there was very little choice. At first, we offered only HND in business studies and Gaidhealtachd studies, then we started offering one-year courses, HNC in information technology and office technology – but again, business was seen as being very important. But it took us years and years, until the early 1990s, before we started other courses, such as in television and in the performing arts. But it's really since we've started our Gaelic courses like the Cùrsa Comais, the Gaelic and communication course, and then when we got our degree programme started in 1997–98, that was really when our student numbers took off.

'I had imagined, and I think this was the way that Sabhal Mòr was planned, I had imagined Sabhal Mòr Ostaig was all about the Gaidhealtachd. I thought that when I came here first. Then, everything was in Gaelic, the first students were all from the Highlands and Islands, they were all fluent Gaelic speakers, and I had this vision of Sabhal Mòr as a Gaelic-speaking college.

'And then, very quickly, we realised that this wasn't sustainable, and that there was an interest out there beyond the Highlands and Islands; and that was a good realisation.

'Back in 1983, when we began, Gaelic wasn't even taught as a subject. Then we started getting a couple of learners. Ina MacInnes was teaching them, and it was just a very informal thing, teaching of language in the evening. She used to do a class for students who weren't quite so fluent.

'But then we said, "Right, we've got to look at our approach here." We recognised that language teaching had to be part of our new curriculum, but it probably took another ten years, well into the 1990s, before we actually started having language courses as such, full-time courses which last a year. We have never had absolute beginners as learners, but people at a certain level, and we brought them on to fluency. These are now the most popular courses. I mean, it's fine to have Gaelic-medium education, but if you don't have people who are fluent enough to benefit from that education – well, you've basically got to grow your own student.

'In 1983, we had seven students. Twenty years later we have over one hundred, and they are mostly learners who have learned the language very well and who are very accurate and confident in using the language. This now accounts for about 70–80 per cent of the student population. When you're talking about native, fluent Gaelic speakers, although they do come to Sabhal Mòr having gone through Gaelic-medium primary education and so on, it's very difficult to get people who are actually very fluent. We've got a few just now who are very good speakers. There are some very good fluent students who come here; but a lot of people come to learn the language, and they do it very well, they're very committed.

'I think we achieved the right mix as far as the courses and the needs of the Gaelic community are concerned. We've got courses which bring people to fluency, they're the only courses which are delivered entirely through the medium of Gaelic, we've got a degree programme, and then there are the vocational courses like the diploma in television and multi-media. We've always gone for courses that are contemporary, because I think at the end of the day we were always of the opinion that we're here to save a language. We're here to give people opportunities to use the language as well and we're very much about educating people to make a living.'

This commercial globalisation of the language fitted many people's view of its future. 'I'm totally convinced,' says Alan Campbell, 'that if Gaelic is going to survive, then it must become reintegrated into community life. Not across the whole of Scotland, that won't happen, but here and there. These pockets would be vitally important energy centres for the language.

'Now, for a long time, I have seen Gaelic as having the potential to play a really significant and very prosperous role in tourism, which is a huge industry for us. As a Sgitheanach [Skyeman], I am one of those who has watched tourism erode our culture. For years and years people tried to pander to this sort of mystical creature, the visitor, that had aspirations nobody seemed to understand; increasingly we fed them exactly the same sort of stuff that they would get anywhere else in the UK. They would only get different scenery up here.

'And in doing that, we deprived them of what was really unique about us, our area and our community: we deprived them of the language, we deprived them of the food – all of the good things that we had to offer. Well, happily, I think there is now an increasing awareness of the unique potential of our market in terms of food, in terms of scenery, music and culture, and we have to add the language into that.

'If Sabhal Mòr and Lews Castle and Inverness College and all the other places that are beginning to develop Gaelic at academic levels and in vocational courses are to succeed, we must look to a world where there is a genuine benefit to the aspiring restaurant manager who can say on his CV that he also speaks Gaelic, that he is going to be able to meet and greet and talk to visitors about the language as well as in the language. The same applies to receptionists, to hotel staff, shop staff, garage staff.

'You can place an advert on the Internet saying something like: "Is your name MacNeil, Neil or O'Neil?" And you've got somebody of that name sitting in Phoenix, Arizona, sweltering under a hot sky looking at the Internet, and they see this advert. It goes on to say: "Because if you are, and you want to know where your people came from, you want to know a little bit about your roots, there's only one place to go, and that place is Barra." And then you show a nice, moist, soft picture of Barra, something that's going to look attractive in Phoenix, and you let these American

MacNeils get their Visa cards out and book themselves a package.

'When you get them here, you feed them the food, you show them the scenery, you give them good quality everything. This is not a market that's going to be sold on cheapness, this is a market that's going to be sold on quality. That doesn't mean that everyone has to be the standard of the Three Chimneys in my home village of Colbost, but you can have a three- and a four-star standard. You can put nice things into the package. You throw in a car, you throw in a driver if they want it, a guide, somebody who will talk to them about Gaelic and in Gaelic. As a part of their experience, you bring in the kids who are learning the skills of music and song in the fèisean and you give these kids the chance to perform and you pay them for it.

'So the whole language experience is beginning to have an economic value; that's the way it's got to be. That's the sort of thing that I hope for, and I think then that the satisfied customer will always be the best salesperson. That potential, that market will grow, and it will feed increasingly into the confidence and self-esteem of a community; parents will teach the children the language because that language is going to be synonymous with regeneration. People will opt for Gaelic-medium education for the same reason, and people, as they go through further and higher education, will see that there is an end-product, a benefit, a career structure.

'People will realise that being bilingual with Gaelic does have advantages, and these are the people who will be bilingual at an absolute minimum but more likely and increasingly multilingual. People will have Gaelic and English automatically; when you go to European countries like Denmark and Finland, you find people with three or four languages and that's the norm, that's basic. That's what I would like to see happening. So, not only will we be able to speak to visitors in Gaelic but we'll be able to speak to them in Gaelic and French without bothering to use English. I would like to look back and say that I had contributed to that. That would be wonderful.'

Andrew Gossen's fellow students at Sabhal Mòr Ostaig in the late 1990s were, as his statistics indicate, fully reflective of Gaelic's increasing transnational appeal. There were students from as close to Ostaig as Camus Croise, a few miles north on the Sleat peninsula. According to his thesis, there was a Lowland Scottish student who had:

> first encountered Gaelic when very young and spending time with his Gaelic-speaking grandfather in Glasgow. Although he did not grow up speaking the language, this early exposure planted a seed of interest that ultimately led him to a degree programme in Celtic and Scottish history at the University of Edinburgh. After his first three years at Edinburgh, he found himself increasingly frustrated by a dearth of instruction in spoken Gaelic – '. . . I was getting one hour a week at the university, one hour a week outside the university, which was at a conversation circle, and apart from that I was paying a private tutor for two hours a week. So four hours a week was about the maximum I was getting, you know, apart from informal attempts in pubs. But nowhere near enough. Nowhere near enough, and that's the reason I chose to come to Sabhal Mòr.'

There was a Canadian student from Cape Breton whose aunt and grandmother had been fluent native speakers. There were the Scottish children of Runrig; one woman who grew up outside Glasgow said:

> 'I guess the first time I ever really heard [the language] was listening to Runrig on the radio. And I must have been 12 or 13, and amazingly enough, I'd never even heard of Gaelic. I remember asking my parents where they spoke it, which is just a ridiculous state of affairs.'

Another came from Denmark. She told Gossen:

> 'Basically, I think it was because I was interested in Scotland. You get a lot of music and such and a lot of knowledge about the culture [in Denmark], and of course I'd seen pictures

from over here. So then I thought, just go and find out whether it's really so nice as I think it is. And because I was interested in Scotland, I got interested in Gaelic.'

Andrew Gossen noted that in 1998, the first year that SMO offered its degree course in affiliation with the new multi-campus University of the Highlands and Islands (UHI), a small division arose between students who were Gaelic learners, who tended to enroll for the degree course, and native Highlanders:

> Although there were a number of native speakers in the student body, they tended to cluster in the HNC/D business course and the television course. The formal academic courses at SMO were populated almost entirely by learners and lapsed speakers.

By the late 1990s, the academic staff embodied a similar variety of backgrounds. Under the aegis of the native Skyeman and head of studies John Norman MacLeod, there laboured an American lawyer who had deserted his practice in the USA to take a doctorate in Celtic at the University of Edinburgh; a lecturer who had cut his teeth as a language assistant at University College, Galway; a Canadian from Alberta who had learned the language at St Francis Xavier University in Antigonish, Nova Scotia. And there were native speakers and native learners, and those who despite their Gaelic background had previously let their first language lapse, only then to discover that it would never really disappear: 'My Gaelic was quite poor when I came down here, but I just had to do my best. And I could make myself understood, more than understood.'

Throughout the 1990s, Sabhal Mòr Ostaig expanded apace. There had been those in the previous decade who could challenge its position as the flagship of any late-twentieth-century renaissance. By the end of the millennium, that reputation was secure.

In 1992, the college established Lèirsinn Research Centre to provide research services to the Gaelic-speaking areas. The Lèirsinn Centre, which partly finances itself through the provision of a wide range of investigative and evaluative projects, is also sponsored by several public bodies and Gaelic agencies. It specialises in research in such areas as Gaelic-medium education, social and economic development, the broadcasting media, language and sociolinguistics. Lèirsinn works in association with other international research centres involved in the maintenance and development of lesser-used European languages. The director of Lèirsinn was the founding convener of the University of the Highlands and Islands Research School in Language, Culture and Heritage, and Lèirsinn's staff contribute to the development of new degree courses, supervise post-graduate research degrees and publish research papers.

In 1992, the college also established Cànan, a company which offers a wide range of services to the Gaelic community and to the wider business sector. Cànan specialises in multi-media productions, publishing, translation, subtitling, marketing and support for Gaelic learners. The enterprise became involved in a number of national and international projects in partnership with other bodies in Wales and Ireland. It has been responsible for the publishing of much of the material used in Gaelic-medium primary education, and Cànan provided all of the publications for students connected with the Gaelic learners' television series, *Speaking Our Language*.

In 1987, Stòr-Dàta was set up to create a Gaelic terminology database. This project developed into a resource which is used by thousands of people every week around the world. It also produced electronic linguistic resources, thesauri, pronunciation dictionaries and other learning resources. The database is also to be found in hard copy throughout Britain and the wider world, and Stòr-Dàta also produced a bilingual English–Gaelic dictionary which was published by Cànan in 1993.

By the end of the 1990s, the college's campus contained one of the best antiquarian libraries of Gaelic and Gaelic-related volumes in the world. The McCormaig and Celtica collections alone – two extremely important portfolios – constitute a resource of international significance, which the college made determined efforts to obtain in order both to maintain their integrity and to ensure their accessibility in perpetuity for scholarship and research.

Sabhal Mòr Ostaig also became the lead partner in Tobar an Dualchais (the Well of Heritage), a major project which aims to digitise – and thus both preserve and disseminate – 18,000 hours of archive Gaelic and Scots audio and visual recordings. Tobar an Dualchais catalogues this immense resource, currently stored on deteriorating film and tape, and distributes the material to the international community through the World Wide Web.

All this, and the ongoing writer's residency, a new musician's residency and the plan to introduce fellowships in the visual arts. Meanwhile, Scotland's only professional Gaelic theatre company, Tosg, became based at the college, employing young actors and commissioning new works as well as providing the Gaidhealtachd with popular touring entertainment.

The old steading was bursting at the seams. In 1993, with the help of that £400,000 donation from Scottish Television and Grampian Television (whose interest was piqued by the need for more qualified young people in Gaelic-medium broadcasting), the old campus site was doubled in size. The television money was used to leverage access to other funds and Arainn Ostaig (the Ostaig Campus) was upgraded to include more teaching and admin space, new student accommodation and a TV studio.

It was still not enough. Sabhal Mòr Ostaig had ceased to be, as one critic of its small annual intake suggested in the early 1990s, 'an exhibition without pictures'. It had become rather a booming justification of the *Field of Dreams* or advance factory unit theory: if you build it, they will come. The extraordinary amount of on-campus activity, the growth in student numbers following the UHI degree course and the massively increased number of applicants for summer schools and short courses (by early in the twenty-first century the number of people taught annually would total over 500) made Arainn Ostaig insufficient for demand within a few months of its completion.

In the words of Glasgow University's lecturer in strategic management Donald MacLean:

With the latest development now behind them, staff at the college began to think of the next phase of expansion. In the interim, it had become clear that one of the founding assumptions of the college was perhaps running up against its limits in that there simply weren't sufficient numbers of native Gaelic-speaking business students to sustain the college in the longer term. In contrast to this, there was growing interest in the Gaelic dimension of SMO's provision both in terms of studying the language and culture in-house, and in developing IT-enabled, access-level material for distance learning.

In some senses, since SMO had exhausted availability of native language speakers, it was dedicating increasing resources to creation of a new supply, and in the process, was en route from its origins as a Gaelic-medium business school to its current position as the steward of, and campaigner for, Gaelic language and culture.

In 1995, Norman Gillies, now director, together with leading figures in the local economic development agency, came to hear about the establishment of the Millennium Commission, which would distribute funds to worthy causes to mark the commencement of the third millennium. The news crystallised a desire to embark on an exciting new project in the hope that funding for it would come from the Millennium Commission.

Norman Gillies, John Norman MacLeod and others came up with a plan and drawings for 'Baile Ur Ostaig' – The New Village of Ostaig. This was an ambitious £20-million development of the current campus which would enable the provision of many more courses in the Gaelic language, developing some of these towards degree level, as well as scaling up the infrastructure to include enhanced student accommodation, state of the art teaching and learning facilities, a theatre, a new broadcast training unit, a research centre and other facilities.

Whilst such a development may sound overly-ambitious for such a small college, staff had become accustomed to thinking on a 20-year time-frame since, by then, the key concern of expanding the Gaelic language and culture was viewed as something which occurred on the timescales of a human generation. Plans had to be laid now for children who were just about to enter Gaelic-medium education at the pre-nursery level.

Commitment to and belief in 'Baile Ur Ostaig' was such that in 1995, a signpost was erected outside the college campus – indicating the impending development. In 1996, staff received news that the bid had been unsuccessful. Part of the reasoning was that SMO would not get the necessary planning consents to secure the development, and that even if this were not the case, the infrastructure around the current campus was simply not capable of dealing with such a development. Just as the SMO development was rejected by the Millennium Commission, the UHI project was given the go-ahead.

In many ways, the University of the Highlands and Islands development was like a much bigger version of the SMO concept, with a similar rationale but without the Gaelic focus. Leading eventually to the establishment of an IT-intensive University of the Highlands and Islands, the UHI-Millennium Institute bid envisaged the coalescence of numerous further education facilities in the Highlands into a networked provider of higher education. Since this would present an attractive local alternative to aspiring students who would otherwise have no option but to leave, the development was seen as key to arresting the processes of erosion of the cultural fabric (and future) of the region.

Whilst the rejection of the SMO bid was something of a blow in the short term, there was some sense that the creation of UHI-MI provided a new level of opportunity in that, if SMO was to become an active part (which has indeed been the case), it would pave the way to operation as an institute of higher (rather than further) education, and provide new sources of funding in the future.

In the mean time, the main funder of the organisation which owned the land around the campus confirmed that it could not sanction any development as it would run counter to its own constitution. However, in a generous move, he offered, for a nominal sum, a six-acre site less than a mile from the current campus, overlooking the sea with superb views of Knoydart and the Scottish mainland. He had purchased this site some time previously with a view to building a family home, but recognised, some years later, that this was unlikely ever to happen. This site was undoubtedly one of the prime locations on the island, with views to rival any in the Scottish Highlands. With this fortunate and generous turn of events, resolve developed at SMO to show the Millennium Commission what a mistake it had made.

The organisation which owned the land around the campus was the Clan Donald Lands Trust. This body had been established chiefly by American MacDonalds within the Clan Donald Society to buy and administer the southern portion of the old Macdonald Estate in Sleat when Iain Noble had bought the rest in 1972. The 'main funder' of that organisation was Ellice McDonald, the son of a family which had fled from famine and clearance in Glen Coe and Knoydart during the nineteenth century. (Although Gaelic had died out in Ellice McDonald's family, memory was still alive; he had been christened after a nineteenth-century Liberal MP named Edward Ellice who was noted for his efforts on behalf of Highland famine relief.)

Donald MacLean concludes:

> Development followed at a rapid rate. A degree programme, which had been launched in 1996/7, signalled SMO's readiness to join the higher education firmament and aligned it for incorporation into the UHI-MI network. A funding package of £7 million was secured from a variety of public and private sources (including the Millennium Commission), and building work for the new campus commenced in late

> 1997. A year later, the first building was opened and the new
> campus, Arainn Chaluim Chille, became operational in time
> for the millennium.

This astonishing new complex, the Columba Campus, on a blunt
headland overlooking the Sound of Sleat catapulted Sabhal Mòr
Ostaig, and much of the Gaelic movement along with it, into the
twenty-first century. Roy Pedersen of the old HIDB was by that
time on the development committee of Sabhal Mòr Ostaig. 'When
the extension to the old building at Ostaig was completed,' he
remembers, 'it was hailed as a major achievement, which of course
it was. It had progressed from a ruined farm steading, to an
upgraded farm steading, to more than doubling in size and
providing modern accommodation for 35 students. So this building
was a major achievement, and everyone hailed it as such. But I
myself had concerns that while it was undoubtedly a great thing, we
still hadn't achieved critical mass for something that was going to be
sustainable. Thirty-five full-time students was barely enough.

'My thought was that, good though this was, we had to look to a
longer-term development of the college, perhaps anticipating 250
students, with a full range of sports facilities and accommodation,
over a 25-year timescale. I felt that it was necessary to put in place
some kind of plan to work towards such a scenario. I discussed this
idea firstly with my friend John Angus MacKay, and then wrote a
letter or a memo to Norman Gillies setting out this proposition.

'He said, "Well, that is a reasonable point, what do you intend to
do about it?" I said, "Why don't we pull a meeting together with a
number of people who might be able to discuss how we take it
forward?" The outcome of that was that a meeting was held in the
Merlin Chinese restaurant in Inverness. Attending that meeting
were Norman Gillies, John Angus MacKay, Lorne MacLeod, who
was then chief executive of Skye and Lochalsh Enterprise, Peter
Peacock, who was the convenor of Highland Council, Mike Grieve,
who was senior planner within the council, and myself.

'If I recall, this was just shortly after the first extension was built.
The outcome of that meeting was that, yes, it was accepted that this

was reasonable – that we should work towards a long-term plan for the development of the college, not just stop where we were. It was suggested by Mike Grieve that the way to start pushing it forward was to produce an accommodation plan. What was meant was, if you're talking about 250 students, the lecture rooms that they would require, the accommodation that they would require, what sort of accommodation in terms of square metreage do you need and how might it be spread on a site? So that was agreed, and HIE was persuaded to fund a study to deduce an accommodation plan. Consultants were brought in, and they developed the concept of Baile Ur Ostaig, the new town of Ostaig, which basically had Sabhal Mòr at its hub. And the next step was – well, Sabhal Mòr didn't own the land, the land was owned by Clan Donald and, of course, where the funds would come from was, as yet, an unknown quantity. But a process was started through the Development Committee which was set up at that time to explore how one would take this plan forward into reality. It was thought at first that it would be a gradual thing over twenty-five years, but two things happened. The first was the establishment of the grant-aiding Millennium Commission. It was realised that that might be a major source of funds for a development of this kind, and so further consultants were employed to develop a bid to the Millennium Commission.

'The second thing was that Norman Gillies and Jim Hunter [then head of Skye and Lochalsh Enterprise] took on the task of approaching Clan Donald, which was really Ellice McDonald at the time; he was the money behind Clan Donald. He can be quite difficult to approach because he lives in America and isn't over very often, but they did manage a meeting with him. Apparently, Ellice was very impressed with the concept but raised questions about where the land would come from, and he basically made it clear that really Clan Donald land was not available for being developed. However, he said that he personally had a piece of land which was overlooking the sea and that he would be prepared to make that available to the college for the price he had paid for it.

'That really is how the Baile Ur Ostaig became a no-no, partly because of problems with Clan Donald land, and then how it transmogrified into Arainn Chaluim Chille, the Columba Campus that we now know, on the site which previously had been Ellice McDonald's proposed retirement home. Sabhal Mòr's bid for Millennium funding, backed up by European funding and other monies, failed. But the UHI's bid succeeded, so, while Baile Ùr Ostaig failed, the concept lived on in a reconstituted form in Arainn Chaluim Chille as part of the UHI Millennium bid.'

In May 1997, with the return to office of a Labour government, Brian Wilson – who had been the MP for Cunninghame North in Ayrshire since 1987 – was assigned to the Scottish Office as the Minister for Industry, Education and Gaelic. Wilson had over the years added a personal fluency in Gaelic to his interest in the language's health. 'I had responsibility for Gaelic at the Scottish Office,' he says, 'but I didn't have the rest of Arts and Culture. I found out that a civil servant in that section was in the habit of slicing off the savings from any underspend at year's end and using it to buy new paintings for the Scottish galleries. Not a bad use of surpluses, when you come to think of it. Anyway, I said to him, "This year, what about something for Gaelic?" And I got it. Well, I got £900,000 out of end of year savings. And that's how the tower accommodation block – that great landmark of the new campus – was built on Arainn Chaluim Chille.'

'If you think,' says Norman Gillies, 'that this college is here only because of Gaels, or even people who speak Gaelic, you're very wrong. There's been a lot of encouragement and a lot of work behind the scenes by non-Gaelic people who have an empathy or sympathy toward the language and what we're trying to do.'

Eight

On 9 June 1997, President Mary Robinson of the Republic of Ireland got to her feet in a lecture theatre in Arainn Ostaig, the extended old campus, and delivered the eighth annual Sabhal Mòr lecture.

It would later be recalled as a seminal, almost a transforming, occasion – as noteworthy in the annals as George Younger's 'road to Damascus' speech at the college 11 years earlier. After Mrs Robinson had sat down again, a lot of things began to happen.

The Sabhal Mòr lectures had been launched as a part of that new relationship between Gaelic, the commercial broadcasting stations and Sabhal Mòr Ostaig. They were routinely delivered in English, and were sponsored, televised and broadcast by Grampian and Scottish Television – although in a slot which moved with the years steadily further away from prime time, until the SMO lectures frequently found themselves competing with Gaelic programmes themselves for the attention of insomniacs and misprogrammed video recorders.

The second lecture had been delivered in 1991 by the managing director of Scottish Television, Gus Macdonald. Macdonald – whose paternal family originated in Skye, just a few miles from Ostaig – employed the occasion to discuss the impending Broadcasting Act and its potential for Gaelic, urging Gaels to seize the employment opportunities shortly to be offered by the Gaelic Broadcasting Fund. He also stressed, in an instructive indicator of commercial television's true future priorities, that Gaelic speakers accounted for just 1 per cent – 37,000 out of 3,700,000 – of Scottish Television's prospective audience and that most of the 99 per cent did not want more Gaelic TV. And he told his audience that the experience of S4C in Welsh-language broadcasting had indicated that its soap operas, such as *Pobol y Cwm*, were most popular across the language divide. 'According to Welsh producers,' said Macdonald, 'the creation of such an idealised community on screen is by far the best way to re-engage Gaels lost to the Lowlands with their Gaelic heartland.'

The stage was thereby set in that Sabhal Mòr lecture for *Machair*, a Gaelic soap opera set in the Hebrides. The overly optimistic prime-time proposals for *Machair* would greatly assist Gus Macdonald's STV in retaining its Lowland Scottish franchise. The soap – which did indeed prove moderately popular with Gaels and many non-Gaels – cost £2 million a year and would eat up the lion's share of the Gaelic Broadcasting Fund for 12 series before being sunk without trace in 1999.

The lectures moved from the accessible to the arcane and back again. The inaugural lecture had been delivered in 1990 by James Hunter, the Highland historian who was then director of the reconstituted Scottish Crofters Union and who would progress to the chair of Highlands and Islands Enterprise. He talked of the future of the crofting community which had sustained the Gaelic language for so long against such enormous odds.

The 'sheer strength of the forces arrayed against them,' said Hunter, had resulted in the historical quietism of the Scottish Gael. 'Thus it comes about that something which most other societies take for granted – that young people should have the right to be educated in their own language – still seems to us to be in the nature of a novel and daring experiment.' The case for crofting in the late twentieth century, Hunter proceeded to argue, was strong. Even in weakness and in comparative decline, crofting kept people on the land, while large-scale farming emptied the countryside. That was 'why the crofting townships of places like Lewis and South Uist are among Britain's most densely-populated rural localities'.

In the years to come, John Goodlad, the celebrated Shetland local politician, drew comparisons with the economic and cultural prospects of his own northern isles and the Hebrides. Dr Una Maclean delivered an important paper on the mental health of island women. Alistair Moffat, by then chief executive of Scottish Television Enterprises, rolled up in 1995 to offer more insights into the future of Gaelic broadcasting. In 1996, the retiring lead singer of Runrig, Donnie Munro, spoke of being part of a generation that had 'suffered a cultural repression and neglect which was institutional and unforgivable. Our language was devalued and almost set aside, our social history all but ignored.'

Two weeks before the first Scottish Parliament elections in 1999, Gordon Brown, the Chancellor of the Exchequer, drove down the old single track road to deliver the lecture and walked into a contrived controversy. Brown had been invited two years earlier and insisted that the event was non-political. 'The Chancellor of the Exchequer,' said a Scottish National Party official, 'one of the most important figures within the Labour Party, is not seeing this as a political event two weeks before an election? Come off it, Gordon, who do you think you are kidding?' Norman Gillies replied: 'We cannot cancel a lecture because some people don't like the lecturer. For anyone to suggest that we should reject the chance to have the serving Chancellor of the Exchequer deliver a lecture at the college, they must be mad.'

At the lectern in the new campus lecture theatre, Gordon Brown said:

> Just as we Scots are a family, so are we a family in Britain. Different relatives, different family members often do things differently – and that too is how it often is in families. In fact, it is that diversity and distinctiveness that with its range of influences strengthens us. What a bland and uniform place this Britain of ours would be if Britishness meant we all spoke the same way, sang, danced and celebrated the same way – in a bland, uniform way.

> The idea of being British in the modern age means a
> nation enriched by the breadth and depth of various cultures
> which can learn from each other – a multinational,
> multicultural country strengthened by each other's
> contributions and weakened by the loss of any.

The following year's lecture was most poignant. In the election which followed Gordon Brown's visit, his party colleague Donald Dewar became the first First Minister of the new Scottish Parliament. It was as First Minister that Dewar arrived in the year 2000, to deliver the 11th Sabhal Mòr lecture in typically laconic style. Donald Dewar was introduced to his audience in Skye by the chairman of the college's trustees, Farquhar MacIntosh, the man from Elgol who had, in the course of a long career, actually taught the young Dewar. ('I had him in history for part of his fifth and sixth year at Glasgow Academy in the early 1950s. I remember him as a rather lonely boy. He was tall and gangly, and everyone in Glasgow Academy had to take rugby and cricket – there was no choice, that was it. But Donald was obviously not built to be a rugby player so he spent quite a lot of his time in the library. At the end of the winter term, we had a general school quiz which carried an award, and I remember, on one occasion at least, Donald winning it. Donald read widely both in history and English. He didn't become a prefect or anything like that, so he didn't shine in that particular way at all . . .')

That September, First Minister Dewar, after confessing his sceptical aversion to 'the peat-fire reek', offered all Gaelic enterprises his assurance of the continued support of the Scottish Executive. In the course of his lecture, Donald Dewar praised the historic contribution made by the Highlands and by Gaelic culture to Scotland. Both the area and the language, he said, had taken great steps in recent years. The population of Scotland as a whole was in 2000 AD exactly the same as in 1970, whereas the population of the Highlands had in the same period increased by 20 per cent. 'Information technology,' he said, 'is helping the Highlands overcome the challenges of location and distances from markets.'

Dewar emphasised the importance of promoting links between Gaelic Scotland and Ireland, as had been achieved by Iomairt Cholm Cille, the Columba Initiative. 'We should view the Gaidhealtachd not as something that is confined to Scotland's shores but as an entity which stretches from the Butt of Lewis to the Dingle peninsula in the south of Ireland,' he said. Recognising the role of Sabhal Mòr Ostaig in sustaining and promoting Gaelic and praising its 'inclusive approach', the First Minister announced additional support for the college of £250,000 a year for each of the next four years.

He stressed the 'welcome' advances made in Gaelic-medium education, and said that the way forward was to develop 'a demand for places . . . We must look to the quality of the service provided to attract parents.' As for Gaelic broadcasting, Dewar acknowledged that under the current system Gaelic programmes carried by the BBC and ITV were 'scattered around the schedule, without any overall coherence to the service'. Digital broadcasting could be significant, providing many more channels and greater opportunities for dedicated Gaelic TV, although no complete transfer from analogue to digital would be countenanced until digital had a thorough geographical spread.

On the vexed question of a Gaelic Language Act to provide 'secure status', the First Minister said, 'I would caution against the view that "legal status" solves all challenges faced by Gaelic.' He doubted that legal status would provide 'the unanswerable and clearly defined route for the recovery and stability we seek'. It could instead provide an unnecessary expense in certain areas, it could waste a good deal of time in unnecessary translation, and it could provoke an anti-Gaelic backlash in other districts.

A month later, Farquhar MacIntosh's bookish 'lonely, gangly' former pupil would be dead at the age of 63.

If Donald Dewar's Sabhal Mòr address was its most poignant lecture, Mary Robinson's three years earlier had been possibly the most seminal. It came about partly through the offices of that tireless campaigner for Gaelic in general and Sabhal Mòr Ostaig in particular, Brian Wilson MP. Wilson's ties with the Scottish Gaelic community were almost matched by his Irish connections. In 1997, while at the Scottish Office, he heard of a planned visit by President Robinson to Stornoway. It was a short walk from there to laying the foundations of the 1997 Sabhal Mòr lecture.

Mary Robinson was in 1997 in her last year as Irish president and had become a figure of international repute. Born in County Mayo in 1944, she had become in 1990 the first woman president of her country. As one of Trinity College's three members of Seánad Eireann, the Irish Senate, the young Mary Bourke first hit the national headlines. She campaigned on a wide range of causes, from women's right to sit on juries and the end to the requirement that all female civil servants resign upon marriage to the right to contraception. When she introduced the first Bill proposing to liberalise the law on contraception in Ireland, nobody in the Seánad would even second it.

She also worked as legal adviser to the Campaign for Homosexual Law Reform with future Trinity College senator and possible future Irish presidential candidate David Norris. Coincidentally, just as Mary McAleese replaced Mary Robinson as Reid Professor of Law and would replace her in the presidency of Ireland, so Robinson replaced McAleese in the Campaign for Homosexual Law Reform.

She decided not to seek re-election to Seánad Eireann in 1989. One year later, however, the Irish Labour Party approached her about the Irish presidency, for which an election was due. She thought she was being asked her legal advice about the sort of policy programme party leader Dick Spring was proposing. As she read the briefing notes, she began to realise that the programme was aimed at her. After a lot of thought, she agreed to become the first Labour nominee for the presidency, the first woman candidate and the first third person to run in what had been a two-candidate campaign since 1945.

Few, even in the Irish Labour Party, gave her any chance of winning. But win she did, and Irish politics changed overnight. She asked groups not normally invited to presidential residences to visit her, from the Christian Brothers, a large religious order which ran schools throughout Ireland, to GLEN, the Gay and Lesbian

Equality Network. She visited Irish nuns and priests abroad, Irish famine-relief charities, attended international sporting events, met the Pope (she was condemned by a young right-wing priest in the *Irish Times* for supposedly breaking Vatican dress codes on her visit; the Vatican insisted she hadn't) and, to the fury of the People's Republic of China, met the Dalai Lama. She famously put a special symbolic light in her kitchen window (which was visible to the public) in Aras an Uachtaráin, the president's official residence, as a symbol of Irish emigrants around the world. Placing a light in a darkened window to guide the way of strangers was an old Irish folk custom. Robinson's light became a symbol of an Ireland contemplating its diaspora, its sons and daughters around the world.

Halfway through her term of office, her popularity rating reached an unprecedented 93 per cent. When she arrived in Lewis and Skye in 1997 as part of a journey in recognition of the 1,400th anniversary of the death of St Columba (521–97) she was perhaps, as one biographer suggests:

> the most popular Irish political leader ever, the most widely recognised president since de Valera, the most popular president of Ireland in the history of the office . . . In the final photocall of her presidency, former taoisigh [prime ministers] and senior government figures stood beside her, beaming with pride at what had been, by any standards, a remarkably successful presidency that had changed the face of the office, the office-holder and Ireland.

Much of what Mary Robinson touched turned to gold. At Sabhal Mòr in June 1997, she attempted the alchemy of reconnecting the old Gaidhealtachds of Ireland and Scotland:

> The past still determines today the links between our countries and the comings and goings of our peoples. I hope that in considering our past we can recognise what we have in common and cherish that. So often, the past has been seen

as a source of division and dissension, and has served to underscore religious and political differences. When I became President of Ireland some six and a half years ago, I spoke of a province of our imagination, a fifth province, a common ground on which we could come together and celebrate what we share.

Perhaps we can create an island space for ourselves to celebrate what Scotland and Ireland share. I'm particularly conscious that this may enable people of both traditions in Northern Ireland to reclaim parts of their inheritance which have been denied them. Too often, in an Irish context, Celtic or Gaelic culture has been identified with Catholicism and nationalism, which has had the effect of inhibiting those of the Protestant and Unionist tradition from claiming part of their inheritance.

It's surely time to insist that our past and our culture is rich, varied and complex; that it cannot be resolved into narrow sectarian compartments and that it's open to each of us to claim what is rightfully ours. In doing so, we don't deprive anyone else of their share; it's something that grows and strengthens and flourishes as more people partake of it. And is it not perhaps a paradox that the island way of life, which is central to what we share, had been consigned by our histories to the margins of our countries and that it's only in recent decades that we've been able to reclaim this precious part of our inheritance?

. . . In the past, it seemed to me, there was a dichotomy between those who saw modernity as a threat to the preservation of traditional values and culture on the one hand, and those on the other who regarded tradition as inhibiting and parochial. Certainly I was aware, growing up in Mayo, of people who would say, 'The Irish language will hold you back, it won't do you any good, it won't get you a job.' You know: 'We have to move on, we have to be modern', and that was a whole sense of what was felt at that time.

Now I believe we're offered a liberating resolution to this dilemma whereby tradition is enhanced and valued and treasured by a modern idiom. I see evidence of this liberation in every sphere of Irish life, a new mood of self-confidence which is invigorating and refreshing. I see young people who are at home in traditional and in modern idioms and who refuse to deny the validity of either. I see a cross-fertilisation of styles, whether in dance or in music, which has found a new popularity not only in Ireland but also around the world.

I read writers who are versed in traditional learning but who are equally immersed in an emerging global culture and find no contradiction in this. The reasons for this new sense of confidence are complex. Some of the factors are due to a young population; about 40 per cent of the population [of Ireland] is under 25. Some are due to rapid economic growth.

. . . I know the experience in Scotland has not been directly comparable to that of Ireland, but I have a real sense here too of change and renewal, reinforced, I may say, by my visit today to the Isle of Lewis and watching the dancing and listening to the singing there. In this process, Sabhal Mòr Ostaig and, ultimately, the University of the Highlands and Islands will have a vital role to play in expressing a life which is yet to find expression.

. . . For the future, Ireland and Scotland have much to learn from each other and to share. There are no two countries in Western Europe which are as close, not only in a shared past but also in what we have in common today. I'm reminded of the words of Sorley Maclean who visited me in Áras an Uachtaráin with a group of Gaelic poets celebrating 25 years of an exchange between the baird and fili of Ireland, and whose passing away last year we mourn deeply. That great poet who loved this island so well. He described the bond between us in words that say it all:

an fheile
nach do reub an cuan,
nach do mhill mìle bliadhna.

the humanity
that the ocean could not break,
that a thousand years has not severed.

Mary Robinson's gently modulated suggestion of a new pan-Celticism to embrace the computer age was beautifully timed. Throughout 1997 and into 1998, the governments of Ireland, the United Kingdom and the United States of America were striving to reconcile the different parties of Northern Ireland in a ceasefire and peace process. Any contribution, however modest, to a sense of unity and progression was welcome. From the Scottish Office, Brian Wilson was able instantly to launch the Columba Initiative to further links between Gaelic Scotland and Ireland – and to base the Scottish end of the scheme – which also has offices in Dublin and Belfast – at Sabhal Mòr Ostaig. In a Scottish Office press release, Wilson said:

> This is a major investment in a project which directly supports Gaelic education while also enhancing the Scottish–Irish connection. It is perhaps ironic that the Scottish Parliament in the seventeenth century should refer to Gaelic as the Irish language. But even that shows how much we have in common within the lands that run from the Ring of Kerry to the Butt of Lewis.

Funding for the Columba Initiative was announced at the same time as Sabhal Mòr Ostaig got the £900,000 extracted from the Civil Service to develop the whole of the new £6,000,000 campus on Ellice McDonald's land. The complex, it was agreed, would be named Arainn Chaluim Chille – the Columba Campus. Iain Noble's first Gaelic centre of higher education since St Columba's monks established themselves in Iona would now be set in concrete and stone. And Gaelic would crop up in unprecedented places: 'The only Gaelic-speaking lifts in the world have been installed in Sabhal Mòr Ostaig college on the Isle of Skye,' reported the Scottish *Daily Record* in October 1998. 'They have been put in to help blind users.'

Iomairt Cholm Cille would under its first Scottish coordinator, Donald Angie MacLennan from North Uist, and his successor, the Mull journalist Alasdair Campbell, proceed to involve itself in a variety of pan-Celtic connections, from introducing Highland crofters to Irish smallholders to sponsoring shinty/hurling fixtures. 'It's the best example I know,' Brian Wilson would say, 'of how, when you have governments behind something, small amounts of money can make a big difference.'

At the following year's Sabhal Mòr lecture, the Irish link was re-emphasised. The 1998 address was co-delivered by the new Minister for Gaelic, Western Isles MP Calum MacDonald, and his Irish counterpart Eamon O Cuív. In the backwash of the Irish peace process and the signing in Belfast of the Good Friday Agreement, even the national tabloid the *Daily Mirror* discovered an interest. On 10 September 1998, the *Mirror* reported:

> The use of the Gaelic tongue in parts of Scotland and Ireland could help the two countries forge a 'special relationship', it was claimed yesterday.
>
> Scottish Gaelic Minister Calum MacDonald said closer links based on similarities such as a shared language could strengthen communities in both countries. Delivering the annual Sabhal Mòr Ostaig Lecture in Skye, Mr MacDonald said: 'In the coming months, we shall be increasing the contacts between the Scottish Office and the Irish Government in order to develop our special relationship.
>
> 'The renewal of Gaelic in Scottish education, broadcasting and the arts is something which is also evident in the new links being forged between Scotland and Ireland. The common history and common culture we share, particularly in the Western Islands and Highlands, constitute a greater

Gaeltacht which can strengthen and enrich our Gaelic-speaking communities.'

Mr MacDonald also said the constitutional and political changes in Scotland, Ireland and Europe made the links between the two countries 'full of potential'.

Iomairt Cholm Cille had the potential to seize imaginations. During one of the intermittent suspensions of the new Northern Ireland Assembly in 2000, the Belfast *News Letter* was able to report that:

A Parliament will be sitting in Northern Ireland within weeks after all! Londonderry is to host a special sitting of a Youth Parliament next month at which the debates will be carried out in Irish and Scottish Gaelic.

Sessions will take place during a four-day festival over St Patrick's Weekend to celebrate the languages and cultures of Ireland and Scotland. While there will be events and concerts around the city from 16–19 March, the core of the Columba Initiative organised festival will be the Youth Parliament which will be attended by students from Northern Ireland, the Irish Republic and Scotland. All the proceedings and debates at each session of the Parliament in Londonderry will be delivered in Irish and Scottish Gaelic.

The Columba Initiative said yesterday that the aim of the Youth Parliament is to bring together undergraduates who are studying either Irish or Scottish Gaelic so that they have a unique opportunity to network and to debate issues that are of common concern. Risteard Mac Gabhann, chairman of the Youth Parliament organisers, said: 'The Parliament is designed to give students experience of speaking in public and to develop key skills such as debating, negotiating, influencing and thinking quickly. These skills will be of practical use to them in whatever careers they follow. That everything will be in Irish and Scottish Gaelic will add an extra dimension.

'One of the primary objectives of the festival is to

encourage the development of both the Irish and Scottish Gaelic languages as well as creating an understanding of and respect of each culture. This festival is designed to be open and inclusive. Everyone with an interest in Irish or Scottish Gaelic will be welcome at the events, particularly the concerts.'

The Columba Initiative is a tripartite body with offices in Belfast, Galway and Scotland. It was set up in 1997 by Eire President Mary Robinson and Brian Wilson, who was Scottish Minister for Education at the time, to 'foster support for the Gaelic language and to develop links between Gaelic Scotland and Ireland'. The Initiative is named after St Columba, who was born in 521 at Gartan, Co. Donegal, and who founded his first monastery in Derry before later taking the message of Christianity to Scotland.

The Irish connection, always energetically pursued and supported by the Hibernophile Brian Wilson during his time in government, would come to manifest itself in a number of ways. It was not, as many recognised, an altogether new development. The related sports of shinty and hurling had met throughout the first third of the twentieth century, and had renewed their brotherhood with increased affection in 1970 after a regrettable 40-year lapse. Mary Robinson had herself paid tribute to the contemporary Irish and Scottish bards who had been exchanging visits and verse since the 1970s.

'The first time I went to Ireland,' says John Norman MacLeod, 'I felt the infrastructure was so terrible – the buildings and the roads – but still I was amazed by the number of people who spoke Gaelic. I was amazed by the different kinds of employment available to them, and the language was so much stronger. The Irish got things done. They would say, for instance, "There's nothing in this community just now, but we're going to build this huge big hall," and when you went back, there it was. We were amazed by all this, and I think all those influences did have an effect.

'Both Scotland and Ireland have benefited from the renewed

connections. There is now a recognition that we are historically very closely related and that we're similar people in so many, many ways. The development of the Columba Initiative has been especially rewarding. It all came down to people who have been influential, like Brian Wilson in particular, you know, with the idea of initially getting Mary Robinson here. But we have to give a lot of credit to Norman Gillies. When he became director he was very outward looking in that sense as well. The Irish connection has been undoubtedly good.'

In 2002, a book was published which did much to celebrate and consolidate Mary Robinson's and Brian Wilson's twenty-first-century pan-Celtic vision. *An Leabhar Mòr*, *The Great Book of Gaelic*, brought together the Gaelic verse of Scotland and Ireland past and present with a collection of illustrations ('illuminations', they used more accurately to be called) specially commissioned from contemporary artists.

It was the first modern Gaelic book to wed words with images. The Scottish and Irish editors' distant ancestors recognised and appreciated the link between the printed word and coloured inks. In his introduction to *An Leabhar Mòr*, one of the volume's editors, Malcolm MacLean of Pròiseact nan Ealan in Lewis, wrote about *The Book of Kells*, an early manuscript which has been popularly associated with early Irish-Gaelic culture, but which was probably prepared at Iona during a time when there were no significant political boundaries between the northern and the southern Gaidhealtachd.

The Book of Kells was a hard act to follow. Most medieval illuminated manuscripts are without compare, and to try to copy them would be as foolish as to attempt to build a modern version of Chartres Cathedral. Malcolm MacLean and his Irish counterpart Theo Dorgan instead adopted the precept of *The Book of Kells* – that words and illustrations combined are more powerful than their component parts – and brought it into the twenty-first century.

Although the Irish and Scottish verse in *An Leabhar Mòr* ranges from the seventh century to the present day, the artists and calligraphers were modern to the core. They were not, most of the time, illustrating the poetry of a contemporary. The verse of Alasdair Mac Mhaighstir Alasdair was as perfectly matched by the art of Anna MacLeod as were the words of former Sabhal Mòr sgrìobhadair Catriona Montgomery by James Morrison's work.

An Leabhar Mòr provoked rumination on the timeless links between Celtic centuries – on Sorley Maclean's 'quality of the Gael permanent'. Gaelic verse and song had been nonsensically caricatured for centuries as limited in its range to sorrow and loss. *An Leabhar Mòr* disproved this at a glance. The service done by the 110 artists and calligraphers assembled was that of matching the vitality and beauty of the words with colour, shape and shade.

A satellite photograph introduced *An Leabhar Mòr* which was as illuminative as any of the graphics that succeeded it. It was of Scotland and the Isle of Man and Ireland, laid sideways, so that Caithness is to the east and Bantry Bay to the west. The seaboard and the islands upon which the Gaels still live lay, in this perspective, flatly along the roof of their world, forming a telling continuum with the bays and lochs of Ireland, Man and the north-west Highlands and Islands. They were no longer peripheral, but overarching.

communications and transport were consistently inferior. This had a very real impact on the confidence, belief and ambition of the area – on the collective psyche that passed from generation to generation. Seventy years ago, history was a nightmare from which the Highlands and Islands was trying to awake. The area was seen as a place with a past, but with no real future. A place that, it was eventually said, was on the conscience of the nation.

But things started to change.

Parliament debated the 'Highland Problem' in the 1960s, when Willie Ross, a Labour Secretary of State, steered through Westminster the legislation that created the Highlands and Islands Development Board. With his colleagues, Willie Ross had the foresight to realise that the HIDB needed more than central government cash. It needed power and responsibility too. The HIDB, and then Highlands and Islands Enterprise, have possessed those uniquely wide-ranging powers ever since: powers to develop communities as well as powers to make grant aid to business; powers to encourage the cultural as well as the economic renewal of the area, forever recognising that economic progress is greater where confidence and belief in community and culture are encouraged to grow.

As everyone here is aware, both the HIDB and its successor have been central in preparing the ground for the cultural and economic renewal that can be witnessed today right across the Highlands and Islands. The effectiveness of Highlands and Islands Enterprise in particular has been driven by an ability to see the whole picture: that economic development, individual confidence, the strength of communities and the quality of life must be intertwined if progress is to happen and be sustainable.

. . . There are many who can take credit for significant developments: the bridges which dramatically cut journey times between the very far north and the south; the introduction of ISDN technology.

Nine

Donald Dewar would not be the last First Minister to deliver the Sabhal Mòr lecture. Just three years later, the third man to hold the office, Jack McConnell, made the obligatory pilgrimage to what had come to be perceived as a rare and inspiring Highland success story and stood on the Sabhal Mòr stage. McConnell had been born in Ayrshire but raised on a sheep farm in Arran, the southernmost link in the Hebridean chain. His address to Sabhal Mòr Ostaig in 2004 was an extraordinary – some would suggest rose-tinted – endorsement of 30 years of activity in the Scottish Gaidhealtachd. The north-west of Scotland as represented in the new campus at Skye's Gaelic college, argued the First Minister, had ceased to be a twilight zone. It was now the land of the rising sun:

In the 30 years since Sabhal Mòr Ostaig came into being, the Sleat peninsula has been transformed – and the college has been absolutely central to making that happen. It is now undoubtedly a hub for the creativity and innovation that can be found not just on this island and the wider Highlands, but also amongst the Gaelic community internationally.

This truly is an inspiring place: one of the finest settings for education imaginable and a physical symbol of the renewed confidence. Sabhal Mòr Ostaig is special not just because of its setting and the excellence it consistently attains, but because of the contribution it makes as the national college for Gaelic.

. . . Today I want to comment on the cultural, economic and social renaissance of the Highlands and Islands. And I want to draw lessons from here for the rest of Scotland. Highland and Island renewal has occurred over 40 years and it is accelerating with devolved government in Scotland. It has been underpinned by government action – local and national. Not a coincidence or a series of accidents, but deliberate choices made to invest and modernise, which have created the conditions for individual and community progress. Government has invested in infrastructure, in education and in culture. And governments have promoted individual enterprise and community responsibility with economic reforms and, crucially, with land ownership reform.

Government cannot succeed alone, but these actions have supported individuals and communities inspired by increased confidence, a strong and proud sense of identity, an openness to new people and ideas and a hunger to succeed here, rather than leave a declining home behind. It is that combination of government action – investment and modernisation – with the celebration of individual and community ambition and enterprise which is the key to a prosperous, just and sustainable future for all of Scotland.

. . . Like the original Renaissance, the one under way in the Highlands and Islands has come after a long period of decline. Depopulation, economic failure and a cultural downturn preceded this modern Scottish renaissance. The Clearances highlighted the very worst in human nature, and they transformed the cultural landscape of the Highlands and Islands forever.

In the space of less than 50 years, the Highlands became one of the most sparsely populated areas in Europe. Communities were devastated, and the settlement pattern

that had served people for more than 1,000 years previously, virtually vanished. Here, on Skye, more than 40,000 people received writs of removal; and, in some places, 1 person was left where there had been 100. In the first 3 years of the nineteenth century, more than 10,000 Highlanders left for Nova Scotia and Canada; by the 1820s, that had gone up to 20,000 a year – most from the Western Highlands, Ross-shire and Sutherland.

. . . The traditional clan structure was lost, and subsequently even the language of the Highlanders was under threat as the education system promoted English in preference to Gaelic. Here and elsewhere, schoolchildren were belted for daring to speak their own language in the playground, let alone the classroom, and were forced to keep their Gaelic for the home. That language and the distinctive view of the world it represented were under serious threat of disappearing.

. . . Seventy years ago, the Highlands and Islands lived under the dark shadow of that decline. Without doubt, i was one of the most deprived and run-down parts of Britain It had been dealt a truly shabby deal by history. This was place where the only way to get on was to get out. Familie were continually separated and communities were neve given a chance to grow.

And those who did stay were born into a culture that ha understandably, lost its confidence. People had been taugh to know their place and to defer to their superiors and believe that their language and culture were worthless ar would hold them back. This was not a place to have ide above your station. It was not a place where people we encouraged to have ambitions. Too many ordina Highlanders were taught not to expect much from life, ar because of that, they weren't disappointed. As Neil Gu once remarked, Highlanders were 'made to despise th language and traditions'.

Housing conditions were poor, and inter

And the many who campaigned and won the argument for resurgence in Gaelic-medium teaching. They redefined the place of the language in the Scottish education system, sending a signal about the worth of the language. And the result is a renaissance in the Highlands and Islands that is nothing short of remarkable. Since 1960, the population of the Highlands and Islands has increased by a fifth, and the number of people in work in the area is up by as much as 50 per cent.

And we need hardly look beyond what is happening here, in Sabhal Mòr Ostaig, and the successes you've had in regenerating your proud cultural heritage in Skye and the surrounding areas. Skye is an island that was once predicted to be in a never-ending spiral of decline, but it is now in its fifth successive decade of population growth. And what is striking about that growth is that it's being accompanied by a flowering of creativity and an enterprising attitude.

Nowadays in Skye, people are not discouraged from having ideas above their station. And they don't let their island location get in the way of their aspirations. Those attitudes of old are being replaced by an enterprising spirit and by a sense that, with the right attitude in place, with confidence, belief and ambition, anything is possible.

. . . For all the achievement of Highland schools in the past, people had to move south to pursue higher education. The development of the UHI Millennium Institute is perhaps the single most important thing we in government can now do for the long term prospects of the Highlands and Islands. The challenge for this decade – like the HIDB was to the 1960s and hydro power was to the 1940s – is to make sure there is a fully fledged, degree awarding University of the Highlands and Islands. My generation needs to deliver that.

Culture for me is more than just the music, the languages and art of Scotland, vital as they are. Our culture helps to define our individual and collective identity. And the greater our confidence in that culture, the greater the sense of our own identity and the greater our positive belief in ourselves. I am not a Nationalist, but I celebrate my Scottish identity. I also celebrate this country's diversity – Gaelic and Scots, Punjabi and English – and I celebrate them positively in their own right, not by reference to our friends and neighbours in the south.

One thing that this college represents is a move beyond the culture of lament and of grievance into a positive, proactive engagement with a globalising world. It is a lesson that all of Scotland can learn. Just look at the thriving literary scene that you now have right across the Highlands and Islands. And just look at recent achievements such as the creation of *The Great Book of Gaelic*; the expanding export market of the Orcadian craft industry; or the highly impressive surge in interest and participation in traditional music by young people.

Look at the enduring popularity of shinty; at the vibrant fiddle scene on the Northern Isles; or at the resurgence of Highland dancing. And look at how the Royal National Mod is still thriving after 100 years; or at the festivals on Shetland which continue to go from strength to strength.

Each year, the area plays host to over 5,000 events, performances and festivals that attract over 1.5 million people. Highlanders are responding to these and other developments – and they are now twice as likely to go to contemporary art exhibitions than people from elsewhere in the country. So the lesson for all of Scotland is that we can celebrate our identity in the context of greater diversity and to positive effect.

But of course, no cultural renaissance here would be complete without a renewal of our proud linguistic heritage. Across Scotland, there are strong and clear links between our geography, our natural heritage, our people and Gaelic. However, Gaelic is about much more than our past and our place names. Gaelic is a living language, and it is the gateway to enter into a culture both ancient and modern. A language that has helped shape many aspects of Scottish life and society, and continues to do so.

Gaelic does much more than just hang on to the fringes of Scottish culture as a barely living echo of the past. Earlier today, during my visit to Sleat Primary School, I saw just how relevant Gaelic language and culture is to Skye's younger generation. It is vital that we do what we can to preserve our Gaelic heritage; to ensure that it not only survives, but has a chance to thrive; to have a vision for the language so that by the middle of this century, Gaelic will be spoken by more people, spoken in more settings and spoken throughout Scotland.

. . . Today, the Highlands and Islands stand proud as a symbol for Scotland's future: a symbol of how the new and old can work together to reinvigorate an economy, a culture and a people. Of course, increased prosperity and renewal are not evident in every corner of this great region; and they bring new challenges too. So our work must go on, in the Western Isles and the far north-west, and in Kintyre and Argyll, to secure that same combination of infrastructure and enterprise, jobs and quality of life which can reverse decline and increase confidence.

And we must, as we will, meet the challenges for affordable housing, for improved communication and for the continual development of Gaelic-medium education and other services. For Scotland though, the lessons are clear. Government must invest for the long term. Transport, communications and education are key. But so too is culture, the environment and our quality of life. The most significant lesson from the renaissance in the Highlands and Islands is that these have to go hand in hand.

. . . Scotland needs a change in attitude. An end to the cringe, the defeatism, the culture of enjoying the failure of others and the embarrassment at ambition and success. We need to instil in young Scots the idea that they should be ambitious, should expect to live in a diverse, welcoming and open country, should celebrate success and achievement, and that they can do this while caring more for others and understanding that strong communities protect the weakest and support the successful.

. . . When Donald Dewar delivered this lecture in September 2000, a month before his death, he summarised the Highlands and Islands' achievements.

'All in all,' Donald said, 'the prospects are good . . . There is a traditional way of life . . . There is a tourist industry . . . there are new manufacturing industries and service-centre growth, bringing prosperity and hope . . . Above all, there are people, in good heart, proud of their inheritance, determined to build a future in which they will flourish.

'Those who read the record,' Donald went on, 'know the Highlands and Islands make an enormous contribution to Scotland and, indeed, given their history, have contributed a great deal more to the life of Scotland than perhaps anyone has a right to expect. I see further progress. I see further movement. I can promise you that efforts to drive forward will have the support of the Parliament and the Executive.'

If Donald could be here today, I'm sure that he'd be greatly encouraged by the progress that's been made since 2000. It is no secret that, in these two and a half years I have been First Minister, I have spent a considerable amount of time here. I have been impressed – and at times inspired – by the strength of community, from Assynt and Ullapool to Alness and Fort William.

I believe that the nature of the relationship between the Highlands and Islands of Scotland and the rest of Scotland has changed for good: no longer are the Highlands and Islands on Scotland's conscience; no longer do the communities of the Highlands and Islands need to be defined by exceptional need; no longer do national politicians need to debate the Highland Problem.

Instead, we come here to be inspired, but also to contribute and play our part. Culturally, economically, demographically, the Highlands and Islands are undoubtedly on the way back – on the way up. Here, there is a sense of collective purpose, ambition and pride in culture. Proving that however shabbily an area has been treated in the past, however deprived it has become, however bleak the future looks, things can be made better. And if ever the corrosive cynicism creeps back in, all we must do is look to that incredible achievement. If it is possible here on Skye, then it is possible anywhere in Scotland.

Clearly, Jack McConnell could not have delivered such a panegyric thirty years earlier; he could not have delivered it ten years earlier. He would have had trouble in phrasing the better part of it in 1997, when President Mary Robinson delivered her Sabhal Mòr lecture in the campus on the old steading at Ostaig.

The implications of Jack McConnell's address were twofold. One was that the political argument for Gaelic had, by the beginning of the twenty-first century, been won. How that translated into practical support and public spending might still be a matter of contention, but across the party lines in Scotland – and indeed in the whole of the UK – barely a politician could be found who would parrot the traditional line about the language being a drag on its users and an anachronism in the modern world. Bilingualism had triumphed, in theory at least.

This achievement, no mean feat in itself, was illustrated by another Lanarkshire politician. In July 2002, the Scottish National Party's shadow minister for lifelong learning, Andrew Wilson, visited Sabhal Mòr Ostaig and returned south to offer the following words to the red-top *Sunday Mail*:

> To allow Gaelic to die would be an act of short-sighted madness from which we would all lose out in financial terms, as well as in the underlying vibrancy of our nation's culture.
>
> So all of us should support sensible plans to help Gaelic flourish. You don't have to be a Gael to want it to work. I visited the Gaelic college on Skye last week. It's called Sabhal

Mòr Ostaig, which sounds terribly romantic until you realise it translates as Big Barn of Ostaig, because it first started in a big barn in a place called Ostaig.

They are doing pioneering work to develop Gaelic teaching in schools and develop the language and economy of the Gaelic communities. The Columba Initiative, based at the college, is making bridges between the Scots and Irish Gaelic communities – a healthy forerunner, we hope, to other joint work such as our Euro 2008 bid.

All of this and the setting is undoubtedly the most stunning educational experience on earth, gazing over the majestic Sound of Sleat. I don't live in the Highlands, but I love the fact that this work is being done on behalf of my country. I am comfortable that a small share of my tax is helping to grow something valuable, not just because I think it has intrinsic value itself, but because I know the economy of my constituency will benefit, too, in the long term.

The second unavoidable conclusion to be drawn from all of these eulogies was that, with so much activity, so much public sympathy, so many initiatives, Gaelic was at last in a condition of robust good health. The language which in the middle of the twentieth century many experts had forecast for oblivion by the early decades of the twenty-first was up on its feet and running into the new millennium.

But both Jack McConnell and Andrew Wilson were aware, in 2004 and 2002 respectively, of the results of the 2001 Gaelic census. They showed the number of Gaelic speakers in Scotland falling from 65,987 to 58,652.

The leading Gaelic analyst Professor Ken MacKinnon by 2002 held appointments at Edinburgh and the Open universities. As we have seen, Professor MacKinnon conducted painstaking analyses of the state of Gaelic in previous censuses.

He was not given to hysteria or hyperbole. While, after the census results were published, much of the Scottish media raged about 'the death of a language', speaking to the *West Highland Free Press*, Professor Ken remained sanguine and considered:

> Although the situation is still one of decline, the rate of
> decline seems to have slowed down – almost to have halved.
> This may be due to improvements in Gaelic education and
> media over the past 12 years.
>
> But the present provision of Gaelic-medium education is
> insufficient to maintain the language. It can only slow down
> the rate of decline.

The 2001 statistics were not as bad as some had feared, and certainly
not so bad as some headlines suggested. The total number of fluent,
self-declared Gaelic speakers in Scotland was always going to fall
from its 1991 figure of 65,987 to below 60,000. The greatest pre-
census concern was that the fall would be as precipitous as between
1981 and 1991, when every year an average of 1,333 speakers were
lost. As it turned out, that decline was substantially slowed down to
755 a year between 1991 and 2001. It was 755 too many, but it
levelled out the total number of current Gaelic speakers at 58,652.

Students of the subject had been aware for some time that Gaelic
was no longer confined to the Gaidhealtachd area of the north-west
Highlands and Islands. Almost half of the Gaelic speakers in
Scotland were in 2001 to be found in the Lowlands and on the east
coast. Districts such as Aberdeen City, Perth and Kinross, and the
Lothians recorded the only increase in numbers in the 2001 census
– a small increase, but one which reflects not only economic
migrancy but also the latterday provision of some Gaelic-medium
education.

The 'heartlands' (Professor MacKinnon preferred the word in
quotation marks) in 2001 supplied just 55 per cent of those 58,652
people.

Close examination of the figures for the Western Isles, Highland
Region, and Argyll and Bute indicated a decline which was almost
commensurate with the overall decrease in population. In 2001,
there were 15,723 Gaelic speakers between Vatersay and the Butt of
Lewis, or almost 60 per cent of the population of the Western Isles.
That contrasted with 19,456 ten years previously, which was 66 per
cent of the population. But the total population of the Isles had

meantime fallen by 3,098 – which was just 750 short of the number of missing Gaelic speakers.

Overall, the population of the Highland Council's vast region had increased to 209,000, while the number of Gaelic speakers had fallen from 14,713 to 12,669. The overall pattern of Highland population change had continued to be one of decline in the west and north, and growth in the east, especially around the Moray Firth. The population of Skye and Lochalsh continued to rise marginally, but the populations of lonely western seaboard communities – for decades the last redoubts of mainland native Gaelic – continued to grow old and to die. In an analysis conducted on behalf of CnaG, Ken MacKinnon made illustrative comparisons between the health of the anglophone Black Isle in the north-east of the region and that of the (formerly Gaelic-speaking) townships of northern Applecross.

Similarly, in Argyll and Bute, the fall in numbers of Gaelic speakers (709) almost precisely mirrored the loss of population (662). Not every single one of the lost 3,000-odd people in the Western Isles and 662 people in Argyll can have been native Gaelic speakers, but given that the Gaidhealtachd had been home in recent times to a larger proportion of older people than elsewhere, and had experienced a steady decline in the size of families, some connection was begging to be made. There seemed to be, in harsh fact, more people dying out of than babies being born into Gaelic communities.

There was a newly introduced section of the 2001 census which did, however, offer real cause for optimism. For the first time it took count of the number of literate Gaels, people who could read and write the language but would not define themselves as fluent speakers. They totalled 65,674, which was 7,022, or 12 per cent, more than the baseline 2001 figure, and almost exactly the same as the 1991 total.

Professor Ken MacKinnon pointed out: 'These 7,022 persons may include – or even largely comprise – Gaelic learners who are confident in reading and writing the language but who would not claim fluent speaking ability. These are closest to the point of becoming fluent speakers.'

And when the figures encompassed those men, women and children who understood Gaelic – who could watch Gaelic television and listen to Gaelic radio and comprehend the conversations of their relatives and neighbours – the total flew up to 92,396.

This figure – more than half as many again as the 2001 baseline total, and almost as many as there had been Gaelic speakers six censuses previously, back in 1951 – clearly represented a mute generation, lost through no fault of its own to fluency.

In the words of Professor MacKinnon:

> This additional 33,744 persons may include some advanced learners but probably represents a large number of 'semi-speakers' who are used to hearing Gaelic in their immediate social environment but who have not been brought up as actively using Gaelic in their home situation. If they had had the opportunity of an active Gaelic education, their passive abilities might have been transformed into active abilities – and this clearly represents a challenge for our education system today.

Education, education, education . . . enough children in the early years of the twenty-first century were receiving the proven benefits of a bilingual upbringing to slow down the 'heartland' decline, but not yet to reverse it. The cold statistics indicated as much. Gaelic-medium education had come a long way in two decades. It was strongest by far in the primary-school sector. In the whole of the Highland Region in 2003, there were 718 pupils in primary-school GMUs. The largest concentration of those was in Skye and Lochalsh – but they still amounted to just 26 per cent of the total number of primary children in the district. (Skye alone performed slightly better, with approximately 30 per cent of the island's primary youngsters in GMUs.)

Throughout the Western Isles, there were 542 pupils on the Gaelic-medium primary rolls. This represented 25 per cent of the total number of 2,173 island primary-age children.

There was, at first sight, a relatively impressive list of GMUs in both council areas – relative compared to 1981. They ranged from Lionel in north Lewis to the Leverhulme School in South Harris, from Staffin to Sleat in Skye, and from Lochcarron to Ullapool on the western mainland. But an examination of the parishes which did not have access to a local GMU was instructive.

Overall, the largest buttons were pressed. There are GMUs in Stornoway; in Sir E. Scott School in Tarbert, Harris; in Balivanich (although not in Lochmaddy) in the Uists and Benbecula; in Daliburgh, Castlebay, Staffin, Portree, Broadford, Sleat, Plockton and Gairloch.

But a remarkable number of apparently obvious candidates did not yet have GMUs in their primary school. Such traditionally Gaelic-speaking islands as Berneray, Scalpay and Raasay were still in 2003 conducting all of their primary education – with the exception of the teaching of Gaelic itself – in English. In the home island of Sorley Maclean, children were still being taught Gaelic as a foreign language. The same applied to such heartland Gaelic parishes as Tolsta in Lewis, Eoligarry in Barra, Carbost and Elgol in Skye, to name just a few.

There was a shortage of suitable Gaelic teachers; there may have been a residual lack of conviction among some parents. Those were good and understandable reasons for the shortfall. But too many local authorities would continue to make the weary justification of proximate GMU. It may have been technically possible to bus under-12s from Scalpay and Raasay to GMUs in Tarbert and Portree, but the request was always unreasonable. Parents with children at a small community school had first of all a deep interest in that school's survival, which meant keeping its numbers up. And besides, if there was any point to Gaelic-medium education in places where Gaelic was still spoken, it was that the teaching should be symbiotic with the children's home community.

The 70 to 75 per cent of Gaidhealtachd primary pupils who were not in Gaelic-medium education did not all live in such Gaelic-speaking parishes. Many of them were in predominantly anglophone centres such as Portree or Stornoway. But by not supplying the option of GMU in those last strongholds of the language, however small they may have been, the real possibility was being lost by the councils of sustaining colloquial Gaelic as a medium of daily exchange at work, at home and in the shops. And the real possibility was opened up that the children of Scalpay, Balallan and Berneray – of all places – would in future censuses join the 33,744 persons who were in 2001 scratching at the windowpane of their culture: who could understand the language but who lacked the confidence and the education to speak it.

The census results which revealed the present state of Gaelic in Scotland did the same for Welsh in Wales. The situation there in 2001 was so strikingly different as to offer hope rather than induce dejection. In 1991, there were 508,000 Welsh speakers in the Principality. By 2001, there were 580,000. The number of Welsh speakers had increased by more than the total number of surviving Gaelic speakers. Ken MacKinnon said:

> I have no doubt why that is. It is due to 30 or 40 years of sustained investment in education and support from a strong Welsh language media.
>
> With only 25 per cent of primary pupils in Gaelic medium in the Western Isles and perhaps around 30 per cent in Skye, even these 'heartland' areas will not maintain Gaelic as a community language without new policies and new philosophies.
>
> This is the challenge for the new Bòrd na Gàidhlig. Any area which claims to be a Gaelic heartland must think seriously about new policies and new practices for Gaelic in the family, in the community and in education.

When the parish-by-parish breakdown of the 2001 census became available, however, one Skye parish above all others was seen to have recorded sensational statistics. Thirty years earlier, in the 1971 census, the southernmost peninsula of Sleat recorded a population of 452. Ten years earlier, in 1991, that had risen to 685. The 2001 figures showed that 780 people lived in Sleat, which was more than at any time since the 1930s.

The parish had achieved this phenomenal growth of 72 per cent over 30 years with a high level of economic activity and a relatively low average age. What was more, despite the fact that 27 per cent of its population was born outside Scotland (the average in Skye and Lochalsh was 22 per cent), 44.4 per cent of Sleat was in 2001 Gaelic speaking – the highest level of Gaelic articulacy in Skye south of Trotternish.

Those unique and apparently magical totems of financial and cultural health were easily attributable to Sabhal Mòr Ostaig, to the pro-Gaelic policies of (the now knighted) Sir Iain Noble's estate, to the local primary school's successful Gaelic-medium unit and to the Clan Donald Visitor Centre of Ellice McDonald.

It was instructive to compare Sleat's neighbouring parishes in the south of Skye. Neither Broadford nor Elgol were in decline, but they paled beside what had happened between Drumfearn and Aird on the Sleat peninsula.

Broadford's population had grown by 9 per cent during the 1990s to a total of 1,237 people, while that of Elgol had remained static at 137. Of Broadford people in 2001, 30 per cent were Gaelic speaking; 37 per cent in Elgol. There was in both of those districts a shortage of people in the 15–24 age range, whereas Sleat, naturally, had the highest percentage of teenagers and young adults in Skye and Lochalsh.

The working population of Sleat was by 2001 as dependent upon educational wages (18 per cent) as that of Elgol was on fishing and fish-farming (18 per cent), and that of Broadford on its hospital and social work (18 per cent). The difference was that both the population and the native language of Broadford and Elgol had survived, but in Sleat both had been revived beyond recognition. The stark figures demonstrated that, more than any other parish in Skye and south-west Ross, Sleat had been transformed. Perhaps most remarkably, its newfound economic health had not come at the cost of its old language. Contrary to most previous official wisdom, one could not have been accomplished without the other.

But every parish in the Highlands and Islands could not

realistically be given a Gaelic college of tertiary education. In other parts of the map and in other areas of activity, the picture was different to that painted and proclaimed by Jack McConnell. Too often in most districts of the traditional Gaidhealtachd, Gaelic was running to stand still. The efforts of its supporters were akin to firefighting.

While the BBC's Gaelic radio provision had continued to offer a vigorous service, Gaelic television – especially in the independent sector – had broadly failed to live up to the promises of the 1990 Broadcasting Act. In 1995, Alistair Moffat of Scottish Television outlined the cheerful, homely manner in which the Gaelic Television Fund was dispensed to broadcasters:

> What happens is broadly this. With no control or advance knowledge of the ITV schedule, the CTG suggest a menu of programme genres to the broadcasters. Who then generally demur, saying parenthetically, let's see what the programmes are like before we decide if and when we schedule them. Then the CTG promulgate this menu to producers, some of whom also have no knowledge of the schedule . . . That this arrangement works at all is a tribute to the good humour of CTG, broadcasters and producers alike.

It worked, he said, because:

> the rigour of the franchise process had encouraged the ITV companies to conduct exhaustive research and to tailor their pre-1993 [when the first CTG-funded programmes were transmitted] programmes accordingly . . . We made Gaelic programmes, very deliberately, about only the good things in life – cookery, cars, fashion and so on . . . it worked because the CTG trusted us. They took a huge risk with [the soap opera] *Machair* particularly – good drama is the hardest thing to do well in television. And it paid off.

It certainly paid off for Scottish Television and Grampian, who were re-awarded their franchises partly on the promise of such prime-time Gaelic programming. But just three years after Alistair Moffat spoke those words, *Machair* was gone – not only from its evening slot but altogether, never to return.

'I'm afraid,' says Brian Wilson, 'Scottish Television's very short-lived commitment to Gaelic in the 1990s was pretty cynical. They had stumbled upon Gaelic's usefulness in securing the Central Scotland franchise which was out to auction at that time. The tactic, which worked brilliantly for them, was to build the myth that peak-hour Gaelic was an essential commitment from anyone who even thought about bidding for this franchise.

'It was a particularly audacious operation since, for 30-odd years, STV had not lifted a finger for Gaelic. Then for two or three years, it was as if they had acquired ownership of the whole Gaelic world. Nothing moved without them being involved. They even published their annual report – for one year only, of course – bilingually.

'As soon as the franchise was awarded to them, without competition and for a nominal sum, they started to back off at a rate of knots. Gaelic had served its purpose. In retrospect, it was an extremely damaging period because it distorted the whole debate about how the Gaelic Television Fund should be applied. One of the few remnants that has survived is the Sabhal Mòr Lecture but even the showing of that has been consigned to the early hours of the morning.'

Two years after the fall of *Machair*, in 2000, Grampian dropped its Gaelic news bulletin *Telefios*. *Telefios*, which had started in 1992, had been the first daily Gaelic news service on television. It offered two daily news bulletins and a weekly news magazine. John Angus MacKay of the Comataidh Craolaidh Gàidhlig (Gaelic Broadcasting Committee), as the Fund's administrators had been renamed when they were enabled to work in radio as well as in television, said:

> We could no longer sustain the funding of *Telefios* in its present slots in the broadcast schedule. This does not mean that we are discarding Gaelic television news from our

portfolio of funded programmes. We will be entering into dialogue with broadcasters and producers to determine the best way to provide a sustainable and affordable Gaelic news and current affairs service during the transition from analogue to digital television and towards a dedicated Gaelic channel as recommended in the Milne Report. Until the optimum solution can be found there may have to be a temporary suspension of daily Gaelic news on television.

The Milne Report into the future of Gaelic broadcasting mentioned by John Angus MacKay had been published earlier in 2000. Alasdair Milne – that former BBC director-general who was a Gaelic learner – had recommended that there should be a Gaelic Broadcasting Authority responsible for the development of a cohesive Gaelic broadcasting service. Within that service there should be a dedicated digital Gaelic television channel.

The report stated that: 'the maintenance of the status quo is not an option' and that the present provision was 'inadequate'. The amounts of money needed to run such a service as was recommended were, according to Milne, 'not insignificant, but they are not overwhelming'.

But the years passed and no dedicated Gaelic channel emerged in Scotland. Soap operas and daily news bulletins a thing of the past, Gaelic television found itself occupying the graveyard slots on independent channels. On 20 October 2004, Western Isles MP Calum MacDonald stood up in the House of Commons to reproach his own government's lack of initiative:

> The Government have produced lots of reports, but there is still no financial backing to underwrite the aspirations contained in them. To the Gaelic community, this is beginning to look like tokenism. What is the point in the new Scottish Parliament opening with a Gaelic psalm if there is no delivery for Gaelic in the decisions being made by that Parliament? What is the point of my constituency in this place being rebranded by the boundary commission with a

new Gaelic name if there is no new funding for the Gaelic Media Service from this Government?

The contrast between the current funding position for Gaelic television and what is needed in order that its aspirations be met is bad enough, but the contrast with past funding is even more embarrassing. I admit this through gritted teeth, and it is a pity that the official Opposition's spokesperson is not present to hear me say this – perhaps that indicates a slackening of their commitment to, and support for, Gaelic under their new leadership – but the fact is that the previous Tory government spent more money on Gaelic television than either this Labour government or the Scottish Executive are managing to do between them.

When the Gaelic Television Fund was created, the then Conservative government found £9.5 million of brand new money to back it. Adjusted for inflation, the equivalent sum today would be almost £13 million. Yet the actual allocation of funding for Gaelic broadcasting in this financial year is only £8.5 million. That is a funding shortfall of more than 30 per cent compared with what the Tories were able to spend.

Funding for Gaelic broadcasting has not increased – not even in nominal terms – since 1997. Yet during that time, total government expenditure has increased by 41 per cent, and the Scottish Executive's budget has increased by a similar amount. By way of contrast, funding for Welsh broadcasting has increased by £16 million in just the past 3 years. During the same period, there have been real-terms cuts for Gaelic. These are indefensible statistics, and the Scottish Executive, this Government and those of us who support them should feel deeply embarrassed about them.

It is no wonder that the Government were criticised by the Council of Europe's committee of experts when it reported in March of this year. It pointed out just how poorly the Government are doing in respect of their broadcasting obligations under the terms of the European Charter for Regional or Minority Languages. I was delighted when we signed up to that charter. It was something that I helped set in motion when I was in the Scottish Office working with Donald Dewar. It saddens me that the progress that we made then has now ground to a halt.

Part of the problem, I acknowledge, is that the constitutional arrangements have obviously changed since I was in the Scottish Office. Responsibility for Gaelic broadcasting is now shared between Whitehall, through the Minister's Department [Culture, Media and Sport], and the Scottish Executive, which is accountable to the Scottish Parliament. Coordination between the two tiers of government is consequently a bit more complicated, but that is no excuse for the failure of either tier to live up to its responsibilities to Gaelic broadcasting.

Gaelic television has become, I fear, a devolution orphan, kept on a starvation diet and forced in consequence to reduce its output each and every year. Not only is the Gaelic Broadcasting Fund too small to deliver the digital channel that was provided for in the Communications Act 2003, it cannot even deliver the basic 200 hours of annual programme output that was anticipated in the Broadcasting Act 1990. Those 200 hours, which we had in the early 1990s, have been cut down to just 137 hours today. Again, that reduction is indefensible and unacceptable.

Calum MacDonald was at this point interrupted by the Plaid Cymru MP for Ceredigion, Simon Thomas, who interjected:

The Hon. gentleman has drawn, quite rightly, on experiences in Wales, and he will also know about the experience of TG4 in Ireland, which runs an Irish-language service with the sort of money that he suggested could run a Gaelic-language service. It happens there in practice. As to declining hours, we have seen S4C in Wales become digital and greatly expand its hours. The Hon. gentleman might like to reflect on the fact that over the 20 years that Wales has had S4C, the number of Welsh speakers, once in decline, was first halted and then increased at the last census, whereas the number of Gaelic speakers has, unfortunately, been on an inexorable decline. Perhaps a Gaelic service would help to protect the language in its heartland in Scotland.

The Western Isles MP agreed:

The success of S4C in stabilising the language is something that we should take careful note of and draw some hope from. The parallel that the Hon. gentleman drew with the Irish position is also interesting, because the new channel in Ireland runs on a similar budget to what is spoken about for the Gaelic service. There are actually more native Gaelic speakers in Scotland than there are native Irish speakers in Ireland. That is a fact that not many people are aware of. Irish is widely used in Ireland, it is learned at school; but when it comes to native speakers – where people learn the language in their own homes – there are more Gaelic speakers in Scotland, as I said.

The game of pass the parcel between the Government here and the Scottish Executive in Edinburgh has been going on since devolution. The result has been the deadlock that I described, which is failing the Gaelic community and, indeed, making a mockery of the spirit of devolution. Both governments, in Westminster and Edinburgh, are to blame for the impasse, but it is the Government here who have reserved to themselves – quite rightly, I believe – the responsibility to legislate for broadcasting. This Government passed the Communications Act last year, so they have a special responsibility to deliver the promises implicit in that Act for the Gaelic Media Service to provide a Gaelic channel.

. . . the Government and all of us must accept that a dedicated Gaelic television service is not a luxury in the context of today's expectations in the twenty-first century. Indeed, it is the minimum acceptable provision for an indigenous British language that has been spoken in these islands for at least one and a half millennia.

The British economy is the fourth biggest in the world. Let us have no more pretence that we cannot afford a television channel for our Gaelic-speaking community. If the Government want to boast that modern Britain is a vibrant, multinational and multicultural society – indeed, a multilingual one – and that they cherish that diversity, they cannot afford not to deliver a Gaelic television service.

The Minister for Sport and Tourism, Richard Caborn, replied:

Funding for Gaelic broadcasting came to prominence in September 2000, when the Milne Committee – to which my Hon. friend the Member for Western Isles referred – produced its report recommending the establishment of a Gaelic Broadcasting Authority to run a dedicated Gaelic television channel at a cost of £44 million.

We reached the view that the Milne Report's core recommendations could not be justified . . .

However, £8.5 million is still a considerable sum of money, and the Gaelic Media Service continues to use it to produce high-quality Gaelic programming. That programming makes an important cultural and economic contribution, especially to the Highlands and Islands of Scotland.

I agree that Gaelic broadcasting has been constrained, and I believe there are two key reasons for that. The first reason is the limited role that the Gaelic Television Committee and, later, the Gaelic Broadcasting Committee – the CCG – were given by the Broadcasting Acts of 1990 and 1996. The inability of those committees to take a more proactive role in commissioning programmes was an area of difficulty, as was their rather awkward arm's-length relationship with the broadcasters that ultimately transmitted these programmes to the public. The CCG could fund programmes, but depended wholly on the BBC and the Gaelic Media Service to broadcast them.

Secondly, Gaelic broadcasting is under pressure because the Scottish Executive has seen education policy and funding as the most effective way of supporting and promoting the Gaelic language. Their ultimate goal – one that we shared when Westminster was responsible for those matters – is to ensure that the Gaelic language continues as a healthy, living indigenous language of the UK.

If there was no immediate sign on the horizon of a dedicated television channel, there would finally, as the politicians had regularly promised, be a Gaelic Act. The new process began with the establishment in 2003 of a semi-autonomous non-governmental organisation named Bòrd na Gàidhlig. Based in Inverness, with Alan Campbell as director and chaired by Duncan Ferguson, one of Sorley Maclean's successors as rector of Plockton High School, the new board's aims would be to:

> Increase the numbers of speakers and users of Gaelic; Strengthen Gaelic as a family and community language; Facilitate access to Gaelic language and culture throughout Scotland; Promote and celebrate Gaelic's contribution to Scottish cultural life; Extend and enhance the use of Gaelic in all aspects of life in Scotland.

More immediately, Bòrd na Gàidhlig's priorities would be to steer through and administer the first Gaelic Language Act in Scottish history. Introduced to the Scottish Parliament in September 2004, the Gaelic Bill will, if established as an Act of Parliament, provisionally require local authorities and public bodies to adopt a Gaelic strategy – or to give Bòrd na Gàidhlig good reasons why they should refrain from doing so.

And on the peripheries, institutions continued to rise out of the ground. In August 2002, *The Herald* reported that:

Islay moved back towards the centre of the Gaelic world with the opening of a £2 million education centre for the language.

They came from all parts of the Highlands and Islands and from many parts of Ireland yesterday to celebrate the unveiling of the Gaelic language, culture and heritage centre on the shores of Loch Indall. It will be a major boost to the island which holds an immensely significant place in Scottish history when almost 700 years ago the Lord of the Isles held court at Finlaggan and was at the heart of Gaelic life. As the children of Bowmore Primary sang ''S ann an Ile' – Islay's national anthem – all appeared convinced something profoundly important for Islay was happening yesterday with the birth of Ionad Chaluim Chille Ile – the Islay Columba Centre.

Robin Currie, the project chairman and local councillor, for one was confident: 'The Columba Centre as the strong heart of the Gaidhealtachd of Scotland and Ireland, will mark the turning of the tide of the regeneration of Islay.' He added: 'For the first time ever, for our youth getting on in life will not mean having to go away from the island. A bright new light has been lit on Islay.'

The centre was opened by Mike Watson, the minister for tourism, culture and sport. It will offer a range of courses in Gaelic language, arts and history, accredited by the Open University.

It will be linked to the University of the Highlands and Islands and overseen by Sabhal Mòr Ostaig, the highly successful Gaelic College on Skye.

Mr Watson said: 'This centre will offer the people of Islay the opportunity to share in the educational benefits and to explore the island's historic cultural connections with the rest of the Gaelic world.'

A special tribute was paid to Brian Wilson, the energy minister who four years ago chaired a meeting of the Glasgow Islay Gathering and first proposed the idea of establishing a Gaelic college on Islay. That was when he was a Scottish Office minister, but his own association with the island went back a lot longer.

Mr Wilson said that while he had nothing to do with choosing the new centre's location at an old cottage hospital at Gartnatra, just east of the main town of Bowmore, it was significant in his own family history. He said: 'My mother was the nurse in charge of Gartnatra during the Second World War and first met my father, who was the public assistance officer on Islay, on the steps of the hospital. So my personal links with the building as well as the project will remain very strong.'

Mr Wilson said the Gaelic language on Islay was struggling with the number of Gaelic speakers having fallen from 50 per cent in 1971, to around 20 per cent today and now 'desperately needs an injection of support'.

It seemed at times like a contradictory, inverted relationship. Sympathy and support for the Gaelic language from outside the Scottish Gaidhealtachd was most fulsome and generous just as the culture at the hearthside and the corner shop reached its lowest ebb.

It was reasonably clear within 30 years of the establishment of Sabhal Mòr Ostaig that the Gaelic language would not, after all, die in the early decades of the twenty-first century. It would survive in some shape or form. The second Gaelic renaissance had at least done what the first had failed to do: it had squeezed a lifejacket over the shoulders of its weakened charge.

Iain Taylor, the director of Sabhal Mòr Ostaig during the Ceartas militancy of 20 years earlier, would occasionally return from his new home in the Irish Gaeltacht to the college as a lecturer in the early 2000s. 'I think that Gaelic,' he would say during one of his visits to the Highlands, 'is in big danger of dying out as a community language, even in the heartland areas, in Lewis and in South Uist.

'I can't see it ever disappearing, but equally I can't see it really continuing as a community language. Just from looking at how Sleat has changed . . . it has in many ways changed for the better, that is undeniable. But Gaelic is effectively dead outwith the college. You can still buy ferry tickets or petrol and do your postal business up in Kilmore in Gaelic, and you can buy drinks in Gaelic, but in general you can't do your shopping in the language, and you just don't hear as much Gaelic any more in Sleat unless you're with college people. I can tell you, I've only heard Gaelic being spoken once in the six months I've been here in 2003–04 where I wasn't part of the conversation or somebody else from the college wasn't part of the conversation. That was my neighbour in Tarskavaig, who is a home help for an older lady in the village; I was waiting for a lift one day at the phone box and I heard her coming into the older lady's house and shouting "Cheerio" to her and all that sort of thing, and it was through Gaelic.

'Even thinking of Tarskavaig, I think it's only used in one house that's not got SMO people in it, and that's at my next-door neighbour's, whose dad, an old man, lives with him. It's maybe used in one other home, but I find it hard to believe, because the two kids there in their 20s don't speak it well. So I think it's down to one house, because the other houses that have Gaelic speakers in them, there's only one person in them so they've got nobody to speak to anyway.

'When I lived in Garrynamonie, in South Uist, every house except one was a Gaelic-speaking house. But I know for a fact that this has changed, because I've still got friends there, and it's just sort of thinned out. And if you can't use Gaelic in a community setting, then it means that people growing up are not going to have the full range of language use. And the language itself suffers.

'It gets to the stage where people have only one word for one thing: everything is *math* [good] or everything is *snog* [nice], there's no more *breagha*, *àlainn*, *eireachdail*, *riochdail*, all of these *boidheach* [beautiful] words. Most Gaelic speakers today have an attenuated vocabulary and a restricted set of structures so they can't use subtlety in the language, and it can't cope – their language isn't at the level that their intellect is, so they have to turn to English to express themselves succinctly and with subtlety and to express nuances.

'That's not to say that there are no young people who can do that in Gaelic, because there definitely are; it's just that there are so few of them. I don't know that Gaelic has a function at a community level that's any better than the state of Irish in Ireland.

'I think it will be an ornament. Even in the Outer Isles now, the default language of young people is their English. It's how they express their individuality, and it's not only because they are teenagers, some of them are older. And you do notice that you're sort of imposing on them if you speak Gaelic to them, because you're forcing them to struggle, and they're not as comfortable.

'A guy who teaches in the Cùrsa Comais here, he says he feels like some kind of controlling parent because he knows that the students want to speak English to one another. He feels that his presence there inhibits them from expressing themselves because they want to do that through English, yet they feel guilty speaking English in his presence because they know his views and they like him. There are a number of students who do speak Gaelic, but I think that if Sabhal Mòr Ostaig is a microcosm of the Gaidhealtachd, then, no, I don't see a very bright future for Gaelic at all, not really, beyond this ornamental 'add-on' role that it can play.

'Maybe I'm wrong. You know, if Gaelic-medium education expands and prospers, then it will be a different kind of Gaelic that we get, but then there's nothing wrong with that. Every language changes and develops. We shouldn't be speaking in eighteenth-century Gaelic because we are not living in the eighteenth century. I don't understand the ultra-Conservative viewpoints about preserving the language as it always was. That will kill off Gaelic as much as any community withering away. I know that it puts me off if I get somebody who says, "Oh, you didn't use a feminine singular dative there." I just think to myself, "Oh, get over yourself."

'I remember reading something that surprised me in a study of American Indian languages. It said not to expect the last fluent speakers to be necessarily sad that their language is dying. I thought that was a weird thing to say, because you'd always imagined such people to be like the great bard Murdo MacFarlane from Melbost, who was very upset that Gaelic was dying. But the argument went on to explain that with the death of a language, with single figures of native speakers, because the language is dying these few remaining people have acquired status. They are now authorities on their language, it's their personal thing. So don't be too surprised if they don't really want to encourage it being brought back, because that would undermine whatever status or authority they have. I can think of examples in Scotland by the barrowload.'

'Communities are changing,' says John Norman MacLeod. 'The world is changing and Gaelic has moved on. The movement in the primary schools is very important. For example here in Sleat, in Tarskavaig, there were very few children in recent years coming to the GMU here, and now there are five or six. And they're Gaelic-speaking children whose parents are also Gaelic speaking.

'You can revive a community, even if it takes a while. I've heard it said here in Sleat by a Gaelic speaker that "Gaelic did very little for me", and there's been a lot of that attitude in older people; they don't really see the value of the language. Although they spoke Gaelic as a community, they were always ready to turn to English when talking to their grandchildren. So it surprises me today when I go into the Co-op in Portree or Broadford and hear a lot of Gaelic spoken.

'People have to want to speak the language. We're finding that as people are growing up, they're using the language – maybe not so much in their community, but they are using it. And I think the language will survive as long as there are people learning the language, as long as people are talking and singing in the language. I'm very hopeful.'

'I think that the major achievement of Sabhal Mòr Ostaig,' says Farquhar MacIntosh, 'has been to alter people's – and by that I mean Gaelic people's – conception of their own language and its standing and status. I said in a letter to Iain Noble in 1973 that I felt that, even under the Education Act as it stood at the time, the authorities were required to make better provision for Gaelic education than they were doing. The fact that the Gaelic college came along and proved to be so successful in using Gaelic as the medium of instruction, proving that it was a viable means of teaching, and showing that we could train people who were then able and willing to get jobs within the Gaelic-speaking areas . . . I think that really altered people's conception of their own culture and language. They could see it as something in which they could take a proper pride. Having taken that first step in seeing the language not as an outgraded or useless subject, not as a hindrance in the modern world, but as a viable means of learning and instruction – that instilled a self-respect in individuals as well as a pride in their language. Once you had individual respect and confidence, then community respect and confidence developed.

'Sabhal Mòr is now, I believe, the biggest employer of people in the south part of Skye. So it has turned the position of Gaelic around, in the sense that people have come to see it as a useful acquisition, and at the same time, they see its real value in reviving communities and creating jobs for those communities. Because there's no point in reviving Gaelic unless you can provide jobs that keep Gaelic people within the areas in which the language is spoken.'

Early in the twenty-first century, the Gaelic Books Council launched a publishing imprint for new Gaelic writing called Ur-Sgeul. It would be in the care of John Storey, the son of that friend of Sabhal Mòr Ostaig and inveterate campaigner for Gaelic within the development agencies, Bob Storey. Ur-Sgeul's job, said John, would be 'to provide an outlet for Gaelic writers who are capable of producing contemporary, exciting new work, and to reach out to Gaelic readers and provide them with a chance to experience these books'.

In 2003 and 2004, John Storey's imprint published two novels from the Uist writer Angus Peter Campbell. The first, *An Oidhche Mus Do Sheòl Sinn (The Night Before We Sailed)*, was received with acclaim tangibly touched by relief – relief that, for all the language's pressing problems, it was still possible for an author to write fiction which spoke to the modern world through the medium of Gaelic.

The second, *Là a' Dèanamh Sgèil Do Là (Day Speaketh Unto Day)*, came out just as *An Oidhche Mus* was shortlisted for the 2004 Saltire Scottish Book of the Year Award.

In the words of its author:

> *Là a' Dèanamh Sgèil Do Là* is a novel which begins in the Torrin/Elgol area of Skye in 2010, when an old man comes to the door carrying a bag of winkles on his shoulders. A young girl, aged about three, answers the door and he asks her in English, 'Is your mum or dad in?' She runs back in to her mum and dad and says in Gaelic, 'There's an old man at the door and he's speaking English.' The father goes to the door and says to the old man in Gaelic, 'You don't need to speak English here; there's plenty Gaelic in this house.'
>
> The novel then becomes the story of who this old man is and who the family are, once the door is opened. He is a Sgitheanach who left in 1940 for the war in the North Atlantic. He has come back to die.
>
> The householder is Seòras Stubbs, from Market Drayton in Shropshire – I just stuck a pin in the map – who came to Skye in 1990 to work as an architect with Skye and Lochalsh Council.
>
> Halfway through the novel, the reader suddenly realises it is not 2010 at all, but some future, unnamed date – perhaps 2040 or 2050 – and Seòras is recalling all this as an old man.
>
> What has really happened is that this architect from Market Drayton is the last Gaelic speaker left in the world, following the globalisation of languages and the new world order.

The book's theme, said Angus Peter Campbell, is 'control and power and freedom'.

Further Reading

Abley, Mark, *Spoken Here: Travels Among Threatened Languages*, Arrow, 2003

Black, Ronald (ed.), *Eilein na h-Oige: The Poems of Fr Allan McDonald*, Mungo Books, 2002

Boswell, James, *The Life of Johnson*, Penguin, 2005

Cameron, Ewan A., *The Life and Times of Fraser-Mackintosh, Crofter MP*, Centre for Scottish Studies, 2000

Cohen, Anthony P. (ed.), *Belonging: Identity and Social Organisation in British Rural Cultures*, Manchester University Press, 1982

Gossen, Andrew Adam, 'Agents of a Modern Gaelic Scotland: Curriculum, Change, and Challenge at Sabhal Mòr Ostaig, the Gaelic College of Scotland', unpublished Ph.D. thesis, Harvard University, 2002

Hunter, James, *Last of the Free*, Mainstream Publishing, 1999

Johnson, Samuel, and James Boswell, *A Journey to the Western Islands of Scotland* and *The Journal of a Tour to the Hebrides*, Penguin, 1984

MacKinnon, Kenneth, 'A Century on the Census: Gaelic in Twentieth Century Focus' in *Gaelic and Scots in Harmony*, ed. Derick S. Thomson, Department of Celtic, University of Glasgow, 1990

Maclean, Calum Iain, *The Highlands*, Mainstream Publishing, 1990

MacLean, Donald, 'Sunshine and Storms on the Isle of Skye: Sabhal Mòr Ostaig and the Gaelic Renaissance' in *Exploring Corporate Strategy*, G. Johnson, K Scholes and R. Whittington, FT Prentice Hall, 2004

Moffat, Alistair, *The Sea Kingdoms: The Story of Celtic Britain and Ireland*, HarperCollins, 2002

Orwell, George, *In Front of Your Nose: The Collected Essays, Journalism and Letters Vol. 4, 1945–50*, Penguin, 1993

Stephens, Meic, *Linguistic Minorities in Western Europe*, Gomer Press, 1976

Stewart, Donald, *A Scot at Westminster*, ed. Mary Stewart MacKinnon, The Catalone Press, 1994

Sorley Maclean's poem 'A Waxing Moon above Sleat' reprinted courtesy of Sabhal Mòr Ostaig.

The quotations from Murdo MacLeod in chapters Two and Three are from 'Gaelic in Highland Education', the *Transactions of the Gaelic Society of Inverness* Vol. 43 (1960-63) pp. 305–34.

Lisa Chipongian's article 'The Cognitive Advantages of Balanced Bilingualism', quoted in Chapter Three, can be found at www.brainconnection.com and is used with the permission of Scientific Learning Corporation.

The author would like to acknowledge the above publications, as well as the newspapers listed below, for valuable assistance in research and background, and is grateful for permission granted for direct quotation.

The *Daily Mirror*, the *Daily Record*, *The Herald*, the Belfast *News Letter*, the *Oban Times*, *The Scotsman*, the *Stornoway Gazette*, the *Sunday Mail*, *The Times* and the *West Highland Free Press*.

Every attempt has been made to trace all rights holders. The publishers will be glad to make good any omissions brought to their attention.

Index

269